Values, Ergonomics and Risk Management in Aviation Business Strategy

Ayse Kucuk Yilmaz · Triant G. Flouris

Values, Ergonomics and Risk Management in Aviation Business Strategy

Foreword by Dr. M. Sani Şener, TAV Airports Holding

Springer

Ayse Kucuk Yilmaz
Anadolu University
Eskişehir, Turkey

Triant G. Flouris
Hellenic American University
Manchester, NH, USA

ISBN 978-981-15-1005-2 ISBN 978-981-15-1006-9 (eBook)
https://doi.org/10.1007/978-981-15-1006-9

This Springer imprint is published by the registered company Springer Nature Singapore Pte Ltd.
The registered company address is: 152 Beach Road, #21-01/04 Gateway East, Singapore 189721, Singapore

For Ayse's Son "Mehmet EFE YILMAZ"
and
For Our Families!
Ayse Kucuk Yilmaz and Triant G. Flouris

Foreword

Three main pillars of management are financial issues, people issues, and technical issues all of which can be perfectly managed by harmonizing the three.

Complex systems management is a difficult task where a manager should run the impeding ingredients, supportive ingredients, and balancing ingredients in parallel. To make this happen, value-based decision-making must be at the center of the business model.

Managers make decisions every day at different levels for choices which must be based on values. Values are the standards by which each member of the organization conducts themselves within the stated corporate culture, and company beliefs and attitudes toward business practices. Fairness, acting with integrity, avoiding an unethical business environment, and respecting social responsibilities will show what your company stands for.

In today's business environment, value-based decision-making, intuitive decision-making, and inspiration are increasingly considered by modern management and strategy techniques. All of these require high ethical standards with human-centered inclusive approaches to sustain success.

Risk management is mainly the management of decision-making and selection processes. In line with the philosophy of the contingency approach, risk management should be inspired by values and human inclusiveness. Enterprise risk management is an important part of management systems and an important framework that supports a corporate vision and mission together with values.

In today's contemporary business world, value-based decision-making is on the agenda of all leaders.

Values Ergonomics and Risk Management in Aviation Business Strategy written by Ayse Kucuk Yilmaz and Triant Flouris is an excellent book for all managers in the aviation sector to improve their value-based risk management and strategy capabilities.

This book has considerable content via a human factor focused approach. As a leader of a leading Airport Company, I believe that this book will make a great contribution to improving situational awareness about both individual and corporate sustainability, because Drs. Kucuk Yilmaz and Flouris believed that management strategies should emanate from values. This book will be a source of inspiration for managers and researchers and offers value to the aviation management and strategy field.

December 2018

Dr. Eng. M. Sani Şener
CEO/Executive Board Member
TAV Airports Holding
http://www.tav.aero

Preface

'Values guide both choices and behaviors in one's individual and professional life.'
'Sustainability is only possible with value-based management.'
Ayse Kucuk Yilmaz and Triant G. Flouris

Our Book Presents Key Values in Management and Strategy Optimization.

We assume that optimization in management and strategy is provided, fundamentally through the implementation of a value-based enterprise risk management with a human-centric approach.

Why should both individual and organizational values be considered in the context of corporate risk management?

Values can be considered to be universal since values are the sources of the virtues. Values are the most vital element of both individual and professional life. For this reason, management and strategy could not be thought of as separate from values. When you integrate your corporate risk management' system with universal values, then your risk management system may serve more support you to achieves strategies.

Values are the issue of management and strategy. Behaviors are shaped and influenced by values and we make choices based on our values; therefore, our decision-making depends strongly on them.

Organizational culture is essential for value-based management. Value-based risk management is in need of a well-established organizational culture. When integrating corporate values with organizational culture, managers then more effectively manage their personnel. Corporate culture has the potential to strong effect on individuals.

The decision as a concept of business management and strategy means that make a "choice" from options. The core of management is decision-making. Managers make choices every day. Value has an impact on effective and timely decision-making. The values which have individuals play a crucial role in decision-making.

Values have the power to impact both individual and corporate viewpoints. When the viewpoint is affected, performance, motivation, and all things related to management and ergonomics may be affected too.

We may evaluate businesses as people. Businesses have the potential to be influenced and affected like humans, and also have limited resources, just like people. At the same time businesses as people have both strong and weak aspects. People are different from each other and perceived differently by others. The same is true for businesses. Businesses consist of people who are affected by their own values which effect, as well, their own decision-making style. It is not possible to obtain original and sustainable results without adding personality and spirit to the mix. This means that each individual brings their uniqueness having a different background, personality, experience, education, and culture components. Considering the human resource in the whole enterprise, this uniqueness can be understood as a whole. Therefore, value-based risk management takes into account the individual; this unique approach to value-based management is a critical aspect of management and strategy.

Management is based on decision-making. Enterprises operate on a daily basis by making decisions and implementing these decisions at both the managerial and individual levels. Executives' decisions are influenced by both the corporate culture and the belief system within the corporate culture. For this reason, decisions are actually resulting from the main ingredients of an organization such as ethical standards, corporate culture, corporate strategy, and risk management.

Equation

$$\boldsymbol{F(Managerial\ decision) = (individual\ values)x + (corporate\ values)y}$$

Values have such a critical role that managers' decisions are influenced by both the corporate culture and the belief system within the culture. In other words, the decisions taken by the managers are the sum of own values and corporate values. Managers reflect own values in their administrative decisions. It is very important that the manager's values are compatible with the organization's values for the optimum performance of the manager. Therefore, values should be taken into consideration as one of the main criteria for selecting managers and personnel in terms of human resources management.

In our view, gap analysis between corporate values and manager values and personnel values should be an important part of the enterprise risk management system. Because values are determinative factors to both high corporate performance and successful risk management practices, the values of the managers and institutions should overlap; manager, employee, and institution values should be compatible with each other.

In order to capture cultural integrity in business, we need common values. As such, values are also vital for corporate sustainability.

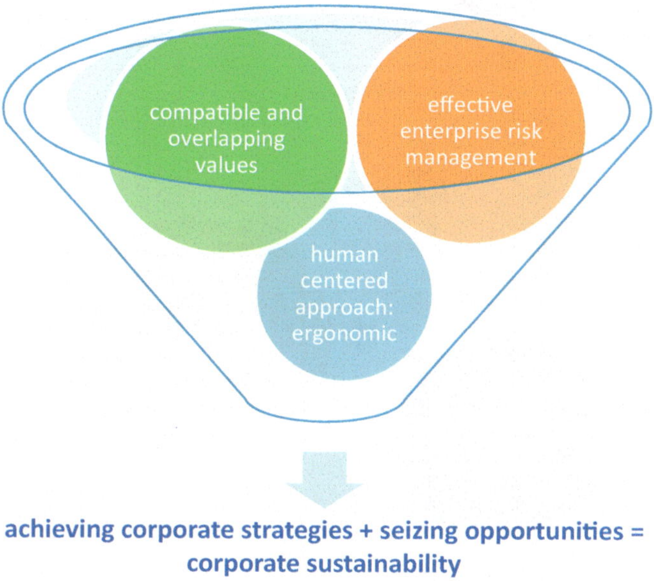

Values play roles in relationship with stakeholders. Decisions are influenced by the manager's point of view and values. Managers usually make decisions under risk and uncertainty. Strategic decision-making process includes the following steps which include multi-criteria decision-making as:

- Identification of corporate objectives,
- assessment and evaluation of alternatives,
- decision-making,
- handling and select options,
- and monitoring (control).

Why Individual Values with Organizational Values are a Risk?

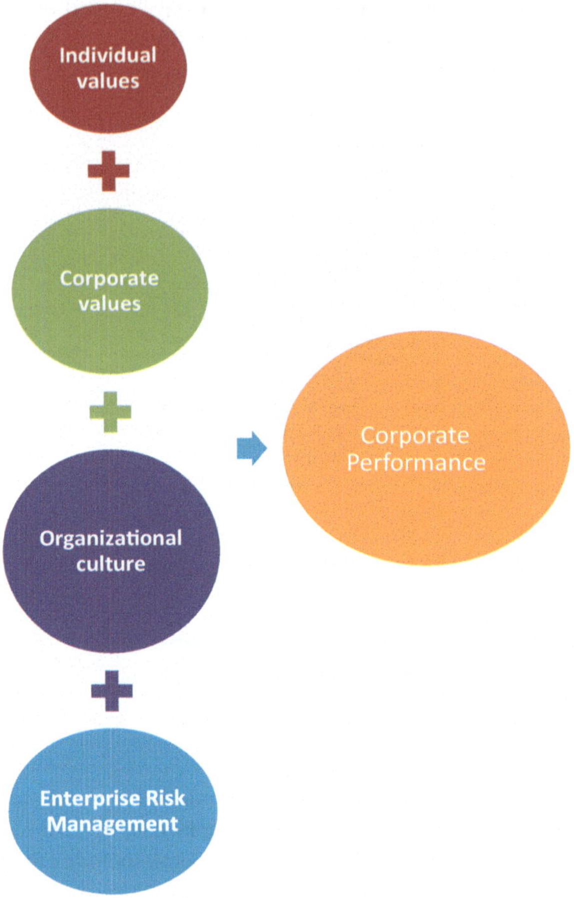

We assumed that corporate performance is comprised of a total of both individual values, corporate values, organizational culture and enterprise risk management.

Values are the source of individual behavior. Values present key points in understanding individual behavior. When managers know the perceptions, motivation, and attitudes of their employees they may understand the holistic value system of them. Values are risks that have a considerable impact on both achieve corporate strategy and related objectives.

Values are determinative in terms of behaviors, both individual and organizational, which means that managerial values are a combination of the two. The harmonization of organizational values and individual values plays an important role in ensuring the integrity in terms of management.

In this book, we are exploring answers to the following questions:

- *"What is the impact of Humanistic Values of Contemporary Management and Strategy?"*
- *"What is the impact of both individual situational awareness of managers and organizational culture on risk management and strategy in Aviation Business?"*
- *"Why international businesses should consider organizational and individual values management?"*

In answering the above research question the book will focus on the following topics:

i. Discussion of the effect on values on both organizational behavior and managerial behavior
ii. Discussion of the vitality of enterprise risk management to both organizational behavior
iii. Discussion ergonomics concept in aviation management and strategy
iv. Discussion **Multi-criteria Decision-making** in the business environment in Aviation
v. Meaning of the **Situational Awareness (SA)** concept in aviation management and strategy
vi. Discussion of the vitality of crisis management to both values and organizational behavior.

The book's main purpose is to present the vital ingredients of contemporary management and strategy in the view of the concept of values, ergonomics, corporate culture, organizational behavior, enterprise risk management, and crisis management. This concept actually is a fundamental part of the management and strategy puzzle. If managers want to achieve their sustainability-based aims via succeeding corporate strategies, they must set a holistic management system based on both enterprise risk management and ergonomics and values.

We make decisions every day since life requires us to constantly make a choice to survive. Decision-making is a routine but also a vital part of managers' daily routine. Especially in aviation, the decision may create considerable results owing to industry-related qualifications with high operational costs. Decisions should be made both carefully and thoughtfully, from the risk management perspective. To manage risk holistically and in a way to support sustainability, we must optimally link SA with decision-making in aviation. Correct and timely decisions produce strategies that help achieve business sustainability.

In this book, we deal with the Meaning of Situational Awareness SA concept in aviation management and strategy. Situational Awareness SA is not only vital to the operational side of aviation such as pilot, ATC, AMT but also has considerable critical importance to managers. To manage both systematically and holistically, managers have to catch optimization in their SA process with decision-making integration. Situational Awareness is not performance; meaning, it should not be understood as performance.

During the analysis of corporate performance, managers should not use the level of SA to evaluate both their managerial and individual performance. But improved situational awareness of managers may support corporate performance and for this reason, SA has an important place in decision-making, and a high level of situational awareness cannot give absolute assurance to high performance in both ergonomics and management.

This book aims to contribute to corporate performance sustainability in aviation by considering a paradigm of enterprise risk management. To achieve this aim, we have embraced an ergonomics-based value-based approach.

- Our approach will raise the awareness level related to organizational behavior and culture as regards enterprise risk management.
- Our holistic approach contributes to the field of management and strategy.
- Managers will gain insight into enterprise risk management in business.
- Managers will gain opportunities to improve their competitive advantage via focusing values at both individual and organizational levels.
- Managers will understand the vital role of ergonomics in their own sustainability.
- Managers may be identifying their situational awareness level in the decision-making process.
- Managers may seize the opportunity to improve their level of situational awareness owing to this book.
- Readers will gain insight into all aspects of enterprise risk management via a contemporary approach.
- Managers will become aware that choices depend on our values, and managerial decision-making, therefore, depends strongly on values.

In terms of corporate risk management, risks have the potential of affecting each other known as "interrelations". This effect may be in the form of triggering or damping of risks. Risk analysis without considering the integrated effect is not sufficient.

Value-based enterprise risk management is crucial for businesses operating in a highly volatile, unstable environment. Because today, the basis of the strategy involves ethical standards and values, basic principles of the management and strategy fields. Value-based Enterprise Risk Management provides reasonable assurance for a timely interpretation of all corporate risks. it offers the possibility of transforming risk events from a threat into opportunity or advantage within the value frame.

Our aim is to integrate the relationship between management style and understanding and internalization with contingency and values and present a new and integrated management and strategy approach.

The writing process of the book is designed in accordance with the value-based risk management philosophy. We have prepared our book by interpreting our individual experience, educational background, personality trait, and contingency approach.

Culture, values, the past, and even personality traits are fully involved in a business. By integrating the culture, risk appetite and risk tolerance in the enterprise management and strategy with a holistic approach, the development, and implementation of the organization-specific risk management system is the first of the key points.

We believe that the value-based approach is both necessary and indispensable for the decision-making process which means making a selection, a choice, based on their values. Each choice requires the management of different risks. This is the basic perspective of this book. We hope that our book will create value in both individual and managerial terms, and that it may contribute to readers' approach to life. Life is already value-based risk management, more aware of all of us we wish more informed and pleasant in our management process.

Organization of the Book

Chapter 1 presents the importance of values that provide a reference to the daily actions and decisions taken by managers. To sustain a business, managers should consider both organizational culture and behavior as risks in their decision-making process in addition to individual values which are a vital risk to the shaping of managerial behavior. Additionally, Chap. 1 discusses organizational values and culture which have a considerable impact on managerial behavior, attitude, and the decision-making process in a multi-business environment.

The contents of the first chapter include Organizational Behavior and Values; Models of Human Relationships; Importance of Managerial and Organizational Psychology; Human Resources Model; Human Resources Development Model; Organizational Culture Models and Humanistic Values of Contemporary Management Theory. Also, in this first chapter, the purpose is to determine what the values are that provide a reference to the daily actions and decisions of the managers.

In Chap. 2, the concept of ergonomics is presented. Human factors are a key element of any business. For effective management, managers should put ergonomics as a top priority in their management agenda.

In Chap. 3, the enterprise risk management concept is presented. The aim of this chapter is to provide both a guideline and a contribution to the literature in support of increasing the level of awareness of enterprise risk management in aviation companies. Due to the sectoral dynamics, the high level of variability and the interest of stakeholders in aviation, the severity of crisis impacts on businesses can be different and of a high level. A crisis that has taken place in any part of the world due to the influence of globalization can directly or indirectly affect the operations of airlines. For this reason, business concerns develop defense mechanisms for institutional sustainability in a sense within institutional strategies for crisis and risk sources. With the development of ERM (Enterprise Risk Management), business concerns have begun to look at risks not only in terms of threats but also in terms of opportunities. Enterprise risk management has a positive impact on corporate value and performance, and it is anticipated that the crisis-specific and risk management systems that are established for the organization play a critical role in achieving corporate strategic objectives.

In Chap. 4, situational awareness has been considered as one of the vital managerial qualifications. To manage, the individual must have a high level of awareness of both the internal and external business environment.

In Chap. 5, decision-making with multi-criteria is presented in view of aviation business management. The decision as a concept of business management and strategy means to choose from different options. The core of management is decision-making. Situational Awareness impacts the performance of both effective and timely decision-making. The values individuals played a crucial role in the decision-making process as decision-making is an essential tenet of both business and personal life. Instantaneous and variable situations in the aviation business are effective in decision-making.

In Chap. 6, strong and well-designed strategies are essential to doing business globally and in a sustainable way. The well-designed and high-performance risk management system presents opportunities to add value to both stakeholders and policyholders while minimizing corporate threats.

The global competition and restructuring pressures not only increase institutional risks but also have implications for management and the organizational structure. Potential events are included within the scope of risk management. Uncertainty and risk are directly proportional, and as the uncertainty increases, the likelihood of the risk occurring increases. While uncertainty includes both negative and positive components, the negative component of uncertainty is a risk and the positive component is an opportunity. But the concepts of risk and uncertainty also have intertwined common features. In order to determine whether an event is a risk or not, the source and the effects of that event must be determined using the right tools and techniques.

Strategic Risk Mapping

In business, defining the most efficient techniques for enterprise risk detection, using and categorizing them under certain groups within the management of defined risks is the main purpose of this stage.

All professional aviators such as pilots, air traffic controllers, technicians, etc. in civil aviaiton system is a key risk source (as both threat and opportunity) in air transportation. Thus errors made by aviators could cause aircraft accidents or incidents or near-miss incidents. In the model that we present in this chapter, human error risks are first categorized into eight groups and then prioritized using the risk matrix. Risk mapping is established to decide which risk management option managers will apply when looking at this map. Managers may use this new risk map to both identify their managerial priorities, share resources to managing and achieve optimal decision-making outcomes on risk handling options.

In Chap. 7, crisis issues are explained. This chapter presents the meaning of crises in the aviation sector. Crisis management is one of these defense mechanisms. Crises management systems and their practices in seven different airline companies operating in different business models are examined. The awareness of businesses in this regard has been researched. Interviews with senior executives of the enterprises were conducted using the semi-structured interview technique. Effective use of resources, seizing opportunities in crises times may be possible with well-designed crises management system. For this reason, business concerns both the performance level of the crises management system and also improving the awareness level of the crisis. Being aware of this nature of businesses, as intended through this study, could also affect their paradigms of crisis and enterprise risk management systems.

Eskişehir, Turkey
Manchester, USA
October 2019

Ayse Kucuk Yilmaz
Triant G. Flouris

Contents

About the Authors

Drs. Kucuk Yilmaz and Flouris have worked together for 13 years, publishing books and articles together. They continue to work on new projects in both aviation the management and strategy field and in enterprise risk management.

Ayse Kucuk Yilmaz (Ph.D. Eskisehir Tecnical University) is Associate Professor in the Faculty of Aeronautics and Astronautics. (*Previously a part of Anadolu University, The Faculty of Aeronautics and Astronautics became a part of the newly established Eskisehir Technical University by Law no. 7141 that was published in the Official Gazette dated May 18, 2018, and numbered 30425*).

Dr. Kucuk Yilmaz's area of expertise is Management and Strategy. Her research interests include enterprise risk management, sustainability risk management, aviation management, international business, multi-criteria problem-solving, decision-making, ergonomics, quality, and strategic management.

Dr. Kucuk Yilmaz is the Airport Business Manager of Hasan Polatkan Airport since Feb 01, 2015. Also, She is Vice Dean responsiblefor operational departments such as Airport, ATC, ATO, AMC. She has authored 11 books, 5 book chapters, and has published numerous academic journal articles in both SCI, ESCI, and indexed journals. She serves as Editor in peer-refereed international journals. She is also a licensed aircraft maintenance technician.

Triant G. Flouris (Ph.D. University of South Carolina) is Provost at Hellenic American University since 2010. Dr. Flouris has served in various faculty and administrative positions (graduate program director, department chair, as well as research institute director) in universities in New Zealand, US, and Canada and has extensive experience in strategic planning and higher education administration. He is the author of 8 books, over 200 refereed journal articles, book chapters, scholarly articles, and public reports. He is a certified professional pilot and flight instructor and holds concurrent appointments as a research associate at the Mineta Transportation Institute, San Jose State University, California, as well as an instructor for the International Air Transport Association. His research interests include project management, sustainability risk management, aviation management, international aviation policy, and strategic management. He is a Commercial Pilot and Certified Flight and Ground Instructor with over 8000 hours of total flight time.

Chapter 1
Organizational Values and Culture: The Management and Organization Psychology

Contents

This chapter aims to form a detailed framework on the importance of values. With this respect, primarily, the theories related to the concept are defined and the values in these theories are stated.

Management Theories and Research

Organizational behavior is a discipline that comprises the study of human behaviors in the organization focused on three levels, individual, group, and organization. (Robbins 1997, p. 2). In the study, primarily, how the organizational behavior showed up (Sargut 2001, p. 23), which development processes it went through, and which contexts supported this development will be presented. As stated by Aycan et al. (2016, p. 21) in order to be ahead in the global arena, cultural context must be taken into consideration. In this respect, organizational behavior theories will be evaluated in accordance with the cultural context. Organizations develop throughout a certain historical process. Aycan et al. (2016, p. 21) summarized this development in their studies as in the following:

- Aycan et al. (2016), stated that the first development idea showed up as a result of the opinion "the employees have to feed themselves" and so the employees' basic needs must be met.

A. Kucuk Yilmaz and T. G. Flouris, *Values, Ergonomics and Risk Management in Aviation Business Strategy*, https://doi.org/10.1007/978-981-15-1006-9_1

- Another idea showed up as a result of the opinion "employees have hearts" and they emphasized that to motivate employees their emotions must be appealed to.
- The other idea was based on "employees have brains". It claimed that the employees' participation in the strategic decisions of the organization will help the organization to attain its goals.
- The last development was based on the opinion "employees have different cultural values, beliefs and behavior patterns", pointing out the fact that these must be taken into consideration to increase the chance of survival in the global competition (Aycan et al. 2016, 21).

Classical Management Theory

"The industrial revolution" that started in England in the second half of the eighteenth century and spread to the other parts of Europe and America is known as an extremely important event with respect to the management idea (Baransel 1993, p. 105). The industrialization, which increased with the industrial revolution, caused the classical management theory that is seeking an increase of the organization's efficiency and productivity to start and the human troubles to emerge (Eren 2007, p. 10). Classical management theory can be explained with three different opinions. These are scientific management understanding, management theory, and bureaucracy model (Heyel 1965, p. 25; Ceylan 2014, p. 12).

Scientific Management

The first idea of classical management theory was Taylorism. The idea of Taylorism belongs to Frederick Winslow Taylor, the leader of this idea. (Eren 2003, pp. 19–20; Aycan et al. 2016, p. 21). It started with Taylor who was interested in behavior in management subjects and his scientific management movement (Yozgat 1978, p. 22; Eren 2003, pp. 19–20; Koçel 2014, pp. 270, 239; Özkalp and Kırel 2016, p. 27). Some of the problems that Taylor observed in the working areas include unproductivity, the absence of the working standards, errors in choosing the employees, and the absence of the duty consciousness (Ceylan 2014, p. 12; Özkalp and Kırel 2016, p. 28).

These deficiencies damage a business in two ways:

- Waste of energy and time because the employee performs a series of activities that are not necessary for the business;
- The decline in productivity as a result of the employee's leaving the job after completing his working time (Birdal and Aydemir 1992, p. 17).

Taylor, moving in accordance with the idea, "the workers have to feed themselves", as Aycan et al. (2016, p. 24) explained, gave place to some principles such as what a work system and work behaviors are. The interest the scientific management approach has for the human factor since a person's performance is one of the considerable variables which have affects on power of produce (Sargut 2001, p. 45; Koçel 2014, pp. 270, 241). That study, specifically, comprises the worker's capacity, that means productive working potential, needed time to achieve a duty, strength for the individual's muscle force (Kelly 1975, p. 11; Rush 1976, p. 14; Northcraft and Neale 1990, p. 41; Eren 2007, pp. 19–20; Taylor 2013, p. 20).

In scientific management, the most outstanding feature is the "duty" idea. The work that all the workers will do are planned by the management completely at least one day before and the written directions that explain the details of the work and the tools to use are handed out. This duty comprises not only what must be done, but also how and how long it must last. In Taylor's model, the director acts as a coordinator, and since the belief is that people are only motivated by money, it has developed a price-rate pay system (Taylor 2013, p. 38). Within a production system close to the rationality and interaction with the environment, an effective production system is carried out according to the rules (Eren 2003, p. 20). What makes scientific management more productive than the old plan is bringing the worker's effort and the management's new role together (Taylor 2013, p. 40).

As a result, there are some principles of scientific management. These are as follows:

- Choosing the employee carefully.
- Motivating and educating the employee.
- Helping the employee to work in coordination with the scientific methods (Taylor 2013, p. 55).

The criticism of the scientific approach is that in this period, nonhuman factors are focused on (Sabuncuoğlu and Vergiliel Tüz 2013, pp. 12–13; Özkalp and Kırel 2016, p. 28).

Management Theory

After Taylor, the French engineer, Fayol (1949) suggested a management theory by developing a number of management rules and techniques in his book entitled: "General and Industrial Management (Sargut 2001, p. 45). Fayol, especially, focused on how organizations will be managed and divided the management process into five sections: planning (Fayol 1949, p. 43), organizing (Fayol 1949, p. 53), direction (Fayol 1949, p. 97), coordination (Fayol 1949, p. 103), and control (Fayol 1949, p. 107).

The difference of this idea from the scientific management idea is that while Taylor developed methods like the efficiency of the simple works at the worker level (Eren 2007, p. 13), Fayol developed methods for the people at top levels (Birdal and Aydemir 1992, p. 18). As the principles of Taylorism, the principles Fayol put forward for the management and organization area were accepted to a great extent.

Table 1.1 Henri Fayol's principles of management (Fayol 1949, pp. 19–20)

Structure principles	Process principles	Result principles
• Division of work • Unit of direction • Centralization • Authority • Scalar chain	• Unit of command • Discipline • Equity • Remuneration • Subordination of individual interests to the general interest	• Order • Stability of tenure of personnel • Initiative • Esprit de corps

Management activities constitute the fundamental focal point of Fayol's studies (Eren 2007, p. 15). Fayol defined 14 management principles as the process, organization's structure, and the result (Kaynak 1995, pp. 13–18) (Table 1.1).

The first part of these principles is related to the structural principles and comprises the factors about how the work will be done. Process principles explain the necessary principles of the work's process. Finally, the principles after the result of the work done are obtained are explained in the principles of the results section (Fayol 1949, pp. 20–40).

Bureaucracy Model

This approach was developed by Max Weber, a German sociologist, and an economist in the early 1900s (Birdal and Aydemir 1992, p. 21). Weber, who focused on organization and management style pointed out that a bureaucratic structure is ideal for efficiency and signified the features of the bureaucratic organization's structure as in the following (Weber 1947, p. 329):

- Goals and targets are stated clearly and accurately.
- The employees of the organization are equipped with authority in a certain way by giving necessary orders.
- Demanding methods are determined, by identifying the qualification and the price of the work the employees are appointed according to their level.
- Expectations of the employees working at each level depending on their levels and their topic.

Man is chosen according to the work.

- Each position is defined by a superior position.
- The subordinates must obey their superiors.
- In a hierarchy, relationships of the units are written.

Bureaucracy model has a number of rules such as founding a strong organizational structure, making people responsible for fulfilling certain duties of this structure as experts in their fields, establishing an objective and realistic management system, and determining the directors to manage the business with a democratic election according to their abilities and experiences (Weber 1947, p. 330). Since this theory ignored human psychology and behavior as well as the emotional side of management, it was exposed to criticism and helped for management psychology to rise (Eren 2007, p. 19; Ceylan 2014, p. 15).

The philosophy of the management theory and the bureaucracy model resemble each other with respect to the formulation of the ideas related to management. Nevertheless, there are various differences between these two models. Although management theorists take care of all the stages of the management activities and behave in a flexible way, in this case, in the bureaucracy model, taking care of the organization and impersonal strict rules and standards were developed. Management theorists try to develop some general principles for individual efficient management (Cole 2004, p. 4). According to Ceylan, although the bureaucratic model defenders are aware of the human factor, they were not able to be efficient enough in dealing with human troubles. They didn't take informal organizational structures into consideration; therefore, they were inefficient in solving the problems (Ceylan 2014, p. 15).

Human-Related Values of the Classical Management Theory

Kara (2011, pp. 89–90), stated the human-related values of the classical management theory as in the following:

- People behave rationally giving particular importance to their economic benefits.
- Since people are lazy by birth and don't like working, they have to be directed with strict supervision.
- People work for their economic benefits. Therefore, when the economic rewards are associated with success, they exert all their efforts and abilities.
- An average employee needs to be directed by others.
- Occupational safety has more importance than decision-making and behaving freely at work for an employer.
- People like simple and ordinary tasks. If a person is employed with occupational standards defined in accordance with a normal person's ability, they not only get efficiency but also it can be changed with something else if needed. That the work must be done is more important and privileged than everything.
- People have importance with respect to the work they do and the contributions they make to the organizations.
- Management troubles are caused by the supervision's failure, failing to associate the price and the rewards with success and inconsistency of the managers.

The organizational values of the classical management theory are as follows (Kara 2011, p. 91):

- Boosting the organization's efficiency, which is completely a technical problem depends on using only the limited resources in the most economical way.

- Systematizing the work to be done in the organization makes the employees more productive.
- Being prepared to get informed of the long-term plans rather than the short-term plans is necessary.
- Management must focus on the problems related to the work, ignoring human behaviors.
- In boosting management efficiency, the employees' specializing is of high importance.
- The decision-making authority must be gathered in top management. The top manager can transfer some of this authority to the directors at lower levels if necessary.
- Management activities must be implemented in accordance with the scientific principles regardless of the human and environmental factors.

Research that Reveal the Importance of the Management and Organization Psychology

Ignoring the human condition comes at the top of the criticisms given for the classical management theory (Koçel 2014, p. 270; Özkalp and Kırel 2016, p. 30). After that, ideas that approach these theories with criticisms have shown up and the research conducted to eliminate these deficiencies are mentioned in this part.

Leadership Research

In this research, the leadership styles of the children and the effects of them on their group relationships and organization's productivity were studied (Baransel 1993, p. 265). Lewin et al. conducted studies in which they tried to determine the leadership styles of children ages 10 or 11. A person who had the first type of leadership had a dominant manner toward his subordinates. While some of the group members obeyed the leader, some didn't like the orders and wanted extra information. In this group, the productivity level was high but the quality of the output (mask) was poor. The person who had the second type of leadership had a flexible manner and gave the others the chance to make masks as they wished.

The group members who couldn't get detailed information made poor quality masks. That the leader couldn't socialize with the group was stated as the reason for it. The person who had the third type of leadership approached his subordinates in a democratic and participating manner. He directed the group members, exchanged information, and wanted them to make masks by getting feedback from them. Within the members of this group, an emotional bond was seen. It was observed that productivity was good in this group, but less than the first one. But the masks produced were at the highest level of quality. The aim of this study is to reveal the fact that humanly behaviors and emotions are important for management (Eren 2007, p. 20).

Hawthorne Researches

A movement that focuses on human factors in the businesses, doesn't consider the organizations as "a machine which operates full time" and claims that the organizations have a structure based on the human factor in addition to the technical and financial factors that emerged (Koçel 2014, p. 273). This movement was called "Human Relations Approach" at first; afterward, since it didn't handle the Classical Theory in detail but gave importance to the human factor, it was called supplementary of the Classical theory in a sense. The most important results of these studies are that instead of the "economic human" concept, a "social human" concept showed up (Aycan et al. 2016, p. 24). Since this new approach is focused on human behaviors, today, it is called Behavioral Management and Organization Theory/Organizational Behavior (Kaynak 1995, p. 7; Koçel 2014, pp. 270, 273).

Between 1927 and 1932, in the Hawthorne facility of the Western Electricity Company, in the USA, a research study that went on for years was carried out on a great number of workers by Mayo et al. (Mayo 1960, p. 55; Rush 1976, pp. 13–14; Northcraft and Neale 1990, p. 45). These studies, known as Hawthorne studies, were determined to be important for the rise of the study of Organizational Behavior. These experiments were organized in groups as follows: illumination experiment, relay assembly test experiments, relay assembly room 2, mica splitting test group, plant interview group, and bank wiring observation group (Baransel 1993, p. 237). At the end of the study, it was observed that no matter how much the mentioned factors are improved, the productivity doesn't increase and even when no improvement is made the productivity increases (Mayo 1960, pp. 53–73).

Therefore, the researchers searched for human factors such as the workers' motivation, satisfaction, and their relationships with each other among others. It revealed that productivity is not only related to physical factors but also social behaviors (Birdal and Aydemir 1992, p. 22). The Hawthorne studies questioned the validity of some basic hypothesis that constitutes the basis of the scientific management approaches for the first time. Since the 1930s, this approach suggested that management must take the aim, wish, and needs of the working individual and groups into consideration, and as long as these are paid attention to, the organization productivity and efficiency will be ensured (Eren 2003, p. 20; Koçel 2014, p. 275; Özkalp and Kırel 2016, pp. 32–33).

Yankee City Research

This research was carried out by the social anthropologist W. L. Warner to study the effects of the technological changes and innovations on people and their relationships. The workers' being members of a trade union urged the researcher to study this case (Baransel 1993, p. 275). Mechanization in shoe production brought the technical ability hierarchy to a standstill and changed the dependence of the ability on age to a great extent. The workers, who were qualified before, turning into semiskilled laborers after technical changes, caused differences between the workers (Baransel 1993, p. 275).

With an increase in the technology used in the production process, it increased the need for different investments and these different partnerships affected the working relationships in the factory (Baransel 1993, p. 275; Eren 2007, pp. 22–23). This study shows that the developments in the social and technological systems can cause changes in the workers' behavior and manners. It was stated that the human factor and its prestige, and statue and relationships in society must be taken into consideration in such changes (Eren 2007, pp. 22–23).

Harwood Manufacturing Operations Survey

Harwood Manufacturing Corporation specializes in pajama manufacturing. Baransel stated that the biggest problem of this establishment is the frequent model changes. The emergence of this problem is that these changes have negative effects on the workers. Among these negative effects, the workers being late for work, an increase in the discontinuity, and an increase in the transfer of the labor are signified (Baransel 1993, p. 276).

In order to prevent this problem, the negativities were tried to be eliminated by implementing three different methods in three different groups. In the first group, no change was made and after the model change, a decline in production was seen and the production didn't turn back to its former level (Eren 2007, p. 25).

In the second group, the employees joined in the decisions and while a decrease in production was seen at first as a result of the model change, it turned back to its former level in a short time. In the last group, the employees completely joined management. Although production decreased at first, in a very short time, it turned back to its former level. In addition to the fact that there were no complaints, it was seen that the employees' manners toward their managers improved. The study showed that when the same employees at the same business are made to work with different management styles, different satisfaction levels form (Eren 2007, pp. 23–25).

Tavistock Institute Research

How miners working in coal mines in England were affected by changes in tools, equipment, and production methods used was investigated by Trist and Bamforth. The small groups worked as rivals following a method known as "short wall" and then changed to a method called "long wall" (Trist and Bamforth 1951). In the long wall method, the workers had to be together with their rivals. Besides, their decision-making flexibility was taken from them, and they were made to work for the machine-bound mass production. It decreased the workforce productivity of the employees who suffered from the monotony and emotional dissatisfaction owing to their working method, and this situation affected the organizational efficiency negatively (Baransel 1993, p. 278; Eren 2007, p. 25; Koçel 2014, p. 347).

Human-Related Values of the Neo-Classic Management Theory

Kara (2011, p. 99) stated the human-related values of neo-classic management as in the following:

- Making an effort is natural for an individual. No antipathy arises by birth.
- Force and sanctions are not successful in getting an individual to move.
- Setting to work to attain a goal depends on the expected reward. Satisfying the ego and the social conditions by attaining this success is the most effective reward.
- Creative ability to solve organizational problems is more prevalent than thought. The important thing is to create an environment in which creativity can be developed.
- If there is a suitable atmosphere, an individual not only accepts his responsibilities but also looks for such responsibilities.
- The productivity of an employee doesn't depend on their physical but rather their social efficiency.
- Nonmonetary rewards and sanctions affect the employees' manners and behavior more than monetary ones.
- Employees generally don't act as an individual but as a member of a group.

Organization related values of the Neo-classic management theory are as follows (Kara 2011, p. 100):

- There is no difference between formal and informal leadership.
- It is important that the employees participate in the decisions that concern them directly.
- It is important to explain employee behaviors and to have communication in general.

- There are outstanding benefits of the democratic leaders who make cooperation attractive, give importance to humanly troubles, are respectful to the rights, and provide impartial management.
- A person acts not only with his biological but also sociological and psychological sides. A manager must take into consideration the many facets of employees.
- For the employees, a duty has meaning. An employee must be expected to make decisions besides developing competence at work.

Some Theoretical Ideas that Form the Basis of the Management and Organization Psychology

X and Y Theories

Douglas discussed both X theories and then Y theories effecting critique on X theories. With reference to the study carried out by Eren (2015), the hypothesis of Douglas' X and Y theories are given below. With this theory, new ideas that the human factor shouldn't be ignored were suggested and these ideas were not developed without mentioning the principles of Y theory (Özkalp and Kırel 2016, p. 34) (Table 1.2).

Table 1.2 Mc Gregor Theory X–Y (Douglas 1960, pp. 33–47)

Theory X
• The average person dislikes work and will avoid it if he/she can
• Therefore most people must be forced with the threat of punishment to work towards organisational objectives
• The average person prefers to be directed, to avoid responsibility, is relatively unambitious, and wants security above all else
Theory Y
• Effort in work is as natural as work and play
• People will apply self-control and self-direction in the pursuit of organisational objectives, without external control or the threat of punishment
• Commitment to objectives is a function of rewards associated with their achievement
• People usually accept and often seek responsibility
• The capacity to use a high degree of imagination, ingenuity and creativity in solving organisational problems is widely, not narrowly, distributed in the population
• In industry the intellectual potential of the average person is only partly utilised

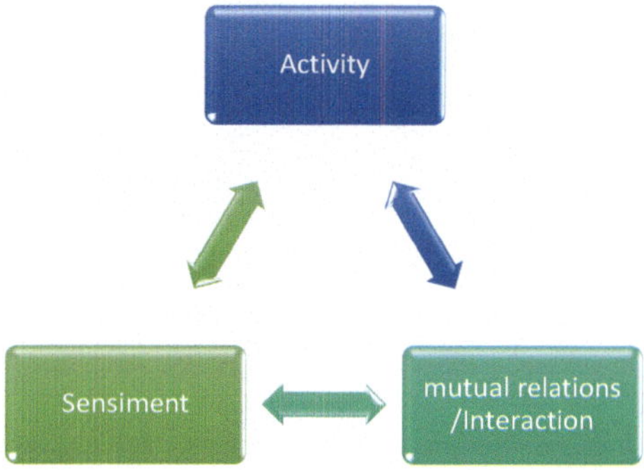

Fig. 1.1 Homans's social behavior (Homans 1950, p. 104)

Human Group Factor

George C. Homans is another researcher who focuses on human groups (Eren 2015). Homans pointed out in his research, Human Group, that organization managers fear informal, powerful groups. Through psychological analysis, Homan conducted research on the reasons for the interdependency of the workgroups and developed a social model consisting of three factors focusing on emotions and social relationships (Homans 1950, p. 104) (Fig. 1.1).

According to Homan's model, in order to talk about a social organization, there occurs an affinity with respect to the activities the individuals of the organization do, the relationships they establish while carrying out these activities and the individuals' emotions in this process. Homan stated that, the group members will develop certain norms and expectations regarding how to behave in certain situations when there is a balance, and when the interdependence of the group reaches an adequate level, there will be a decline in the group members' wish for leaving the group (Homans 1950, p. 107).

Maturity Theory

According to the Mature and Immature Person Model by Chris Argyris, as people develop, they change from having an immature person's characteristics into having those of a mature person (Koçel 2014, p. 280). This model's features are as follows (Fig. 1.2).

According to Argyris, boosting the person's responsibility area matures a person more. So, the person must be given the chance to do activities beneficial for himself and the business (Argyris 1957, p. 66).

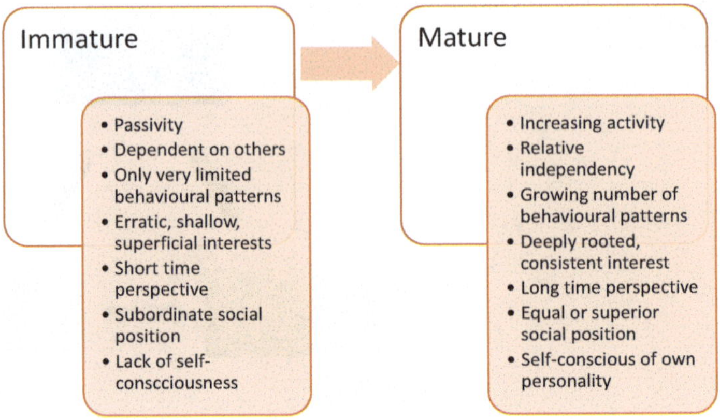

Fig. 1.2 Chris Argyris's model of maturity (Koçel 2014, p. 281)

Human Needs Theory

Maslow observed people's behaviors in the business. He searched why employees work at a business and how they obey in accordance with the orders of the other people. At the end of his studies, he revealed that people, as a biological, social, and psychological beings, act in this way as a result of some needs (Maslow 1954, p. 35). These needs are physiological, safety, belongings, love, esteem needs, and self-actualization (Fig. 1.3).

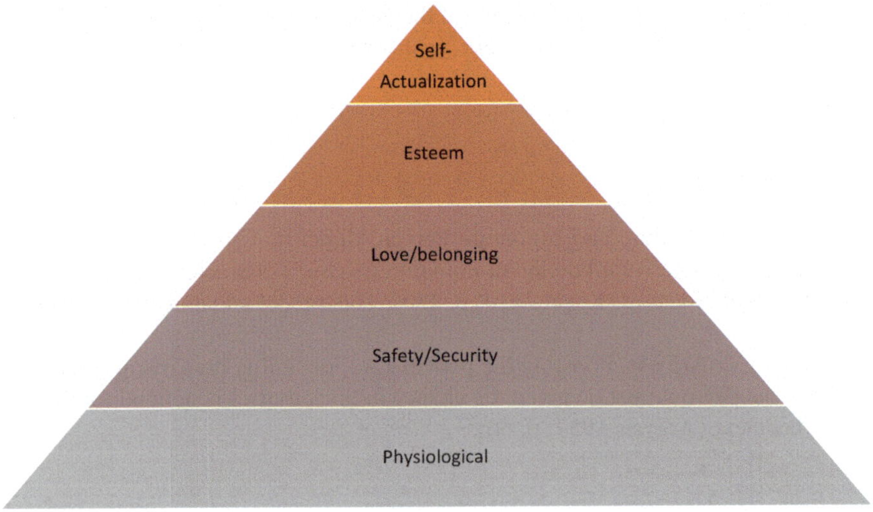

Fig. 1.3 Maslow's hierarchy of needs (Maslow 1954)

Two-Factor (Motivators-Hygiene) Theory

At the end of the studies carried out by Herzberg et al., the workplace conditions to make people work efficiently and productively were revealed (Herzberg et al. 1959, p. 11). They determined the conditions of working efficiently and productively studied the effects of hygiene and motivators on employees. Hygiene conditions are general business policy and management, the technical knowledge and skill of the closest manager, the relationship between the directors and the subordinates, wage, and salary conditions, physical working conditions, and occupational safety.

Motivators include completing the work and feeling satisfied with the success, being well-known at the business, loving work, gaining authority, and responsibility, gaining social status, and improving oneself in terms of work. It was revealed that providing only hygiene conditions is not enough and that motivators must also be provided to employees (Herzberg et al. 1959, pp. 113–119).

Rensis Likert's Management Systems Approach

Likert and his friends carried out research on the factors needed for the efficient management of human and capital sources. As a result, they developed organizational change programs. According to Likert et al., while the losses in the capital sources can be cleared easily, the losses in human resources cannot be cleared easily (Likert 1967, p. 258). Developed organizational change programs directed the organizations to help pass from X theory to Y theory (Eren 2007, p. 35) (Fig. 1.4).

Kurt Lewin's Force Field Analysis

Force field analysis is an approach to understanding group behavior by providing the evaluation and discussion of a planned change and a list of the various powers against this change (Burnes 2004, p. 981). Analyzing all the forces that affect the change, weighing its advantages and disadvantages help to look at the big picture (Raven 1999, p. 164; Lewin 2007). In order to minimize and support the effects of the determined forces, certain strategies can be developed (HTTP-1). The basic premise of the directors who want to try to understand the organization and balance these powers is behavioral sciences and psychology (Lewin 1945, pp. 27–129). There are two types of forces in an organization: motivators and restrictive forces (Fig. 1.5).

Lewin stated that, in order to reach balance, the total number of the motivators must be equal to the total number of the restrictive forces (Lewin 1951).

Blake and Mouton's Management Styles

Blake and Mouton developed a management styles model called Managerial Grid and used it in explaining managers' behaviors. This model comprises the efficient

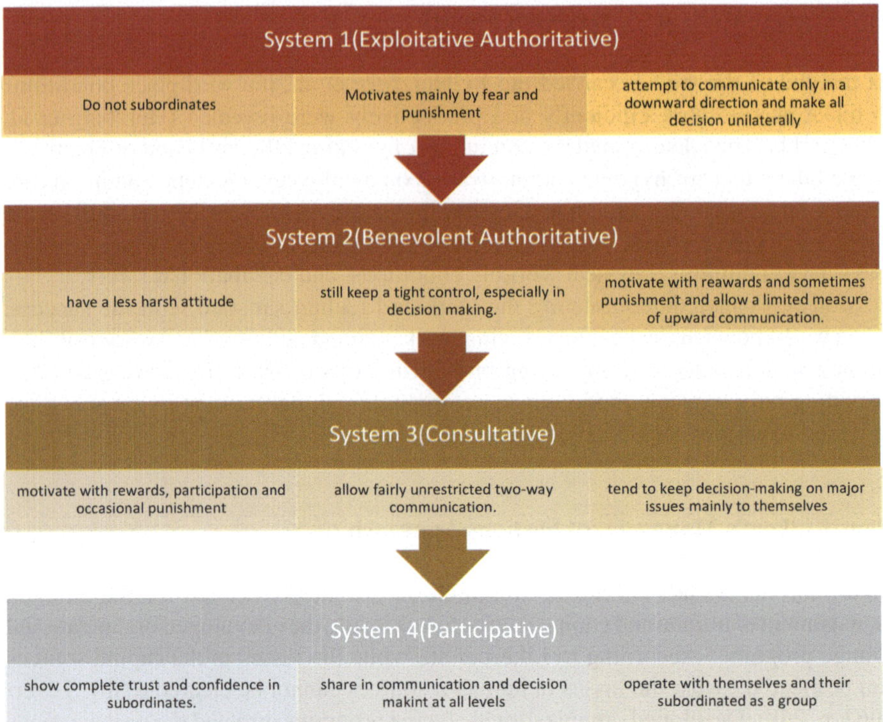

Fig. 1.4 Likert system 1–4 model (Koçel 2014, p. 684)

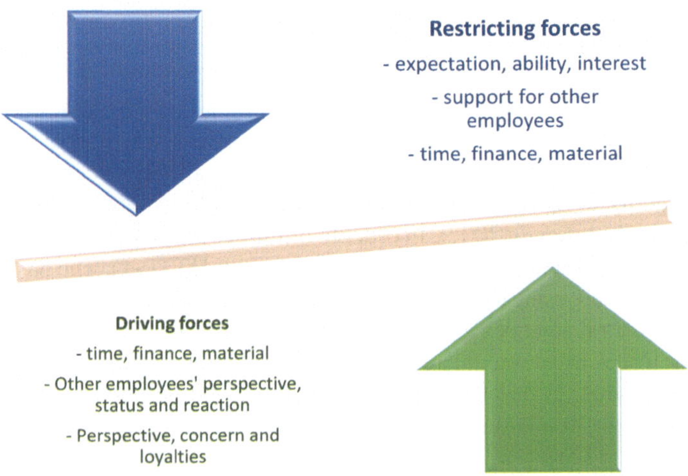

Fig. 1.5 Kurt Lewin's force field analysis (HTTP-2)

and productive use of a human source which is the factor that provides a competitive advantage for the organization. In the grid, production and human orientation are important in understanding management style (Blake and Mouton 1985, p. 11). The manager explaining himself/putting himself into somewhere on the grid is based on the ideals that provide him to manage the results, beliefs, and values (Blake and Mouton 1985, p. 14) (Fig. 1.6).

In this model, the first aspect that was given attention to is the human orientation in the manager's behavior and the second is production orientation. The benefit of the managerial grid is that it provides the determination of the conceptual background. Since it defines all the important approaches, it is extensive. The managerial grid lets us evaluate each leadership type's results in terms of satisfaction, career success, creativity, and productivity. Therefore, the managerial grid that defines the management styles is used in explaining the managerial behaviors and it shows that the leaders' values affect the management style (Blake and Mouton 1985, p. 17).

Second Section

Organizational Culture

When successful management applications are searched (Birdal and Aydemir 1992, p. 41) certain studies appear (Aycan et al. 2016, p. 26). With reference to the foresight that the source of this success is the management applications integrated with the cultural values (Morley and Chen 1996, p. 2), culture, and cultural values are tried to be given place in this part.

Culture

Culture, although it has been defined by many disciplines, comes out as one of the most complicated words in English (Jenks 2001). A working definition of culture was first made by Charles A. Ellwood, who defined culture as a common name used for all behavior patterns taken and transferred socially. Therefore, culture not only comprises the concepts such as language, art, science, law, management, and religion, but also the material means by which the cultural achievements are embodied, as well as buildings, machines, and communication tools by which mental culture features are practiced, or the things made by human hand (Kroeber and Kluckhohn 1952, p. 33; Berger 2011, p. 142). Kroeber and Kluckhohn defined culture as "mind's education, developing and subtilizing, tastes, behavior patterns, and thus the conditions of being educated and refined; intellectual side of civilization" (Kroeber and Kluckhohn 1952, p. 33).

Concern for People	High			
	9 8	1.9 Country Club Management: Thoughtful		9.9 Team Management: Work accomplishments
	7	attention to the needs of the people for satisfying relationships leads to a comfortable friendly organization atmosphere and work tempo.		from committed people; interdependence through a "common stake" in organization; purpose leads to relationships of trust and respect.
	6 5 4		5.5 Middle of the road management: Adequate organization performance is possible through balancing the necessity to get work out while maintaining the morale of people at a satisfactory level.	
	3 2 1	1.1 Impoverished management: Exertion of minimum effort to get required work done is appropriate to sustain organization membership.		9.1 Authority compliance management: Efficiency in operations results from arranging conditions of work in such a way that human elements interfere to a minimum degree.
		1 2 3	4 5 6	7 8 9
	Low			High
	Concern for production			

Fig. 1.6 Managerial grid (Blake and Mouton 1985, p. 12)

Culture, which is composed of many factors such as religion, values, social behavior, and customs, eating and decision-making habits, esthetics, and nationalism; is shortly defined as an integrated system composed of characteristic behavior models of the society members and just like it affects many things within the national boundaries, it affects the management perception and applications deeply, too (Taş and Cevrioğlu 2013, p. 419).

"Culture is everything that a person produces" (Nalçaoğlu 2004, p. 5). According to Bennet (1998, p. 17) "it is applied results, values or the thing that is related to social topics." Ergur (2015, p. 3) defined culture, as the human's skill to think about his existence, symbol producing activity that emerges as a result of changing the nature in accordance with his interpretation of his own existence.

When Gokalp defined culture, he mentioned two meanings and stated them as national culture and reclamation. While national culture is the nation's traditions, customs, oral and written literature, language, music, religion, morals, esthetics, and economic products, reclamation is unique to real highbrows with high education and good manners. It was pointed out that while national culture is national, reclamation is international and that a person gives importance may be just to his nation's culture under the effect of the national culture, but if he had reclamation, he will respect the other nations' cultures as well (Gökalp 1990, pp. 104–105). It is handled as a consistent system composed of basic values that differentiate it from another group with its choices as a unique and unchangeable event (Gagliardi 1990, p. 278).

Similarly with Gokalp's definition, King (1998, p. 17) define culture considered as a feature of people either it is material or symbolic. What differentiates the members of a group or category is the common programming of the minds (Hofstede et al. 2010, p. 6). A group's culture is the basic hypothesis learned by the group members. It is a factor that must be taken care of at the time of solving the adaptation problems inside and the newcomer's adaptation problems (Schein 2010, p. 18). The cultural structure can be defined with values, symbols and norms (Tanase 2015, p. 849). A culture's basic measurable factors are values, norms, beliefs, manners, personal perceptions, cognitive skill, behaviors, and clichés (Minkov 2011, pp. 4–9). According to Öğüt and Kocabacak (2008, p. 147), culture means a society's knowledge, belief, art, morals, traditions, and every type of skills and habits. It was seen that the basic underlying factor of the organizations' failures and successes is based on the culture they have (Yeşil et al. 2016, p. 151).

Organizational Culture

When the definitions of organizational culture are studied, it is seen that they rank from the most general to the most specific, resembling too many culture definitions in anthropology to a great extent (Şişman 2002, p. 82). The organizational culture concept was first suggested by Pettigrew (1979) (Hofstede et al. 1990, p. 286); it is a culture, based on the society's culture, but has different value and norms from this culture, unique to the organization society. Every person develops a value system unique to itself with the cultural values they internalize. From the window of this value system developed, the individual looks around and produces value judgment. For organizational behavior, it is more important to understand what the culture is rather than define it (Başaran 2008, pp. 396–397). Organizational culture is defined as "shared values," (Peters and Waterman 1987; Ülgen and Mirze 2013, p. 418) "a behavior regulator," "style of what is done at the organization," (Deal and Kennedy 1982) "values and ideologies shared by the organization members," (Arogyaswamy and Byles 1987) "a network of meanings comprising value, norm and ideologies," (Trice and Beyer 1984) "a system of the meanings shared in a group at any time," (Pettigrew 1979), and "a system of meanings and symbols shared by the group members" (Robbins 1997; Schein 2010).

Managers use symbols, customs, ceremonies, and stories to reinforce the company's organizational culture (Boone and Kurtz 2013, pp. 235–236). Organizational culture ties the organization's members (Barney 1986, p. 656; Karahan 2008, p. 549). Culture, because of this importance, forms the working area of many sciences such as anthropology, sociology, social psychology, and economy (Mullins 1996, p. 715; Ceylan 2014, p. 132).

Organizational culture is composed of myth, ceremony, and symbols that provide belief, value, and communication between the organization workers (Ouchi 1981, p. 41). Organizational culture symbolizes the complicated and deep side of an organization that will affect the organization members strongly (Hofstede et al. 1990, p. 286). Since organizations are composed of individuals that have different cultural values, these individuals who have come together with functional criteria, are different from the other organizations, but in themselves have relatively more common belief and values system (Eren 2015, p. 135).

Employees help adaptation to the organizational society occur by internalizing the values of the culture that the organization society developed (Thompson 1990, p. 328), and because of the changes in their personality, cause a change in behaviors (Başaran 2008, pp. 396–397). Mullins states that a person's personality is affected by the values of the social culture in which he grew up (1996, p. 715). The values a person gets from their culture form the basis of their personality.

Basaran suggested that these values settle in a person's personality, and as long as there is no suspicious event, the person doesn't doubt these values (Başaran 2008, pp. 387–388). Besides, small differences in cultural values reflect on the behaviors in a bigger way as a result of this direction (Adler 2008, p. 19) (Fig. 1.7).

Factors That Form Culture

Some universal factors tied to culture are mentioned in the literature as cultural output includes beliefs, values as well as actions and behavior. These are norm, symbol, hero, ceremony, language, and technology (Şişman 2002, p. 3; Hofstede et al. 2010, p. 7; Slocum and Hellriegel 2009, p. 458) (Fig. 1.8).

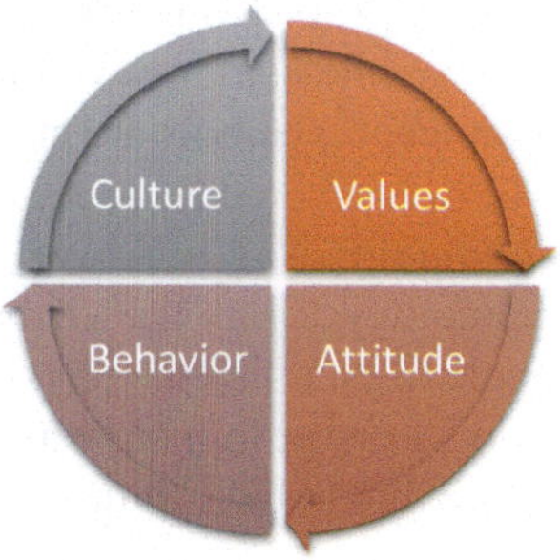

Fig. 1.7 Circle of culture (Adler 2008, p. 19)

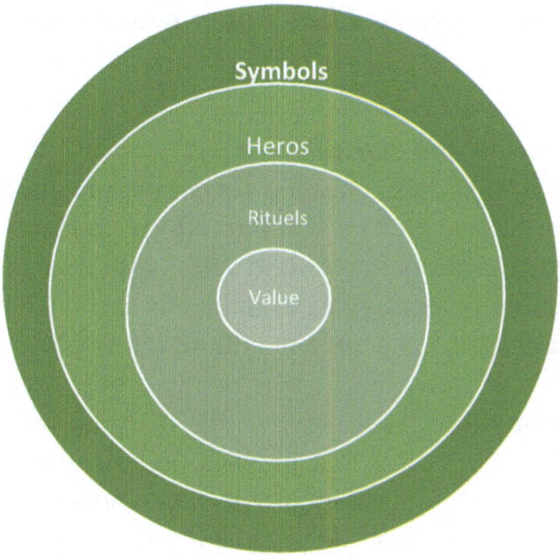

Fig. 1.8 Onion model (Hofstede et al. 2010, p. 8)

Cultural belief

Şişman (2002, p. 3) defined the cultural belief as a common cultural idea of how the world operates, which is commonly accepted and shared by the people. Basaran explained it as accepting one value true and holding on to it (Başaran 2008, p. 391).

Cultural norms

Cultural norms are rules, measures, and scales used in measuring and judging at what level the thing, internalized as a value, is (Başaran 2008, p. 392). Norms are defined as non-written rules that determine how people must behave. Norms are based on values and shape according to those values (Şişman (2002, p. 4).

Symbols

A symbol is an object, picture, activity, and event that helps the culture to settle and take root and has a meaning for the employees (Hofstede et al. 2010, p. 8). Owing to the symbols, the emotions of an organization's members change and there may be an increase in their excitement level while implementing their roles. Symbols intervene in group members' getting to know each other, getting closer and cooperation (Eren

2015, pp. 136–137). They are the most extensive factors of culture (Şişman 2002, p. 4). Symbols are one of the four factors of culture. Symbols complete the culture component. symbols are an integral part of culture.

Technology
Technology forms the visible, material dimension of a culture. Technology helps people to establish the physical, psychological, and social environment and thus has an effect on the human behaviors and relationships. Just as it is a product of a certain culture, it can be a culture's factor itself (Şişman 2002, p. 4).

The Factors That Form the Organizational Culture

Heroes and stories
The first factor needed for an organizational culture to take root and get stronger is heroes. Heroes form an ethical values model with their behaviors and help the organizational culture to settle with related stories (Eren 2015, p. 137). Heroes are, living or nonliving, examples in terms of real or imaginary behavior, pacemakers, and awarded people in culture (Hofstede et al. 2010, p. 8).

Slogans
Another factor that touches organization members and helps them to reveal their energy by increasing their excitement is the slogan. The slogan is a cultural factor that shows that the organizational culture is internalized and is ready to be applied in needed fields by organization members (Eren 2015, p. 137).

Ceremony
Another factor that has an important role in the organizational culture‘s taking root is a ceremony. It is defined as a planned activity made for the group members that have come together for a special purpose (Hofstede et al. 2010, p. 9, Eren 2015, p. 138).

Culture's importance
A culture's importance comes from the power the people have for shaping their working style, work density and environmental relationships (besides their decision-making and behaviors). Decisions made by people and their application conditions are strictly tied to the person's cultural value judgments (Aydınlı 2003, p. 88). Aycan et al. emphasized the importance of paying attention to the cultural context in order to learn more and to be ahead in the global arena as regards organizations and management in the cross-cultural context (2016, p. 19). Since culture is not just a tendency, it changes usual human behaviors, as it directly affects what people decide they will or will not do (Schein 2010, p. 7).

Organizational Culture Models

Parsonian Model

Social psychologist, Talcott Parsons focused on the social values and their contributions in studying and forming the organizational culture. Parsons expressed the complexity of the social systems and stated the intersystem correlation and relationship. The model developed by Parsons has four functions: adaptation, goal attainment, integration, and latency and can be found in the literature under its acronym "AGIL".

Parsons stated the necessity of adaptation to the environment, attaining goals, integration of the systems, and being believed by the individuals of the society in terms of laws in the current system. In the Parsonian model, the most important means to achieve these activities is defined as cultural values (Parsons 1991, p. 92).

Schein's Model

According to Schein, there are three functions of the organizational culture:

- The first function of the organizational culture is adapting to the outer environment and, in order to continue its existence, solving the problems (Schein 2010, p. 23).
- The second function is carrying out activities to solve the integration problems. Common language and concept unity, belonging to a group, etc. can be signified among these functions (Schein 2010, p. 25).
- The third function is reducing anxiety. Reducing anxiety lessens an organization's level of uncertainty (Schein 2010, p. 27).

Kilmann's Model

Kilmann defines the organizational culture as having social energy that can activate everything. Organizational culture fills the gap between what is defined as ideal and what is applied. Since the common culture and climate reflect on the employee's behaviors in an organization, the organizational culture affects the organization's decision system and the efficiency of the employees. In this context, the organizational culture has two aspects. The first of these is bureaucratic and the second is innovative culture. In bureaucratic culture, the authority and responsibilities of the employees are defined clearly. The organizations that have a bureaucratic culture are among those businesses which have attained the maturity level of the life curve. Those that have innovative cultures, however, can adapt to the changing environment and needs of the globalizing world (Karaköse 2013, p. 18).

Quinn and Cameron's Model

Quinn and Cameron pointed out that a model can be created with culture types. They called this model "Competitive Values". Four culture types were defined: Clan, Adhocracy, Hierarchy and Market Culture. In Clan culture, the employees are strictly tied to each other. The leader and the managers of the organization are accepted as mentors. In hierarchy culture, values, rules, and regulations are given priority. In Market culture, the employees are objective-focused and competitive and in Adhocracy there is a lack of standard rules and procedures (Yılmaz 2010, p. 40).

Byars' Model

The organizational culture scale, developed by Byars, is two-dimensional. The first dimension, is related to the participation feature, while the second is related to the activity's feature shown to the environment (Leblebici and Karasoy 2009, p. 285) (Table 1.3).

The first dimension, participation feature, refers to a culture with strong communication, at a level that can answer both the employees' and the customers' desires. Those who have the opposite features are a part of a nonparticipant culture. With respect to the activities shown to the environment, there emerge four culture types. Systematic cultures are in the organizations that are nonparticipant and have reactive activities against the environment.

In a systematic culture, focusing on the system in the application of the procedure and policy is the case. Interacting cultures are the organizational culture types encountered in participative and reactive featured organizations. The organizations that have this culture, aim to meet both the employees' and the customers' needs. Competitive cultures are culture types at nonparticipating and perlocutionary organizations. They are at organizations that are open to new products and services. Integrated culture is a culture type encountered in organizations that are both participative and perlocutionary. The main duty of the organizations that have this culture is changing the employees' and the customers' needs. It is known as the culture type that human relations are given importance in (Durmaz 2010, p. 25).

Table 1.3 Organizational culture (Eren 2015)

People	Non-participate	Systematic	Entrepreneurs
	Participate	Interacting	Integrated
		Reactively	Affective
		Activities	

Table 1.4 Four different culture types

	Fast	Slow
High-risk decision	Tough Guy, Macho	Be-your company
Low-risk decision	Work hard/play hard	Process

Deal and Kennedy Model

This model is separated into four different culture types with respect to the success feedback of the risk level and the strategies of the organization's main activities (Table 1.4).

Tough guy, macho culture; this culture comes out in the occupations that need high-level risk decisions and fast feedback. In this culture type individualism is prioritized. Work hard, play hard; in this culture type, fast feedback and low-level risk decisions are needed. Here, teamwork and every person's individual superiority are given importance. Be-your company; in this culture type, feedback is slow, and risk decisions high, focused on the long-term. Process; feedback in this culture is slow, the risks are low. Since the feedback is low, focusing on how it was done, rather than what was done is the point (Deal and Kennedy 1982, p. 101).

Miles and Snow Model

Miles and Snow gathered the features of the organizations under four culture groups according to their customs and habits and explained this culture's contributions to creating the strategy (Miles et al. 1978, p. 550):

- Protective Culture: The organization has conservative beliefs and value judgments. Low risk and operating in safe markets is preferred.
- Constructive Culture: This kind of organization is defined as innovative. The managers of such organizations tend to produce new products, get into new markets easily and have high-risk levels.
- Analyzer Culture: In such cultures, there are two different aspects: balance and change. Balance is about creating formal structures and searching for efficiency. Change is defined as cautious strategies developed by controlling the opponents' activity and strategies. Out of these strategies, balance is prioritized.
- Responsive Culture: In such organizations, opponents and the surroundings apply pressure for change. The managers that cannot keep up with this change find themselves in such a situation where while struggling to survive, they try not to go bankrupt (Miles et al. 1978, p. 553).

Quichi's "Z" Culture Model

William Quchi, in his book *Z Management Theory*, took care of the value judgments of Japan and the US and (Peters and Waterman 1987, p. 23), for the first time, tried to explain Japan's management style's applications. He continues by explaining how this management style can be adapted to the American management style (Ouchi 1981, p. 10), pointing out that if American business managers want, they can apply Japan's successful management style, creating an advantage to them and their businesses by developing the Z-type management culture in their organizations.

In Z-type organizational culture, long-term employment, participant management style in critical cases, slow evaluation, and promotion, open office system, vertical and horizontal rotation are applied. At the bottom of this system, the employees are handled with their families and their dependency on the surroundings. Thus, renewing the employees' feelings of being alone and independent, an attempt is made to strengthen the emotion of belonging to the business (Ouchi 1981, p. 58) (Table 1.5).

Table 1.5 Types of organization (Eren 2015, p. 159)

Type A organization	Short time employment and high employee turnover
	Individual decision making
	Individual responsibility based on merit
	Rapid evaluation and rapid promotion
	Explicit with formalized measures and emphasis on bureaucratic type control
	Specialized career path, bureaucratic control of individuals requires specialties and sub-specialties to reduce the interdepence
	Segmented concern and non-personal task oriented concern
Type Z organization	Longterm employment and moderate employee turnover
	Consensus decision making
	Individual decision making
	Slow evaluation and slow promotion
	Mixed control, implicit control and informal control with explicit formalized measures
	Moderately specialized career path
	Holistic concern for employee's well being
Type J organization	Lifetime employment and low employee turnover
	Consensus decision making
	Collective decision making
	Slow evaluation and slow promotion
	Implicit, control, subtle control and emphasis on clan type control
	Non-specialized career path
	Holistic concern for employee's well being

Peters and Waterman's Excellence Model

Tom Peters and Robert Waterman searched success secrets for the USA business managers and gave place to eight common attributes that made the businesses succeed in their book *In Search of Excellence*. As a criterion for success, financial and economic success criteria such as the high increases in the businesses' decisions and sales incomes compared to their rivals and developments in their annual growing speed compared to their assets were regarded. According to the writers, eight successful behaviors are given below (Peters and Waterman 1987, p. 51) (Table 1.6).

Human-Related Values of the Contemporary Management Theory

The human-related values of the contemporary management theory are given below (Kara 2011, p. 101):

- When the conditions are suitable, work is as natural as a play for the individual.
- In attaining the goals of the organization, an individual must control himself.
- The individual's self-control with the organization's goals is the function of the rewards that satisfy the ego and the social needs as well as basic nutrition need.
- The creativity capacity to solve the organizational troubles range from person to person to a great extent.
- In organizations, people's creativity capacity is used completely.

Organization-related values of the contemporary management theory (Kara 2011, p. 102) are as follows:

Table 1.6 Common features of successful companies (Peters and Waterman 1987, pp. 46–51)

Action was a strong emphasis upon experimentation; people were encouraged to try out new ideas and approaches
They were dependent on their customers for their continued success
They valued and fostered innovation and risk-taking
They viewed employees as the key sources of ideas for improvements in quality and productivity
Top managers tended to see their role as that of managing the values of their organizations
They stayed close to what they knew and could do well
They kept corporate staffs small and do not use a complex matrix structure
A high degree of autonomy and a great deal of emphasis given in individual initiative

- Authority emerges from the organization's formal and informal resources, moves up and down and sideways.
- Observation is general, control field is extensive.
- A manager shouldn't ignore the individual and his biological, social and psychological sides as a whole in working conditions.
- Duty is meaningful as a whole. Besides different surroundings it provides, it will entail mastership and judging.

Values

Value has been defined as a belief related to the quantity and quality that determines the benefit, goodness, beauty, accuracy, the desirability of a person, object, belief, operation, opinion, process, and action (Şişman 2002, p. 4). Values are defined as criteria that have no specific feature and used in discrimination of the good–bad, beautiful–ugly, normal–abnormal, and rational–irrational related to behavior, manner, and opinions (Hofstede et al. 1990, p. 291; Schwartz 1999, p. 24; Ros et al. 1999, p. 51; Sabuncuoğlu and Vergiliel Tüz 2013, p. 47).

Values are considered as the most important factor in explaining a culture. According to sociologist Milton Rokeach, the value is "a belief that has continuity related to the preference of a certain means or final result or a means or results in the opposite position individually or socially" (Rokeach 1973, p. 35; William 1995, p. 16). Greves pointed out that values must be handled with the person's socialization levels (Greves 1974, p. 73). Values are the criteria that the people use to evaluate the events, themselves, people, to choose the actions and justify (Özkalp et al. 2016, p. 8).

In TLA, values are explained as the whole of the material and spiritual factors that comprise the social, cultural, economic and specific values a nation has (HTTP-4). In order to understand the human behaviors in an organization, values must be defined (Organ and Hammer 1982, p. 3; Chiaramonte 2011, p. 152).

Just like people, organizations have value, too. In order to be efficient in an organization, it must be analyzed whether the person's values are compatible with the organization's values (Drucker 2006, p. 13). Many individuals in interactive relations that share common values, unite in a sense to defend the values against threats. This helps the organization to be more efficient (Alexander and Seidman 2013, p. 57). Values form one of the most important factors of dependency on the goals of a group or the system (Katz and Georgopoulos 1976, p. 384).

Thus, culture, class, occupation, religion, and political judgment differences can cause differences underlying the value and value systems (Rokeach 1973, p. 26). Culture, defining the behavior with the values and manners it foresees, presents the relationship between the culture and the values (Sargut 2001, p. 20). According to Hodgkinson, the most important function of the values is providing private standards that guide behaviors in various situations (Vurgun and Öztop 2011, p. 218).

The values are thought to affect the behavior (Sverko 1999, p. 93). Values refer to both content and density. Referring to the content emphasizes that the behavior styles or the existence's aims are important, referring to the density states how these are important. If a person's values are graded with respect to their density, that person's value system is obtained (Robbins and Judge 2015, p. 145).

Managerial Values

Depending on the Turkish culture, the managers' values tend to develop and orient under the effect of the culture's general features. The managers, with the common sense the professionalism provides, must fulfill the responsibilities the society culture imposes on them. Among these orders, the values have an important role (Kara 2011, p. 50) According to Nicolai Hotman, "nobody can tolerate living in a world that scraped off its values and lost its holiness." Values provide stability in the rapidly developing world (Özgener 2000, p. 175). Basic differences between cultures reflect on the human that is the main factor of the societies. İf the people are not in accordance with the environment they live in, they have difficulty in attaining their goals.

Therefore, people are equipped to comply with the environment they live in, by their cultural surroundings. The education process that foresees and supplies the equipment starts with the birth of the human and continues throughout his life. Values are desired positions, aims, targets, or behaviors (Elizur and Sagie 1999, p. 74).

Values can guide decision-making (Desson and Clouthier 2010, p. 2). Values affect our decisions and accordingly our lives as the interior references we consult continuously. It was claimed that values in groups differ significantly according to the demographic features and cultural differences (Rokeach 1973, p. 95; Tuulik et al. 2016, p. 152). Therefore, it is important to define the differences in the groups as well as the values.

The main features of the values (Özgener 2000, p. 173) are as follows:

- Values express a personal decision and preferences.
- Since values are organized by a human group, together, they are social.
- Values differ within the groups.
- Values are the product of the experience that is conveyed from generation to generation and has continuity in a certain time period.
- Values can change and change.

According to Smith, Kline, and Beecham, the reasons that make the values important are as follows (Özgener 2000, p. 175):

- Values present a guiding framework in relation to the behaviors and decisions.
- Values help build an ethical culture.
- Values have the potential to affect an organization's success. If the business' vision and strategic plans are compatible with the values, the business becomes successful.

- Values are first degree motivators. Values can be a strong source of a business' continuous competitive advantage.
- Values not only hinder managers from giving inappropriate orders continuously, but also prevent the employees from implementing the inappropriate orders.

The arrangement and the strategies are formed to a great extent under the effect of the cultural understanding and values system shared by the organization members. As every society has a culture unique to it, it is impossible to isolate the concept, principle, process, and applications related to the management from this cultural context. In this case, besides some universal facts, some local differences unique to each culture can be the point (Şişman 1996, p. 296). As Paul H. Appleby pointed out, all human organizations are in search of various systematical values.

The operation of the organization becomes more and more important as a side of the value search (Emre 2000, p. 18). One of the dimensions that prioritize the culture in management and organization science literature is the modern management and organization models‘ appearance in parallel with industrialization developing and accordingly having the western culture's features. Industrializing countries get into the process of industrialization by taking an example of the management and organization models that are developed in both industrialization and western.

This process creates trouble since the exemplary management and organization models aren't compatible with the industrializing countries' cultural features. These troubles caused different ideas related to the topic to appear. İdeas that emerged within this framework is gathered in three groups. The first of these ideas consider industrialization as an indicative factor in creating the management and organization model and defends that industrializing countries managerial and organizational applications and values will resemble each other in parallel with the industrialization process.

The second idea defends that management and organizational values will differ owing to the local cultural features and the third idea defends that different from the exemplary country culture and local culture's features, a hybrid of managerial and organizational values will appear (Ralston et al. 1999, p. 659; Grupta and Wang 2004, p. 38; Ralston et al. 2008, p. 11; Sabuncuoğlu and Vergiliel Tüz 2013, p. 47; Yüksel and Durna 2015, p. 296).

The Classification of Values

The categorization of values in the literature is given below.

Rokeach's value survey

Rokeach separated the values into two groups as terminal values and instrumental values.

Terminal values represent the goals a person would like to achieve during their lifetime, while instrumental values represent the means of achieving the terminal values (Çalışkur and Aslan 2013, p. 89) (Table 1.7).

Table 1.7 Rokeach value survey (Çalışkur and Aslan 2013, p. 89)

Terminal values		Instrumental values	
A world at peace	True friendship	Ambitious	Broadminded
Family security	A sense of accomplishment	Capable	Cheerful
Freedom	Inner harmony	Clean	Courageous
Equality	A comfortable life	Forgiving	Helpful
Self-respect	Mature love	Honest	Imaginative
Happiness	A world of beauty	Independent	Intellectual
Wisdom	Pleasure	Logical	Loving
National security	Social recognition	Obedient	Polite
Salvation	An exciting life	Responsible	Self-controlled

Graves Values Levels

Graves classified the values at seven levels (Aktürk 2009, p. 17).

- Level 1—Reactive: This level is the one at which the person reacts to his or her basic needs.
- Level 2—Tribal: At this level, the dependency of the people is high, and they generally try to abstain from the pain by obeying the traditions and the authority.
- Level 3—Egocentric: It can be defined as a highly individualistic level where the individual doesn't react to the organization's needs.
- Level 4—Conformist: These individuals have a low threshold level of tolerance for the people who don't share their values. They expect the values internalized by them to be accepted easily.
- Level 5—Materialist: These people try to direct the people and the extent in order to attain their goals.
- Level 6—Society Centered: This type of people care about being loved and getting on with others rather than developing; the indicator of the success is being loved by the others.
- Level 7—Existentialist: It is used for the type of people that have a high level of uncertainty and the people who have different values approach with tolerance. Objecting to the restrictive adjustments, statutory expressions and using the authority randomly, it only cares about the welfare of the people.

Scott's Value Classification

Scott developed a scale with a 12 value field to rate personal values. These fields are: being intellectual, courtesy, social skills, loyalty, academic success, physical development, statue (leadership), honesty, religious commitment, self-control, creativity, and independence (Scott and Bruce 1995, p. 820).

Table 1.8 Schwartz's value survey

Value types	Values they contain
Power	Social power, authority, wealth
Achievement	Success, capability, ambition, influence on people and events
Hedonism	Gratification of desires, enjoyment in life, self-indulgence
Stimulation	Daring, a varied and challenging life, an exciting life
Self-direction	Creativity, freedom, curiosity, independence, choosing one's own goals
Universalism	Broad-mindedness, the beauty of nature and arts, social justice, a world at peace, equality, wisdom, unity with nature, environmental protection
Benevolence	Helpfulness, honesty, forgiveness, loyalty, responsibility
Tradition	Respect for tradition, humbleness, accepting one's portion in life, devotion, modesty
Conformity	Obedience, honoring parents and elders, self-discipline, politeness
Security	National security, family security, social order, cleanliness, reciprocation of favors

Schwartz's Value Classification

Schwartz combined 56 values, which were defined before, in 10 primary categories. These values are stated in Table 1.8 (Yiğittir 2012, p. 4).

Lifestyle and Individual Value Classification

Values are expressed as lifestyle and individual values. The primary starting point of this approach is detecting the differences and the inequalities in the organization (Kara 2011, p. 76) (Table 1.9).

Hodgkinson's Value Classification

Hodgkinson presented a classification that separates the values into three categories. According to their order of importance, he signified these categories as follows:

- Transrational (Type 1) values are based on the principles.
- Rational (Type 2a) values depend on the individual's perception of the truth and his or her evaluation style of the result. (Type 2b) Rational values are based on how the individual perceives the truth; but this time on evaluation style of the reconciliation.
- Lower rational (Type 3) values are related to the individual preferences or the situations that are perceived accurately (Razik and Swanson 1995, p. 119).

Table 1.9 Lifestyle and individual values

Values	Individual features
Opponent	They do not care about themselves and other people, they are just trying to get rid of their physiological needs
Tribal, holder	They are very influenced by the traditions and authority that are dependent
Egocentric	These individuals are aggressive and selfish individuals who believe in strict individuality
Compliance provider	Individuals who are difficult to tolerate and who cannot tolerate ambiguity are different from their own values
Manipulative	They are individuals who have succeeded in using other people
Sociocentric	These individuals are individuals who are not loved and choose to get along with others. They run at the level of self-esteem and high status and recognition
Existentialist	These individuals are harmonious with people who have great endurance to ambiguity and who have different values

Prencipe and Helwig's Value Classification

In the study carried out by Prencipe and Helwig (2002, p. 845), values are separated into six categories

- Directly Ethical Values: The values that comprise the others' welfare and rights.
- Ethical Character Values: The values that comprise the individual characteristics besides directly ethical values.
- Nonethical Character Values: The values that comprise only the individual futures.
- Political Ethical Values: Democratic values in the policy world.
- Traditional Political Values: Values like patriotism.
- Religious Values: Values of faith and faith practice.

Nelson's Value Classification

According to Nelson, the values are separated into three categories:

- Individual Values: The values that are related to personal preferences.
- Group Values: The values that are shared by the group members.
- Social Values: The values that help the individual to continue his/her existence in the current social structure (Doğruel 2013, p. 52).

Fichter's Value Classification

Fichter (2006, pp. 173–175) separated the social values into three groups. These are the following:

- Classification with respect to their compelling levels: In this group, the values are signified according to their influence levels on the personality.
- Classification with respect to the continuity: These are the values that have importance in collaboration and action.
- Classification with respect to the relationships in the organization: These are the values, which the individuals who share in the organization, must obey.

Cevizci's Value Classification

Cevizci classified values in six types. Each type of value has positive and negative sides. Hedonistic Values: Pleasure and pain; Esthetical Values: Beautiful and ugly; Ethical Values: Good and bad; Pragmatic Values: Useful and useless; Religious Values: Sin and good deed; Logical Values: Right and wrong (Doğruel 2013, p. 46).

Kinnier, Kernes, and Dautheribes' Value Classification

Common values were stated in the study carried out by Kinnier et al. (2000, p. 13) These values are as follows:

- Devotion to a superior thing,
- Seeking the truth and justice,
- Protecting oneself,
- Respecting to oneself,
- Having individual responsibility,
- Not being egocentric,
- Being responsible for the behaviors,
- Behaving in accordance with the conscience,
- Helping the others,
- Being respectful, tolerant, and merciful, and
- Not hurting the others and protecting the other living creatures.

Spranger and All Parts Value Classification

Taking the human types into consideration, Spranger grouped the values in six groups (Uyan 2002, p. 52). These values are as follows:

- Esthetical Values: The values that care shape and harmony.

- Theoretical Values: The values that suggest that the main goal of life is getting information.
- Economic Values: The values that are based on economic benefit.
- Political Values: The values that care to have power over the others.
- Social Values: The values that care courtesy, sympathetic and devoted behaviors.
- Religious Values: The values that are based on understanding the whole universe.

Ozgener's Value Classification

While some of the values are shaped by the environment, some are shaped by the tendencies of social, economic, legal, and cultural structure. Ozgener classified the values into four groups as: economic, social, individual, and ethical (Özgener 2004, pp. 128–130).

De Bono's Value Classification

De Bono separated the values into six categories (Bono 2007, pp. 44–46).

- Human Values: Feeding, sheltering, health, and respect.
- Enterprise Values: Values such as serving well, decreasing the complaints and simplifying the operations which can vary according to the enterprise's aim.
- Quality Values: Customer values, service quality.
- Glass Medaled Values: Values that are related to productivity, innovation, and simplicity.
- Environmental Values: Values that are generally related to the environment.
- Perceptive Values: The group of values which state that the world we live in is the world we perceive with respect to the aspect that even if the perceived thing is not real, perception is reality.

Evin and Kafadar's Value Classification

Evin and Kafadar separated the values into two groups: national and universal (Doğruel 2013, p. 49) (Table 1.10).

Sarnoff's Value Classification

Sarnoff separated the values into seven and combined them into two groups. In the first group, there are values of power, in the second group, there are values of human relationships.

Table 1.10 Evin and Kafadar's value classification

National values	Universal values
Nation	Democracy
State	Human right and independence
Homeland	Civilization
Army	Peace
Republic	Equality
National Symbols	Science and scientific thinking
Heroism	Art
Language	Environmental awareness
Traditions and customs	Love values

- Values of power: financial potential, power, and prestige
- Values of human relationships: esthetics, equality, intelligence, and being humanistic (Doğruel 2013, p. 50).

Ennulo and Turnpuu's Value Classification

Alas et al. (2006, p. 274) classified the values into 10 groups: business' ideological values, leadership and ideological values, social values, individual values, private-related values, professional values, cultural values, values unique to the lifestyle, organizational legal values, and ethical values.

Basaran's Value Classification

Basaran (2008, p. 393) signified the values according to their strength. Basic Values: They define the universal values that form the basis of the culture and are accepted by the majority of society. Private Values: The values whose importance vary according to the region, occupation, the interests. Optional Values: The values that are used in time and place is desired by the members of the culture and the organization. Permanent Values: The values that are used by a certain group for a certain time.

Altas' Value Classification

Altas separated the values according to the goal attributes (Altaş 2004, pp. 35–36). These are entertainment, safety, success, self-direction, restrictive–obedience compelling, prosocial, power, and maturity.

Beck's Value Classification

Beck's study on values took universal values into consideration. According to Beck, there is no exact-absolute value. Values symbolize both the means and the end. Beck explained the value systems under the main headings given below (Yıldırım 2011, p. 20).

- Basic Human Values: These values appear in accordance with the important human needs, such as surviving, health, happiness, and friendship.
- Ethical Values: Being attentive, courage and responsibility.
- Social and Political Values: Tolerance, participation, and loyalty.
- Intermediate Values: Sheltering, amusement, and keeping fit.
- Specific Values: Having a car or a certificate.

Tezcan's Value Classification

Tezcan classified values into six groups (Doğruel 2013, p. 52). These are the values of the family institution, educational values, economic values, religious values, political values, and the values of spare time.

Mike Eskew's Value Classification

Mike Eskew classified values under the headings given below as the characteristic value. These are the values that don't change and that are needed when making a decision even if the strategy and the aims change in time (Vurgun and Öztop 2011, p. 221). Values are categorized as follows:

- Inseparable Values: Doing only the right thing.
- Humanistic Values: Taking the family and society seriously rather than oneself.
- Leadership Values: Telling that you will do, doing what you have said.
- Respect Values: Giving chance to people by behaving fairly and reputably.

Aldemir, Arbak, and Ozmen's Value Classification
Aldemir et al. (2003) separated values into two groups western sourced and local values of managers (Table 1.11).

A Sample for Values from Aviation Business: TAV Airports Company

Individual and organizational values affect a manager's viewpoint toward individual and organizational success, their relationship with individuals, his decisions, his viewpoint, and solutions toward problems (Vurgun and Öztop 2011, p. 220).

Table 1.11 Aldemir, Arbak, and Ozmen's value classification

Local values	Western sourced values
Family Ties	Being fair
Dependence	Rationalism
Oppressiveness	Give importance to detail
Live today	Success
Sordidness	Information sharing
Friendship	Scientific
Sensuality	Give importance to the rights and freedoms of the Individual
Religion	Diligence
Honesty	Discipline
Traditionalism	Entrepreneurship
Confidence	Initiative
Know one's place	Tolerance
Protectionism	Foresight
Factionalism	Voluntarism
Hypocrisy	Cooperation
Wasting	Obey the rules
Do the job well and smoothly	Stingy
Frugality	Competitive
Fatalism	Risk-taking
Frugality	Intuitiveness
Rigidity	Responsibility
Nepotism	Interrogator
Centralism	Agreeableness
Nationalism	Be open to innovations
Give importance to rank and Authorities	Perfection
Loyalty	
Continuity	
Laziness	
Unpretentiousness	
Disloyalty	

TAV has a leading organization in Turkey, and they have both holistic and systematic enterprise risk management systems which depend on strong values, organizational culture. For this reason, their statements about how the best presentation of values from companies may prove useful. They have strong partners and also the mentality of partnership. TAV Airports applies an integrated business model, which is focused on new and profitable business opportunities all over the world in the coming period. They have strong situational awareness in view of both top managers and throughout the holding.

TAV Airports have tailored a strategy for their sustainability. Their strategy is based on both values, risk management and three pillars: Organic growth, Inorganic growth, and Growth of the service companies.

Three Pillars of TAV Airports' Growth Strategy (TAV 2018a, b, c):

(1) **Organic growth: Present operations are focused on the fastest-growing aviation markets in the world**

Our primary market, Turkey, has been one of the fastest-growing aviation markets in the world. According to projections of Airbus, Boeing, Eurocontrol, and the State Airports Authority of Turkey, growth is poised to continue in the next 10 years. In addition to Turkey, almost all of the airports that we operate are located in emerging economies with a well-established track record of above-average growth.

(2) **Inorganic growth: An extensive track record in disciplined bidding for new airports**

Our main focus in inorganic growth is value creation by generating a return above our cost of capital. To this end, we carefully screen countless airport operation projects around the world with very sophisticated financial and operational models, project an expected return and keep our bidding within the parameters of these calculations. We have a solid track record in discontinuing tenders where we believe the implied IRR has fallen below our acceptable return threshold.

(3) **The growth of the service companies outside the TAV ecosystem**

We have defined the growth of our auxiliary service companies as the third pillar of TAV Airports' growth strategy. Since the definition of this mandate, service companies in our portfolio have won numerous concessions around the world in tenders for duty-free, ground handling, IT, and lounge services.

The following information from TAV Airports holding point to best practices in regard to the use of values:

Samples of Corporate Value TAV AIRPORTS (TAV 2018a, b, c)
http://www.tavyatirimciiliskileri.com/en-EN/Pages/OurVisionMission.aspx.

Our Vision
To be the pioneering and leading airport operating company in our target regions (Europe, Russia and the Commonwealth of Independent States, Middle East, Africa, and India).

Our Mission
To create the highest value for all stakeholders in airport operations through our customer-oriented management approach.

Our Corporate Values

Professionalism: We perform our duties with the utmost diligence and at the highest standards, following global developments related to our work. We consider our jobs and job-related priorities in all our interactions.

Respect: We act in line with ethical standards as a fundamental rule, prioritizing respect for people, the environment, laws, and regulations. We behave in an honest, transparent, fair and responsible manner in all our endeavors.

Dynamism: Having adopted the principle of a dynamic and flexible work ethic, we work in an efficient, result-oriented manner, no matter what the circumstances. Constantly remaining aware of environmental conditions and monitoring change, we respond and adapt to change promptly.

Innovation: We continually create opportunities for improvement and innovation in all processes, with an emphasis on customer satisfaction. Being aware that difference stems from innovative practices, we employ our best efforts to ensure that our services are contemporary and creative.

Teamwork: Being aware that cooperation, mutual commitment, expertise, and knowledge sharing are the building blocks of success, we also consider teamwork the assurance of personal success and we support teamwork in all endeavors.

TAV Value Chain

Value creation: As TAV Airports Holding, we will continue to generate value for our shareholders with our energy and determination.

Regional player: We will proceed on our way as one of the strongest regional players of Europe, Russia and the Commonwealth of Independent States, Middle East, Africa, and India.

Customer satisfaction: With our vast know-how, highly qualified human capital and advanced technology, we will maintain our service mentality based on customer satisfaction in operations and management.

Human capital and teamwork: We aim to fortify our distinguished position we have achieved with our young and dynamic team, formed by the most qualified professionals in Turkey, and to generate value through our highly qualified workforce, our most valuable asset.

Performance: We have served approximately 451 thousand flights and 53 million passengers annually. Hereby, we are one of the leading airport operating companies in the world.

Growth: We are moving forward with determination toward our target of "Serving an average of 100 million passengers annually by 2017" as an international brand with ever growing business volume.

The Company expands maximum effort to be sensitive to its social responsibilities in its operations. It complies with all regulations regarding the environment, consumer and public health, as well as ethics rules, and directs and supports its subsidiaries to behave in the same manner. The Company's terminal operating subsidiaries conduct their operations in compliance with environmental legislation, directives, and guidelines of international aviation organizations such as the ICAO,

ECAC, EUROCONTROL, and IATA, as well as the Equator Principles of the World Bank (TAV 2018a, b, c).

Management of Strategic and Operational Risks

(http://www.tavyatirimciiliskileri.com/external/tav_faaliyet_raporlari/2016/en/risk-yonetimi-ic-denetim.html, *tarih yok).*

The Company continuously undertakes improvement and development related activities at all airports operated by TAV Airports Holding in order to ensure efficient and safe operations amid the demands of growing passenger traffic. Medium and large scale problems that the Group may be exposed to within the expanding and evolving aviation industry are assessed by the Risk Committee and senior management on an ongoing basis and long-term strategies are formulated promptly to counter potential risks. Primary operational risks the Company may be exposed to include unexpected business interruptions, deterioration in service quality standards and the inability of aging terminal buildings to meet the Company's needs. In accordance with its high-quality service strategy, TAV Airports ensures that its service quality standard is maintained at the same high level by way of regular maintenance, repair, investment, renovation and extension related projects at the terminals. The Company constantly monitors, updates and practices emergency operations plans against contingencies, preventing potential business interruptions and minimizing their impact on passengers. The infrastructure of the terminal buildings has been designed in accordance with specific standards against force majeure events; the Company is appropriately insured against losses from natural disasters and business interruptions. While it is impossible to fully eliminate risks, the Company takes these measures in order to minimize their consequences and impacts (TAV 2018a, b, c).

Strategic management has primary importance for companies and relates decision-making about future orientation of organizations and implementation decisions. Effectiveness on selecting the right strategies and implementation for companies provide organizational success. Strategic analysis process includes to collect and assess knowledge both internal and external environments. The air transportation sector is one of the most growing sectors and privatization of airports has increased their interests to catch opportunities in the new sector for companies. In this paper, the case of TAV company will be examined. It recognized changes in the aviation sector and utilized opportunities from privatization of airports. It succeeds in strategic planning and strategic implementation. The ten airports of TAV are comprised of four airports in Turkey, two in Georgia, two in Tunisia, and two in Macedonia. Among the seven services of TAV Airports there are TAV Security, HAVAŞ Ground Services, BTA Food & Drink, ATÜ Duty Free, TAV O&M, TAV Information Technologies, and the recently established TGS (a Ground Service Company in partnership with THY) TAV has achieved success by implementing a unique business model that is based on both horizontal and vertical integration. TAV not only designs, manages, and operates its airports, but also offers important services such as duty-free and regular retail outlets, passenger and aircraft ground handling, food and beverage services, aviation security, and airport IT systems. No other airport operator around the world has implemented this type of business matrix structure, which leads to significant operational and financial synergies. In TAV 10th year, five of their companies managed to place among the 500 largest companies in Turkey (AKPINAR 2011).

References

Adler, N.J. 2008. *International dimension of organizational behavior*, 5th ed. Boston: Thomson Learning.

AKPINAR, A.T. 2011. Ali Talip Akpinar. *Kocaeli Üniversitesi Sosyal Bilimler Enstitüsü Dergisi (21) 2011/1:150–161*, pp. 150–161.

Aktürk, Y. 2009. *Temel Değerlerin Sürdürülebilirliği ve Performans Değerleme İlişkisi*. İstanbul: Doğuş Üniversitesi Sosyal Bilimler Entitüsü.

Alas, R., J. Ennulo, and L. Türnpuu. 2006. Managerial values in institutional context. *Journal of Business Ethics* 2006 (65): 269–278.

Aldemir, C.M., Y. Arbak, and Ö. Özmen. 2003. Türkiye'de iş görme anlayışı: Tanımı ve boyutları. *Yönetim Araştırmaları Dergisi* 3 (1): 5–28.

Alexander, J.C., and S. Seidman. 2013. *Kültür ve Toplum: Güncel tartışmalar*, 1st ed. İstanbul: Boğaziçi Üniversitesi Yayınevi.

Altaş, S.S. 2004. *İş değerleri, örgütsel vatandaşlık davranışı ilişkisinin bireysel iş performansı ve işten ayrılma eğilimi üzerindeki etkisine yönelik bir araştırma*. Kocaeli: Gebze Yüksek Teknoloji Enstitüsü.

Argyris, C. 1957. *Personality and organizayion: The conflict between system and the individual*. New York: Harper & Row.

Arogyaswamy, B., and C.M. Byles. 1987. Organizational culture: Internal and external fits. *Journal of Management* 13 (4): 647–658.

Aycan, Z., R.N. Kanungo, and M. Mendonça. 2016. *Kültürel Arası Bağlamda Örgütler ve Yönetim*, 85–121. İstanbul: Koç Üniversitesi Yayınları.

Aydınlı, Hİ. 2003. Örgüt kültürünün yönetim açısından önemi. *Bilgi* 7 (2): 79–99.

Baransel, A. 1993. *Çağdaş Yönetim Düşüncesinin Evrimi*. İstanbul: İşletme Fakültesi Yayınları.

Barney, J.B. 1986. Organizational culture: Can it be a source of sustained competitive advantage? *Academy of Management Review* 11 (3): 656–665.

Başaran, İ.E. 2008. *Örgütsel Davranış: İnsanın Üretim Gücü*. Ankara: Ekinoks Yayınları.

Baubakary. 2015. The influence of the personal values of the leader on the growth of SME's in Cameroon. *International Strategic Management Review* 3(1–2): 15–23.

Bennett, T. 1998. *Culture: A performer's science*. Sidney: South Wind Productions.

Berger, A.A. 2011. *Kültür eleşririsi: Kültürel kavramlara giriş*. İstanbul: Pinhan Yayınları.

Birdal, İ., and N. Aydemir. 1992. *Yönetim Teorileri*. İstanbul: Sistem Yayıncılık.

Blake, R.R., and J.S. Mouton. 1985. *The managerial grid III*. Houston: Gulf Publishing Company.

Bono, E.d. 2007. *6 Değer Madalyası: 21. yüzyılda başarının anahtarı*, 1st ed. İstanbul: Remzi Kitabevi.

Boone, L.E., and D.L. Kurtz. 2013. Bir İşletmede Yönetsel Hiyerarşi Nasıl İşler? *Çağdaş İşletme*, 215–250. Nobel Yayıncılık: İstanbul.

Burnes, B. 2004. Kurt Lewin and the planned approach to change: A re-appraisal. *Journal of Management Studies* 41 (6): 977–1002.

Ceylan, A. 2014. *Yönetimde İnsan ve Davranış*, 3rd ed. İstanbul: Kuşak Matbaası.

Chiaramonte, P. 2011. Values and attitudes at work. *Organizational behavior in a global context*, 149–204. Toronto: Broadview Press.

Cole, G.A. 2004. *Management theory and practice*. London: Geralding Lyons.

Çalışkur, A., and A.E. Aslan. 2013. Rokeach Değerler Envanteri Güvenirlik ve Geçerlik Çalışması. *Balıkesir Üniversitesi Sosyal Bilimler Enstitüsü Dergisi* 16 (29): 81–105.
Danışman, A., and H. Özgen. 2008. Organizational subcultures and resources: An empirical research in an industrial firm. *Journal of Development* 35 (December): 277–304.
Deal, T.E., and A.A. Kennedy. 1982. Corporate cultures: The rites and rituals of organizational life. *Reading*, 98–103. Boston: Addison Wesley.
Desson, K., and J. Clouthier. 2010. *Organizational culture—What does it matter?* 1–9. Vienne.
Doğruel, H. 2013. *Yönetsel Değerlerin Önem Düzeyi ile İş Performansı Arasındaki İlişkinin İncelenmesi*. Gaziantep: Gaziantep Üniversitesi Eğitim Bilimleri Enstitüsü.
Douglas, M. 1960. *The human side of enterprise*. New York: McGraw-Hill.
Drucker, P.F. 2006. *Klasik Drucker*. İstanbul: Bahçeşehir Üniversitesi Yayınları.
Durmaz, O. 2010. *Örgüt Kültürünün Örgüsel Bağlılık Üzerine Etkisi: Analitik Bir İnceleme*. İzmir: Dokuz Eylül Üniversitesi Sosyal Bilimler Enstitüsü.
Elizur, D., and A. Sagie. 1999. Facets of personal values: A structural analysis of life and work values. *Applied Psychology: An International Review* 48 (1): 73–87.
Emre, C. 2000. Kültürel değerler, ahlak ve Türkiye'de kamu yönetimi. *Mülkiye* 26 (236): 15–32.
Eren, E. 2003. *Yönetim ve Organizasyon: Çağdaş ve Küresel Yaklaşımlar*. İstanbul: Beta Basım A.Ş.
Eren, E. 2007. *Örgütsel Davranış ve Yönetim Psikolojisi*, 10th ed. İstanbul: Beta Yayınları.
Eren, E. 2015. *Örgütsel Davranış ve Yönetim Psikolojisi*. İstanbul: Beta Yayınları.
Ergur, A. 2015. Kültürün önemi. In: *Kültür sosyolojisi*, 2–23. Eskişehir: Anadolu Üniversitesi, Açık Öğretim Fakültesi Yayın.
Erkenekli, M. 2013. A value-centered integrated culture model for social culture resear. *Journal of Defense Scie* 147–172.
Fayol, H. 1949. *General and industrial management*. London: Pitman Press.
Fichter, J.H. 2006. *Sosyoloji nedir*, 8th ed. Ankara: Anı Yayıncılık.
Gagliardi, P. 1990. The creation and change of organizational cultures: A conceptual framework. *Organizational behavior and management*, 203–287. Boston: PWS-KENT Publishing.
Gökalp, Z. 1990. *Türkçülüğün Esasları*. İstanbul: Milli Eğitim Basımevi.
Greves, C.W. 1974. *Human nature prepares for momentus*, 72–85. Issue April: The futurist.
Grupta, V., and J. Wang. 2004. The transvergence proposition under globalization: looking beyond convergence, divergence and crossvergence. *The Multinational Business Review* 12 (2): 36–57.
Herzberg, F., B. Mausner, and B.B. Snyderman. 1959. *The motivation to work*. New York: Wiley.
Heyel, C. 1965. The value and dignity of human beings as a basis indusrtial cooperation. *International handbook of management*, 25–38. New York: McGraw-Hill.
Hofstede, G., G.J. Hofstede, and M. Minkov. 2010. *Cultures and organizations: Software of the mind: Intercultural cooperation and its importance for survival*, 3rd ed. New York: McGrawHill.
Hofstede, G., B. Neuijen, D.D. Ohayv, and G. Sanders. 1990. Measuring organizational cultures: A qualitative an quantitive study across twenty cases. *Administrative Science Quartely* 35 (2): 286–316.
Homans, G.C. 1950. *The human group*. New York: Harcourt Brace and Company.
http://www.tavyatirimciiliskileri.com/external/tav_faaliyet_raporlari/2016/en/risk-yonetimi-ic-denetim.html. n.d. [Online].
Jenks, C. 2001. *Culture: Key ideas*. New York: Taylor & Francis.
Kara, H. 2011. *Yönetsel ve örgütsel değerler*. Bursa: Ekin Basım Yayın Dağıtım.
Karahan, A. 2008. Çalışanların örgüt kültürünü algılamalarına yönelik ampirik bir çalışma. *Selçuk Üniversitesi Sosyal Bilimler Enstitüsü, Issue* 20: 457–478.
Karaköse, S. 2013. *Spor Yönetiminde Örgüt Kültürü*. Konya: Selçuk Üniversitesi Sağlık Bilimleri Enstitüsü.
Katz, D., and B.S. Georgopoulos. 1976. Organizations in a changing world. *Organizational behavior: Readings and cases*, 383–401. New York: Macmillan.
Kaynak, T. 1995. *Organizasyonel Davranış ve Yönlendirilmesi*. İstanbul: Alfa Baım Yayım Dağıtım.
Kelly, J. 1975. *Organizational behavior*, Revised ed. London: Richard D. Irwin.

King, A.D. 1998. *Kültür, küreselleşme ve dünya sistemi*. Ankara: Bilim ve Sanat Yayınları.
Kinnier, R.T., J.L. Kernes, and T.M. Dautheribes. 2000. A short list of universal moral values. *Counseling and Values* 45 (1): 4–16.
Koçel, T. 2014. *İşletme Yöneticiliği*, 270. İstanbul: Beta Basım A.Ş.
Kroeber, A.L., and C. Kluckhohn. 1952. *Cultur: A critical review of concepts and definitions*. Cambridge, MA.
Leblebici, D.N., and A. Karasoy. 2009. Örgüt kültürünün algılanan hizmet kalitesine etkisi: Kamu ve özel öğrenci yurtlarında karşılaştırmalı bir araştırma. *H.Ü. İktisadi ve İdari Bilimler Fakültesi Dergisi* 27(1): 279–304.
Lewin, K. 1945. The research center for group dynamics at Massachusetts Institute of Technology, 126–136 (American Sociological Association).
Lewin, K. 1951. *Field theory in social science*. New York: Harper & Brothers.
Lewin, K. 2007. Forcefield analysis. Available at: http://cannexus.ca/wp-content/uploads/2014/04/Where-In-The-World-Non-Canadian-Experience-Counts-Too-Neault-41.pdf.
Likert, R. 1967. *The human organization: Its management and value*. New York: McGraw-Hill.
Maslow, A.H. 1954. *Motivation and personality*. New York: Harper & Row.
Mayo, E. 1960. *The human problems of an indusrial civilization*. New York: The Viking Press.
Miles, R.E., C.C. Snow, A.D. Meyer, and H.J. Coleman. 1978. Organizational strategy, structure, and process. *Academy of Management Review*, 546–562.
Minkov, M. 2011. *Cultural differences in a globalizing world*. Bingley: Emerald Publishing.
Morley, D., and K.H. Chen. 1996. Introduction. In *Critical dialogues in cultural studies*, ed. D. Morley and K.H. Chen. London: Routledge, Chapman and Hall.
Mullins, L.J. 1996. *Management and organizational behavior*, 4th ed. London: Pitmon Publishing.
Münch, R., and N.J. Smelser. 2014. *Cultural theo* (C. Atay, Trans.). Istanbul: Pales Publications.
Nalçaoğlu, H. 2004. *Kültürel farkın yapısökümü*. Phoenix: Ankara.
Northcraft, G.B., and M.A. Neale. 1990. *Organizational behavior*. Orlando: The Dryden Press.
Organ, D.W., and W.C. Hammer. 1982. *Organizational behavior: An applied psychological approach*. Texas: Business Publications.
Ouchi, W.G. 1981. *Theory Z: How American business can meet the Japanese challenge*, 4th ed. Massachusetts: Addison-Wesley.
Öğüt, A., and A. Kocabacak. 2008. Küreselleşme sürecinde Türk iş kültüründe yaşanan dönüşümün boyutları. *Türkiyat Araştırmaları Dergisi* 1 (23): 145–170.
Özgener, Ş. 2000. Değer yönetimi: İmalat sanayiindeki Türk yöneticilerinin yükselen değerlerine iilişkin bir araştırma. *Muğla Üniversitesi SBE Dergisi*, 173–189.
Özgener, Ş. 2004. *İş ahlakının temelleri: yönetsel bir yaklaşım*, 1st ed. Ankara: Nobel Yayın Dağıtım.
Özkalp, E., and Ç. Kırel. 2016. *Örgütsel Davranış*, 6th ed. Bursa: Ekin Basım Yayın Dağıtım.
Özkalp, E., A.A. Özdemir, and E.C. Duyan. 2016. Değer tipleri ve öznel iyi oluş arasındaki ilişkide örgütsel vatandaşlık davranışının aracılık rolü. *İş, güç endüstri ilişkileri ve insan kaynakları dergisi*, 1–22.
Parsons, T. 1991. *The social system*. London: Routledge & Kegan Paul.
Peters, T.J., and R.H. Waterman. 1987. *Yönetme ve Yükselme Sanatı*. İstanbul: Altın Kitaplar Yayınevi.
Pettigrew, A.M. 1979. On studying organizatioal cultures. *Administrative Science Quarterly* 24 (4): 570–581.
Prencipe, A., and C.C. Helwig. 2002. The development of reasoning about the teaching of values. *Child Development* 73 (3): 841–856.
Ralston, D.A., D.H. Holt, R.H. Terpstra, and Y. Kai-Cheng. 2008. The impact of national culture and economic ideology on manegerial work values: A study of the United States, Russia, Japan, and China. *Journal of International Business Studies* 39 (1): 8–26.
Ralston, D.A., N.V. Thang, and N.K. Napier. 1999. A comparative study of the work values of north and south Vietnamese managers. *Journal of International Business Studies* 30 (4): 655–672.
Raven, B.H. 1999. Kurt Lewin address: Influence, power, religion, and the mechanism of social control. *Journal of Social Issues* 55 (1): 161–186.

Razik, T.A., and A.D. Swanson. 1995. *Fundemental concepts of educational leadership and management*. New Jersey: Merril Prentica Hall.
Robbins, S.P. 1997. *Essentials of organizational behavior*. Upper Saddle River, NJ: Prentice Hall.
Robbins, S.P., and T.A. Judge. 2015. *Örgütsel Davranış*. Ankara: Nobel Yayıncılık.
Rokeach, M. 1973. *The nature of human values*. New York: The Free Press.
Ros, M., S.H. Schwartz, and S. Surkiss. 1999. Basic individual values, work values, and the meaning of work. *Applied Psychology: An International Review* 48 (1): 49–71.
Rush, H.M. 1976. The world of work and the behavioral sciences: A perspective and an overview. *Organizational behavior: Readings and cases*, 3–14. New York: Macmillian.
Sabuncuoğlu, Z., and M. Vergiliel Tüz. 2013. *Örgütsel davranış*. Bursa: Aktüel Yayınları.
Sargut, S.A. 2001. *Kültürler Arası Farklılaşma ve Yönetim*, 2nd ed. Ankara: İmge Kitabevi.
Schein, E.H. 2010. *Organizational culture and leadership*. San Francisco: Wiley.
Schwartz, S.H. 1999. A theory of cultural values and some implications for work. *Applied Psychology: An International Review* 48 (1): 23–47.
Scott, S., and R.A. Bruce. 1995. Decision-making style: The development and assessment of a new measure. *Educational and Psychological Measurement* 55 (5): 818–831.
Slocum, J.W., and D. Hellriegel. 2009. *Principles of organizational behavior*. South Western: Cengage Learning.
Sverko, B. 1999. The work importance study: Recent changes of values in Croatia. *Applied Psychology: An International Review* 48 (1): 89–102.
Şişman, M. 1996. Yönetim Kuramı ve Kültürlerarası Farklılaşma Açısından Yönetim Uygulamaları. *Eğitim Yönetimi* 2 (2): 295–308.
Şişman, M. 2002. *Örgütler ve Kültürler*. Ankara: Pegem A Yayınları.
Tanase, I.A. 2015. *The importance of organizational culture based on culture transfer*, 848–852. s.n.: Bükreş.
Taş, A., and E. Cevrioğlu. 2013. Ulusal kültürü oluşturan değerler tipolojisi-stratejik yönetim ilişkisi: kültürel kodların işletmelerin stratejik yönelimlerine etkisi üzerinde bir araştırma. *AİBÜ Sosyal Bilimler Enstitüsü Dergisi* 13 (2): 417–435.
TAV. 2018a. Invester relations. Available at: http://www.tavyatirimciiliskileri.com/en-EN/Pages/StrategicPriorities.aspx. Accessed 22 Feb 2018.
TAV. 2018b. Sustainability report. Available at: http://www.tavyatirimciiliskileri.com/en-EN/Pages/CorporateSocialResponsibility.aspx. Accessed 2018 02 2018.
TAV. 2018c. TAV investment relations annual report. [Online] Available at: http://www.tavyatirimciiliskileri.com/en-EN/Lists/Annual%20Reports/Attachments/16/TAV_FRAE_2016_MTB.PDF Accessed 22 Feb 2018.
Taylor, F.W. 2013. *Bilimsel Yönetimin İlkeleri*, 6th ed. Ankara: Adres Yayınları.
Thompson, K.R. 1990. Organizational culture: A behavioral perspective. *Organizational climate and culture*, 319–344. San Francisco: Jossey-Bass Publishers.
Trice, H.M., and J.M. Beyer. 1984. Studying organizational cultures through rites and ceremonials. *Academy of Management Review* 9 (4): 653–669.
Trist, E.L., and K.W. Bamforth. 1951. Some social and psychological consequences of the longwall method of coal getting: An examination of the psychological situation and defences of a work group in relation to the social structure and technological content of the work system. *Human Relations* 4 (1): 3–38.
Tuulik, K., T. Õunapuu, K. Kuimet, and E. Titov. 2016. Rokeach's instrumental and terminal values as descriptors of modern organisation values. *International Journal of Organizational Leadership* 5 (2): 151–161.
Uyan, G. 2002. *Öğretmenlerin iş değerleri, kişilik özellikleri ve iş tatminleri arasındaki ilişkilerin incelenmesi: MEB'na bağlı resmi ve özel eğitim kurumlarında gerçekleştirilen bir uygulama*. İstanbul: İstanbul Üniversitesi Sosyal Bilimler Enstitüsü.
Ülgen, H., and S.K. Mirze. 2013. Stratejilerin Uygulanması-2: Yönetim Biçimleri, Paylaşılan Değerler, İnsan Kaynakları ve İşletme Yetenekleri. *İşletmelerde Stratejik Yönetim*, 408–435. Beta Yayınları: İstanbul.

Vurgun, L., and S. Öztop. 2011. Yönetim ve örgüt kültüründe değerlerin önemi. *SDÜ İktisadi ve İdari Bilimler Fakültesi Dergisi* 16 (3): 217–230.

Weber, M. 1947. *The theory of social and economic organization*. New York: Oxford University Press.

William, F.C. 1995. *Values, nature and culture in American Corporation*. North Carolina: Oxford University Press.

Yeşil, S., İ.F. Doğan, and Ö. Doğan. 2016. Örgüt kültürünün girişimcilik yönelimi ile örgütsel performans üzerindeki etkisi: Kahramanmaraş ili tekstil sektörü örneği. *Yönetim ve Ekonomi Araştırmaları Dergisi* 14 (1): 150–172.

Yiğittir, S. 2012. İlköğretim 5. sınıf öğrencilerinin değer yönelimlerinin Rokeach ve Schwartz Değer sınıflandırmasına göre değerlendirilmesş. *Dicle Üniversitesi Ziya Gökalp Eğitim Fakültesi Dergisi* 19: 1–15.

Yıldırım, A. 2011. *İlköğretim okullarındaki örgüt ikliminin yönetici ve öğretmenlerin değer sistemleri bakımından incelenmesi*. Konya: Selçuk Üniversitesi Eğitim Bilimleri Enstitüsü.

Yılmaz, P. 2010. *Örgüt kültürü ve finans sektöründe bir uygulama*. İstanbul: Bahçeşehir Üniversitesi.

Yozgat, O. 1978. *İşletme Yönetimi*. İstanbul: Nihad Sayar Yayınları.

Yüksel, Y., and T. Durna. 2015. The adaptability of management models across cultures. *Uluslararası İktisadi ve İdari İncelemeler Dergisi* 7 (14): 295–316.

Chapter 2
Value-Based Enterprise Risk Management: Ergonomics, Ethics, and Organizational Structure Considered Approach

The Corporate sustainability is only possible owing to the value-based management.
We need strong values, ethics and structure to be sustain.
Ayse and Triant G.

Contents

In terms of system approach, enterprises are open systems. Open systems have the potential to be affected and influenced by both internal and external factors. Businesses, such as individuals, have to keep up with the external and internal environments in which they are maintained. The internal and external environments of the enterprises have to manage their risks based on a situational approach in order to continue their lives because they are constantly changing. How can sustainability be possible when there is a continuous change in environment? Therefore, it is considered as a strategy to support sustainability by updating the organizational objectives with a situational approach and using the resources with correct and timely allocation. In this context, value-based risk management requires a flexible and development-free structure. Therefore, values are one of the key elements of corporate sustainability.

Management is based on decision-making. The enterprises are operated every day by making decisions and implementing these decisions at both managerial and individual levels.

A. Kucuk Yilmaz and T. G. Flouris, *Values, Ergonomics and Risk Management in Aviation Business Strategy*, https://doi.org/10.1007/978-981-15-1006-9_2

Values

The decisions of the executives are influenced by both the corporate culture and the belief system within the corporate culture. For this reason, decisions are actually resulting in the main ingredients of an organization such as ethical standards, corporate culture, corporate strategy, and risk management.

When supported by a psychological and sociological approach, values are effective in concluding both institutional and individual efforts in a desirable way, with both individual and cumulative impact.

Values have such a critical role that managers' decisions are influenced by both the corporate culture and the belief system within the culture. In other words, the decisions taken by the managers are the sum of both their values and corporate values as the following equation:

Our New Equation to best decision-making:

$$\boldsymbol{F}(\text{Managerial decision}) = (\text{individual values})\boldsymbol{x} + (\text{corporate values})\,\boldsymbol{y}$$

Values have such a critical role that managers' decisions are influenced by both the corporate culture and the belief system within the culture. In other words, the decisions taken by the managers are the sum of own values and corporate values. Managers reflect own values on their administrator decisions. It is very important that the manager values and corporate values are compatible with the optimum performance of the manager. Therefore, values should be taken into consideration as one of the main criteria for selecting managers and personnel in terms of human resources management.

In our view, gap analysis between corporate values and manager values and personal values should be an important part of the enterprise risk management system, because values are determinative factors to both high corporate performance and successful risk management practices.

Therefore, the values of the managers and institutions should overlap. Manager, employee, and institution values should be compatible with each other.

The necessity of adaptation in today's business environment required the value-based enterprise risk management application, which is supported by the contingency approach. The changing external environment conditions require a rapid and accurate change of the internal conditions due to the situational approach. Therefore, the internal and external environment is constantly developing and changing. In today's business conditions, the effects of the risks on each other and their relationship with each other must be taken into consideration. Therefore, business managers should see the whole picture in classical terms. Managers should follow the optimal decision-making process by systematically analyzing the analysis of potential events with value-based risk management and adapting to changing conditions in a short time; because value-based Enterprise Risk Management is a systematic management approach that is consistent with Organizational Culture and Personality.

In order to capture cultural integrity in business, we need common values. Briefly, values are also vital for corporate sustainability. Every institution, organization, and business, the largest and most important source for the company is the human resource that makes decisions by using other sources.

We believe that there is a serious relationship between values and corporate performance indicators (see figure). The companies that can integrate their values with management systems gain a competitive advantage in terms of both stakeholder and stakeholder relations in terms of both stakeholder and financial value. For these reasons, value-based risk management is essential for today's business management.

Values are also essential components of the organization's personality. In order to achieve the mission, the organizational personality and corporate values must be intact because the organization develops by inspiring from its values in personality.

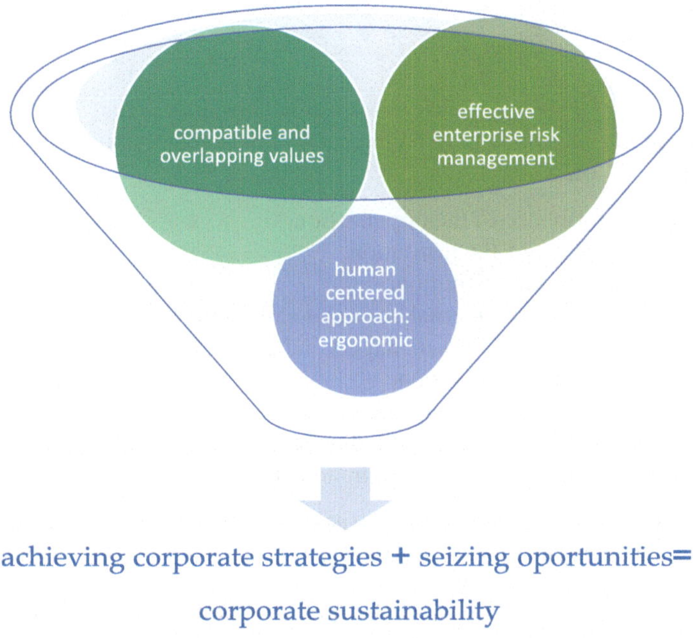

In this point, value-based risk management is a holistic and systematic structural system created to identify potential events with resources, to manage these risks in accordance with the corporate values, risk-taking appetite, tolerance, and profile, and to provide a reasonable level of assurance regarding the company's strategy.

Values determine the way of doing business on both a managerial and individual basis, the decision-making criteria and the ethical field that directs itself. Values are also fundamental to the stability of shareholder relations. The purpose of the entity and the strategies it wants to achieve must be compatible with and reflective of the corporate values.

Aim: improved corporate performance

Values inspire everyone in the organization and thus improve corporate performance.

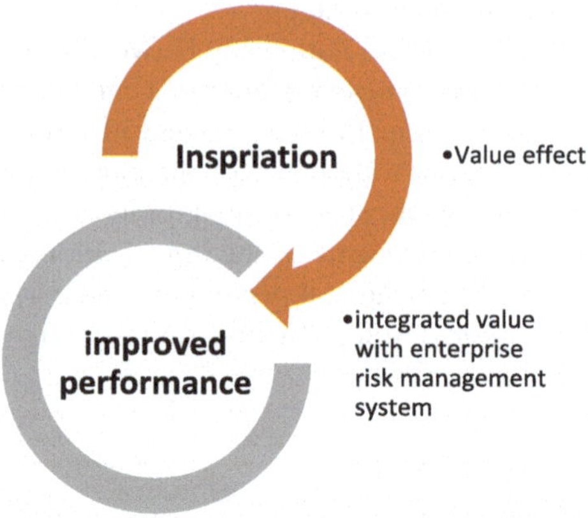

Values are vital since they have an impact on fundamental issues in management and strategy as follows:

- increase the performance of the organization,
- increase the efficiency of the institution,
- increase the profit of the institution,
- provide both external and internal customer satisfaction,
- increase the motivation of both managers and employees,
- strengthen the corporate reputation,
- strengthen the culture of the institution,
- create a common belief and understanding shared by all employees, and
- increase the sense of ownership of shareholders.

If the value system in the institution is weak, it cannot be holistic. Corporate sustainability cannot be mentioned for a company that does not have value. Values have an integrative and integrative effect. Thus, the value-based approach will contribute to the achievement of corporate risk management objectives by increasing the performance of risk management implementation.

Corporate values enable employees to work effectively in line with corporate objectives. Nowadays, firms perform their activities in a business environment which requires them to implement such a system of indicators that illustrates value and profitability in a better way (Bukvič 2014, p. 196).

In today's contemporary environment of management and strategy field, value-based risk management gains interest via focusing ethic and strategy with a *contingency approach*. Every entrepreneurial activity and in particular, every long-term strategic decision involves risks (GleiBner 2005, p. 480).

The International Organization for Standardization (ISO) is a worldwide organization. ISO 31000 is the international standard for risk management and was published in 2009. This standard assists companies in risk analyses and risk assessments by providing comprehensive guidelines (BSI 2016, p. 2). According to the ISO Risk Management standards, risk is defined as a combination or result of the effect of uncertainty on targets, which may be positive, negative, or deviated from the expected (KIWA 2016, p. 1).

In our value-based view, risk (especially in mean as threat) is about directly related with deviated from the core values. America, Canada, Australia/New Zealand, and the UK have remarkable practices in risk management. Especially in Australia, New Zealand, and the UK, risk management models have been developed considering ISO 31000 standards. The models are fundamentally different from each other in terms of principles, and processes while arguing that risk management should be effective throughout the organization (Kızılboğa 2014, p. 82).

A winning strategy is about exploiting an area accompany performance better in from anyone else. Ambitious goals for creating value entail taking on risk. Thus, the execution of any strategy is governed by the willingness of management and the Board to accept the risk and the organization's capacity to bear and manage risk (Deloach 2015, p. 1).

Risk management provides a competitive advantage to enterprises that are able to interpret and manage risks even better than other enterprises, especially during periods of severe increases in uncertainty and in times of crisis (Müller et al. 2014, p. 12)

Values are the basic principles that shape the behavior of all of us. Each society and each organization have their own values of importance and priority. Attitudes and values of people play a key role in making accurate and timely decisions. In the decision-making process of the managers, the evaluation criteria are the values.

Values are the unchanging beliefs that determine the desired behavioral patterns for the organization. At the same time, values affect the behavior preferences of people who are motivated to act consistently. While personal values affect people's intentions and behaviors, organizational values determine the goals, policies, and strategies of organizations (Bilegt 2012, p. 5).

Enterprise risk management is a continuous process designed to help identify strategies and objectives that are consistent with an organization's vision and mission and that support these two elements.

Enterprise risk management philosophy assumes that every organization exists to both provide and maintain values for shareholders. Every organization/business is confronted with uncertainty. All managers are in need of making a decision regarding how much uncertainty will be accepted when trying to increase shareholder value. The risks which include threats and opportunities have considerable potential to both erase and strengthen corporate value. Enterprise risk management enables the institution to strengthen its capacity to create value by dealing effectively and efficiently with risks and opportunities.

According to literature, in the historical background of human societies, developmental characteristics, forms of production, and social relations are the way of life of a society. The different way of life of each society differentiates cultures. The reason for this difference arises from the fact that cultural elements are not similar (Şahin 2010, p. 22).

For a good risk management practice, all employees of the organization, from senior management to the lowest levels, should be familiar with the risk phenomenon, risk management, and corporate risks. This implies the necessity of institutional risk culture. The formation of this culture requires a wide-ranging education (Derici et al. 2007, p. 171). In order to assimilate the business, it is necessary to establish a culture and language based on long-term risk (Topçu 2013, p. 67). For this purpose, it should be ensured that individual values are taken into account together with managerial values and organizational culture should be improved.

According to Kizilboga (2012), who transmitted it from COSO, risk culture is the belief and attitude of how the organization perceives the risk in every job it does, from strategy determination to daily practice activities (Kızılboğa 2012c, p. 85).

Culture inspires and is inspired by shared values and beliefs in the organization. Culture is one of the most important elements of social environmental conditions surrounding organizations. Organizational culture has considerable effects on the life and development of organizations; it is a paradigm that is an intellectual structure that allows the organization to be seen.

The paradigm of the organization provides shared structures, common language, and references to individuals, and provides a similar approach to a solution to a problem within the organization. According to this paradigm approach, organizational culture is a system of norms, behaviors, values, beliefs, and habits. For this reason, culture has the power to direct both people's behavior, attitude, and work style within an organization.

Actually, values are dominant influencers in shaping organizational behavior. For this reason, effective risk management must be set according to the values of corporates. Integrated value, ethic, and enterprise risk management in the ergonomic concept is the key lever to increase shareholder value holistically. Strong culture is actually based on values which are clearly organized and shared throughout a corporation.

Values are fundamental for all individuals in the organization to believe and share; they are and will continue to be an important element of culture. All of these values constitute the basic understanding system in the organization. The organization uses this basic understanding in both internal and external adaptation and decision-making process. A central element in the value-based approach is to start by examining the organization's strategy and build a model to calculate an internal valuation of the firm based on achieving the strategic plan (Moody 2009, p. 74).

In view of value, Enterprise Risk Management (ERM) is the process by which organizations assess, control, exploit, finance, and monitor risks from all sources for the purpose of increasing short- and long-term value for stakeholders (Segal 2005, p. 1).

It is the risk manager's success to both control and manage an out-of-control environment. The principles of risk management are well-established across large businesses, which clearly recognize that they need to manage uncertainty in order to meet their strategic objectives (Baes et al. 2016a, b, p. 32, p. 1). In achieving corporate strategies in times of turbulence, managers should utilize corporate-shaped value-based Enterprise Risk Management (ERM). This kind of enterprise risk management system supports both high ethical standards and corporate reputation in addition to creating an innovative internal environment.

ERM is a widely adopted framework used to manage the full range of corporate risks. According to Segal (2005, p. 2), Value-Based ERM is an approach that makes the quantification of value central to all aspects of the ERM process. This value-centric focus has two key advantages:

- Quantifies the impact of ERM on shareholder value.
- Creates a common "language" that unifies otherwise disparate ERM processes.

When an organization integrates value in their ERM process, both a manager's attitudes and decisions are affected via this integration. Organizational decision-making process works according to assumed organizational and managerial values. At this point, it should be noted that values are fundamental determinatives in both organizational and managerial decision-making. So, the organization will close to corporate sustainability with sounded ethic structure.

We may evaluate businesses as people. Businesses have the potential to be influenced and affected by humans. The enterprises also have limited resources, just like people. At the same time, businesses—as do people—have both strong and weak aspects. People are different from each other and perceived differently by those outside themselves. The same is true for businesses. Businesses consist of people who are affected by their own values, which has an impact on their decision-making style.

It is not possible to obtain original and sustainable results without adding personality and spirit to the work. This means that each individual brings their uniqueness into operation, adding to a company's uniqueness with their different backgrounds, personalities, experiences, education, and cultural components. Considering the human resource in the whole enterprise, this uniqueness can be understood as a whole. Therefore, value-based risk management takes into account the individual. So, this unique approach to value-based management is a critical aspect of management and strategy.

Value-Based Risk Management (VBRM) is all about responding to change and dynamically focusing risk management efforts where they deliver the most value to the business. There are four main pillars to the approach which are discussed in detail in the sections that follows (Baes et al. 2016a, b, p. 32):

(i) Maintain strategic alignment: Keep risk management aligned with changing business strategies.
(ii) Focus on vulnerabilities: Support to rising awareness level as corporate level, present more clear holistic picture as like SWOT Analysis.
(iii) Facilitate decision-making: Support all systems with timelly decision making.
(iv) Build a dynamic risk culture: Develop risk capabilities to enable resilience to change.

Value-Based ERM creates a consistent approach by unifying multiple processes through a focus on value. This minimizes friction, aligns incentives, and encourages value-enhancing decisions and behaviors. Every member of the enterprise is "rowing in the same direction" of value creation (Segal 2005, p. 3).

Strategic Viewpoint

Integration of values with enterprise risk management is a strategic topic since this integrated approach has a considerable effect on both corporate reputation and its innovative business environment.

As a concept, "sustainability" is a subject that we all pause upon when we hear individually. The concept of achieving sustainability in this life of this concept, which is not easy to pronounce, requires both perspective and a strategy as well as a sound method.

A strategic view of risk management adding value focuses on the Board of Directors and executive management to satisfy themselves that the strategy is realistic and does not result in unacceptable execution risks. There are three things the Board and management do to realize this strategic view (Deloach 2015, p. 2). TAV Airports Holding has a strategic view to enterprise risk management and their management system is based on values. This is a considerable sample from global business organizations. So, "every manager is the value driver".

Enterprise risk management has a remarkable philosophy and values on which it is built. This set of values represents the paradigm of enterprise risk management. With this contemporary paradigm, value-based risk management is based on interactive system. this interactive system has double side communication as both from the individual to the enterprise and from the management to person in both the inductive and deductive manner. With its value-based risk management approach, it has the potential to influence all aspects of organizations. Because of this feature, it is considered as an up-to-date management system that affects the organizational structure and shapes the organizational structure.

It is important to develop the right strategies for creating value in management. In line with this strategy, managing enterprise-wide risks is critical to protecting and enhancing business value. Corporate risk management, strategy, people, process, technology, and information integrated with values can be applied successfully.

Complexity, interrelations, uncertainties, and risks are increasing due to changes and developments in the real sector such as liberalization, privatization, commercialization, and competition structures throughout the world. The success of organizations depends to a large extent on their capacity to identify, prevent, mitigate, and manage their risks. Enterprise risk management provides an effective structure for these requirements.

Risk management has direct interrelation with values. Since the culture of risk is the belief and attitude of how the organization perceives the risk in everything it does, from strategy determination to daily practice activities. The risk culture reflects the working style of the institution, determines how corporate risk management elements are implemented, how risks are defined, which risk is acceptable, and affects the management of risk (Kizilboga 2012, p. 85).

As a matter of fact, today's needed management system is value-based corporate risk management that integrates both the internal environment and external environmental risk factors with both contingency approach and values.

Enterprise risk management helps management achieve the entity's performance and profitability targets and prevents loss of resources. Enterprise risk management helps ensure effective reporting and compliance with laws and regulations and helps avoid damage to the entity's reputation and associated consequences. In sum, enterprise risk management helps an entity get to where it wants to go and avoid pitfalls and surprises along the way (COSO 2004, p. 1).

It should be noted that COSO emphasizes the ethical issue in their ERM framework. COSO's ERM framework based on values. COSO is dedicated to guiding executive management and governance entities toward the establishment of more effective, efficient, and ethical business operations on a global basis (COSO 2018, p. 2). Here are four themes that are vital to effective integration of ERM (Opgenorth 2017, p. 1):

1. Implementation with strategy.
2. Integration with performance.
3. Lay a strong foundation with risk governance and culture.
4. Tie risk considerations into decision-making processes.

Value-based risk management processes and systems "encourage" managers and employees to behave in a way that maximizes the value of the organization (Koller 1994, p. 11). This is one of the unique qualifications of both ERM and Value-based risk management. This feature of risk management makes it superior to other management systems.

Inappropriately large amounts of resources tend to be allocated to the first two phases (identify and analyze) at the expense of the final two phases (mitigate and control). By correcting this imbalance—and by incorporating benchmarking and grading into the traditional risk management process—Value-Based Risk Management (VBRM) produces higher quality results with a reduced expenditure of time and other precious resources (Curran 2006, p. 17). An important part of VBM is a deep understanding of the performance variables that will actually create the value of the business—the key value drivers (Koller 1994, p. 11).

The number, quality, and effects of the factors affecting the management style and system of the organization vary from organization to organization. Every organization is unique because the conditions of each organization are unique. According to the contingency approach, the status, activity, and environment of each organization vary. Since the conditions that affect the organizations and the internal situation of the organization are different, the management and organization form and system of each organization will be different and distinctive (Ozturk and Arslan 2016, p. 130).

Values have a considerable effect on vision and mission. Actually, corporate mission and vision are both identify and inspires according to corporate values. For example, TAV Airport Holding states their values with their vision and mission as follows (TAV Airports Holding 2018).

TAV Airports Holding Management Philosophy

Our Mission: To create the highest value for all stakeholders in airport operations through our customer-oriented management approach.

TAV Corporate Values: Professionalism, Respect, Dynamism, Innovation, Teamwork. As seen in statements, TAV Holding has value-based management. Their vision and mission is consistent with their values. Specifically, their missions also depended on value-based approach. Their approach has two main ingredients as ethical standards and ergonomic.

> We act in line with ethical standards as a fundamental rule, prioritizing respect for people, the environment, laws, and regulations. We act in an honest, transparent, fair and responsible manner in all our endeavors. (TAV Airports Holding 2018)

Like TAV Airports Holding, "values" that are understood, embraced, and internalized by all personnel in an organization are an integral part of the corporate culture. Businesses with this principle make decisions based on value and incorporate this into all business processes.

In other words, VBRM optimizes human and financial resources to dramatically improve the risk management process, particularly the highly critical mitigation and control phases (Curran 2006). If the value system in the institution is weak, it cannot be holistic. Corporate sustainability cannot be mentioned for a company that does not have value.

Values have an integrative effect on organizational performance (corporate performance). Thus, the value-based approach will contribute to the achievement of corporate risk management objectives by increasing the performance of risk management implementation.

Ergonomics have a key role in Value-based risk management in, especially, two types of ergonomics: **cognitive** and **organizational** ergonomics.

Cognitive ergonomics is concerned with mental processes, such as perception, memory, reasoning, and motor response, as they affect interactions among humans and other elements of a system (Relevant topics include mental workload, decision-making, skilled performance, human–computer interaction, human reliability, work stress, and training as these may relate to human–system design.) (IEA 2018, p. 1).

This field is also critical to identify risk sources such as skill performance, interaction, stress, design, perception, attitude, and individual values which may affect on decision-making.

Organizational ergonomics is concerned with the optimization of sociotechnical systems, including their organizational structures, policies, and processes (Relevant topics include communication, crew resource management, work design, the design of working times, teamwork, participatory design, community ergonomics, cooperative work, new work paradigms, virtual organizations, telework, and quality management.) (IEA 2018, p. 1).

There is a critical approach of value-based risk management that is a holistic approach to ergonomics with cognitive and organizational domains. İf managers identify human factor based risks in both cognitive and organizational ergonomics sources, then managers achieve optimization of risks.

Risk Management Perspective in Aviation Management

Risk is related to future events and their consequences (outcomes). The objective of risk analysis is to predict unknown physical quantities such as the explosion pressure, the number of fatalities, cost, and so on and assess uncertainties. Risk analysis contains technical, social, and economic issues. Probabilities and expected values are used to express risk. A common approach to risk defines it as probability multiplied by consequences, i.e., what is called the expected value in probability calculus. However, the use of probabilities can generate poor predictions as these are based on conditional specific background knowledge and do not necessarily provide a sufficiently informative picture of the risk. The aim of the risk analysis is to establish a risk picture for a given activity or a given system and through this, to provide a basis for decision-making concerning the selection of solutions and measures.

Furthermore, the author concludes that the main component of risk is uncertainty and not probability and there is a need to adopt a broader approach to risk beyond the expected values and the probabilities and fundamental concepts need to reinterpret. Risk analysis as a tool for assessing uncertainties about risk and risk estimates and probability is a measure of uncertainty through the eyes of the assessor and based on a background knowledge (Aven 2008, p. 204). The large and relevant database may provide more precise probabilities, which may be able to provide accurate predictions of future events.

The objective of the analysis is to identify the important contributors to risk and describe the effect of possible measures on the risk. The author pointed out that we should describe system performance as a whole, where the steps and the stages on the way to the accident are seen as parts of a whole rather than as distinct events.

However, it is difficult to include all factors contributing to risk, including human performance and organizational, management and social factors, to incorporate human error and complex decision-making and to capture the nonlinear dynamics of interactions among components, including the adaptation of social and technical structures over time.

The author stressed that none approach is able to meet the expectations with respect to all aspects. However, the causal chains and event modeling approach is continuously improved, incorporating human, operational and organizational factors. The applied models are judged not only with their ability to represent the real world but also their ability to simplify the world (Aven 2008, p. 204).

Risk management includes all the necessary measures and activities which are placed on many levels and carried out to manage risk and assist the organization to achieve its goals and vision. The risk management task is divided into three main categories: (a) strategic risk, (b) financial risk, and (c) operational risk. Some significant issues to ensure success are: (i) establishment of a strategy for risk management, (ii) establishment of a risk management process for the firm (formal processes and routines), (iii) establishment of management structures (roles and responsibilities), and (iv) implementation of analyses and support systems (risk analysis tools, recording systems for occurrences of various types of events, etc.), communication, training, and development of risk management culture.

Risk analysis has an important role in risk management and can follow a basic structure independently of its area of application. Risk assessment can include both the risk analysis and risk evaluation. Risk assessment is followed by risk treatment and represents the process and implementation of measures to modify risk, including tools to avoid, reduce optimize, transfer, and retain risk. The risk matrix is suggested using categories for both probability and consequences (such as highly probable to unlikely and insignificant to very large).

The first step of risk analysis is to define the objectives of the risk analysis and these are based on a problem definition, as well as limitations to the scope of analysis such as lack of available resources, time limits, and lack of data and information. A working group must be established that has a piece of knowledge about risk analysis and about the system. Also, it is important to make clear how the analyses are to be used in the decision-*making process.*

The selection of analysis method depends on the phase, ease of access to information, the system's significance and its complexity and other factors. The selection of analysis method is also choosing between a forward and backward approach; in the first, the risk analysis begins with the initiating events and in the later, the risk analysis begins with the identification of the resulting events or situations.

The first phase of the execution part of risk analysis is the identification of initiating events (hazard identification) and this should be carried out in a structured and systematic manner with persons who have the necessary competence involved. Cause analysis monitors what is needed for the initiating events to occur. Experts on the systems and in-*depth understanding of the system are normally required.*

Consequence analysis for each initiating event is carried out, addressing the possible consequences the event can lead to, such as financial losses, loss of lives and environmental damage. Using probabilities is difficult to transform uncertainty into probability figures. Thus, in a consequence analysis, one consequence value is specified, although different outcomes are possible. This value is normally interpreted as the expected value should the initiating event occur.

The risk picture is established based on the cause analysis and the consequence analysis. The objective and the type of analysis defines whether the risk picture can be limited to some defined areas and issues.

To be completed, the risk picture needs sensitivity and robustness analyses. These analyses present to what extent the results are dependent on important conditions and assumptions and what it takes for the conclusions to be changed. The depth of these analyses depends on the decision problem, the risks that are analyzed and the available resources. The risk analysis and the discussion of the results will be able to give their message (the risk picture and risk presentation) and then the management can be able to focus on the decision-making.

The main disadvantage of the cost–benefit analysis is the transformation of noneconomic consequences to monetary values. Thus, the value of security and safety is not adequately taken into account by the approach. Selecting the alternative, the risk analysis will provide a basis for arriving at measures that can modify the risk. These measures could be either probability reducing or consequence reducing. It is important to identify the areas and factors that contribute the most to risk. One way of doing this is by looking at the change in risk if this area or factor had contributed insignificantly to the risk. So, if the change is large, then this area or this factor is important.

If the target is to satisfy the risk acceptance criteria or tolerability limits and the criteria and limits are relatively easy to meet, then there may be little incentive for identifying risk-reducing measures. Also, a measure that has a positive expected present value should be implemented immediately.

Assessing risks compliance with principles and standards will be among the first reference points. Risk management processes need formal guidelines or criteria (i.e., risk acceptance criteria and cost-effectiveness indices) to simplify the decision-making. It is a managerial responsibility to make decisions under uncertainty, and management should be aware of the relevant risks and uncertainties.

The risk can be described by injury and accident statistics, risk indicators based on hazard situations, barrier indicators, risk analyses, interviews, surveys of coworkers, and expert groups. In addition, risk analysis includes the identification and analysis of initiating events, cause analysis, consequence analysis, and risk description.

The most basic methods for risk analysis are as follows:

1. Coarse risk analysis, which can provide a crude risk picture, with relatively modest effort and performed by dividing the analysis subject into sub-elements and then carrying the risk analysis for each of these sub-elements in turn. This method identifies the most important risk contributors, and then the causal picture and/or the consequence picture can be accessed in detail using more detailed analyses.

2. Job safety analysis—a simple qualitative risk analysis methodology which is used to identify hazards that are associated with a work assignment that is to be executed. This is usually checklist based.
3. Failure modes and effects analysis that aims to reveal possible failures and to predict the failure effects on the system as a whole. The method is inductive, investigating what happens if a component fails and this takes place for each component of the system. The advantage of this method is that it provides a systematic overview of the important failures in the system and it forces the designer to evaluate the reliability of his system.
4. Hazard and Operability studies—a qualitative risk analysis technique that is used to identify weaknesses and hazards in a processing facility and is used in the planning phase (design). This method is a systematic analysis of how deviation from the design specifications in a system can arise.
5. SWIFT (Structured What—If Technique) uses the lead question—what if—systematically in order to identify deviations from normal conditions. The method utilizes a predefined checklist of the elements that are to be reviewed.
6. Fault tree analysis, which is one of the most used reliability and risk analysis methods and is a logical diagram that shows the relation between system failure, i.e., a specific undesirable event and failures of the components of the system. The undesirable event constitutes the top event of the tree and the different component failures constitute the basic events of the tree and the different component failures constitute the basic events of the tree. A fault tree comprises symbols that show the basic events of the system, and the relation between these events and the state of the system. The top event consists of the starting point when constructing the fault tree and then we must identify the possible failures (events) that can be the direct causes of the top event. Qualitative (based on an identification of the minimal cut sets, since system failure occurs when all the events in at least one minimal cut sets occur) and quantitative (must determine probabilities for the basic events of the fault tree) analysis of the fault tree can take place.
7. Event tree analysis is used to study the consequences of the initiating event of a bow tie diagram. The method can be used both quantitatively (the method provides a picture of the possible scenarios) and qualitatively (probabilities are linked to the various event sequences and their consequences).
8. Bayesian networks consist of events (nodes) and arrows. The arrows show dependencies, i.e., causal connections. Each node can be in various states and the number of states is selected by the risk analyst.
9. Monte Carlo simulation. This technique is to generate a computer model of the system to be investigated, for example, represented as a reliability block diagram, and then to simulate the operation of the system for a specific period of time.

The author pointed out that the use of quantitative analyses should take place with extra care, in particular when cases with large uncertainties are examined and these analyses provide a rather narrow risk picture, through calculated probabilities and expected values. On the other hand, qualitative approaches are appropriate in some case, as a "broader" risk description is required.

These approaches take place when there are different views related to the values to be protected and the priorities to be made. The main issue is the value judgments, but they must be supported by solid scientific analyses, also showing a broad risk picture. Also, if one tries to support that the acceptance of risk is rational, on a scientific basis, a too narrow approach to risk has been adopted. As uncertainty is the main component of risk it is essential to implement risk management. Also, the author pointed out the need to specify whether we are concerned about risk or vulnerability and then refer to risk critical system or a vulnerability critical system.

Risk analysis is a useful decision support tool regarding a choice of solutions and measures and provides a risk description that will provide a basis for the choice of solutions or measures.

The author defines risk as the severity of an event combined with the probability or likelihood of the occurrence of that event. Also, combining the severity of all loss events associated with a system and their estimated future probability or likelihood provides a metric for risk. It is difficult to effectively handle risk as the introduction of new technologies and the continuous change of them increase complexity and human errors. The other problem that the study shows is that many of the indicators in the errors of the leading events are not stochastic and therefore it is difficult to estimate their likelihood using a probability type methodology.

The author proposes a new and different approach to identify system-specific leading indicators and provides guidance on developing a risk management structure to generate, monitor and use the results. In addition, a management process should be established when the leading indicators show that action is necessary. Leading indicators and performance metrics can provide a measure of the risk in the current state of the process and the safety control structure. Also, leading indicators provide important signals about the potential for an accident. The suggested approach is based on the STAMP (System-Theoretic Accident Model and Processes) model of accident causation. The last extends current accident causality to include more complex causes than simply component failures and chains of failure events or deviations from operational expectations.

In addition, STAMP focuses on basic principles of systems thinking and systems theory and not on traditional reliability theory. The model includes nonlinear and indirect relationships and can better handle the levels of complexity and technical innovations, anticipating the risk-related consequences of change and adaptation over time. It is necessary to define effectively and a small number of leading indicators in order to identify the increasing risk of an accident. STAMP supports that accidents occur when the safety constraints of the system are violated. The author proposes the use of anew hazard analysis method STPA (System-Theoretic Process Analysis) which can be used to identify safety-critical assumptions that can then shape the basis for a leading indicator program.

The STPA method examines the control loops in the safety control structure in order to identify scenarios or paths to accidents. STPA can be implemented in the physical system, management structure, and organizational design. STPA hazard analysis identifies scenarios leading to the violation of the safety constraints. Assumptions can be technical (engineering), managerial, and organizational. The first basic set of safety-related assumptions is that hazards will not occur in an efficiently designed and operated system. The creation and use of effective leading indicators will require ways to control the psychological biases and to take into account organizational culture and politics that influence likelihood and vulnerability (Leveson 2015, pp. 19–34).

This work is based on the hypothesis that useful leading indicators can be identified through the assumptions underlying safety engineering practices and on the vulnerability of those assumptions and these contain social and managerial issues. The identification of leading indicators will not be necessarily associated with the assumptions about the occurrence of an accident. If the likelihood is not zero, then the assumption needs to take into account for inclusion in the leading indicator program. It is important to identify the safety-related assumptions in order to be included in a leading indicator program.

Risk is used in engineering in many ways, including determining how much effort and resources should be applied during the development of an engineered system to prevent particular types of hazards or loss events in order to provide an acceptable level of risk in the operational system. (Leveson 2015, pp. 19–34) Assumptions may provide important information if included in a leading indicator program. In addition, the "safety culture" provides important assumptions. The identification and understanding of the causal scenarios can lead to better decisions to be made about vulnerability and even likelihood.

A leading indicator is a warning signal that shows when the validity or vulnerability of an assumption is changing. While the traditional accident causality models explain accidents in terms of a chain of directly related events that cause the accident. Control is provided by engineered systems, direct management intervention, policies, procedures, shared values, and other aspects of the organizational culture. This mentioned concept is state as "safety culture" (Leveson 2015, pp. 19–34).

The Leveson defines "safety culture" as the set of values and deep cultural assumptions upon which safety-related actions are taken and decisions are made in the safety control structure. Safety considerations are the most important in technical decision-making. Also, safety decisions are associated with programmatic considerations, including cost and schedule. These decisions must be based on correct, complete and up-to-date information. The core organizational safety values must be documented along with providing the relevant education and buy-in by all employees. Models of the controlled systems may become incorrect due to missing or inadequate feedback and communication channels (Leveson 2015, pp. 19–34).

After the identification and documentation of safety-related assumptions, they can use as the leading indicator program. This program contains three aspects: (i) identification of appropriate and effective leading indicators, (ii) creation of a safety indicator monitoring program, and (iii) embed this monitoring system within a risk management program (Ibid.).

The monitoring of leading indicators can be done partially through the established organizational accident/incident analysis process and error reporting systems. Also, all accidents and incidents must be investigated in-depth. Periodic performance audits should take place. Checking occasionally the safety constraints that are being enforced by a process is suggested and that the process is being carried out as designed rather than continually checking the failure of each individual assumption. The assumptions are used to determine what must be checked, how, when, and what actions should be taken if the checking shows an assumption is no longer valid. The next step is to generate leading indicators that will monitor when these assumptions are no longer valid. Also, the vulnerability of these assumptions must be determined. Each leading indicator must be specified along with the: (a) associated assumption(s); (b) how it will be checked; (c) when it will be checked; (d) the action(s) to take if the indicator is true (the assumption is violated). The documentation is an important issue (Ibid.).

The assumptions should be recorded and used to plan operations, to design the data and feedback that must be collected and to design the overall leading indicator program. Leading indicators can be similar for different firms only in the case that the hazards, safety constraints, system design, and safety control structure are similar. The leading indicators must reflect the specific physical or organizational they are implemented (Ibid.).

The aim of this work is to identify leading indicators and operationalize them as a means of shaping and hedging actions and warning signals. Leading indicators should be integrated into the risk management program, in order to encourage effective action. These leading indicators must be communicated to the appropriate decision-makers and detailed action plans for critical scenarios have been developed and triggers specifically for implementing those action plans (Leveson 2015, pp. 19–34).

Human Factor Risk Analysis: Ergonomic and Value-Based Perspective

Despite all the gaps between real and ideal the disruption of plans, crises, difficult situations, and the effort to continue in spite of all the constraints of resource allocation and usage, business continues perpetually.

In general, the goal of ergonomics is to fit the task to the individual, not the individual to the task (Fernandez et al. 2018, p. 229). The goal of ergonomics can be summarized as maintaining the health of a person working in a machine system, ensuring safety, and increasing the quantity and quality of work done. Simply, it is possible to define Ergonomics as a branch of science that examines the interaction between man and his object and the environment in which he works. Human beings, being a complex entity with its physical, mental, spiritual, social, and cultural structure, constantly changing needs and expectations, necessitates continuity of ergonomic design studies, and conducting in parallel with the philosophy of Continuous Improvement (Bagis 2013, p. 11).

Ergonomics (or human factors) is the scientific discipline concerned with the understanding of interactions among humans and other elements of a system, and the profession that applies theory, principles, data, and methods to design in order to optimize human well-being and overall system performance (IEA 2018, p. 1).

Look at Background of Ergonomics (Human Factors)

Ergonomics today is growing and changing. Development stems from increasing and improving knowledge about the human and is driven by new applications and new technological developments. To be more specific, researchers defined Ergonomics (also called Human Factors or Human Engineering in the United States) as the discipline to study human characteristics for the appropriate design of the living and working environment. Its fundamental aims are that all man-made tools, devices, equipment, machines, and environment should advance, directly or indirectly, the safety, well-being, and performance of humans. Thus, ergonomics has two distinct aspects:

(1) The study, research, and experimentation, in which we determine specific human traits and characteristics that we need to know for engineering design;
(2) Application and engineering, in which we design tools, machines, shelter, environment, work tasks, and job procedures to fit and accommodate the human. This includes, of course, the observation of the actual performance of human and equipment in the environment to assess the suitability of the designed human–machine system and to determine possible improvements.

Ergonomics adapt the man-made world to the people involved because they focus on the human as the most important component of our technological systems. Thus, the utmost goal of ergonomics is "humanization" of work. This goal may be symbolized by the "E & E" of Ease and Efficiency, for which all technological systems and their elements should be designed. This requires knowledge of the characteristics of the people involved, particularly of their dimensions, their capabilities, and their limitations. There is a hierarchy of goals in ergonomics. The fundamental task is to generate "tolerable" working conditions that do not pose known dangers to human life or health.

This basic requirement assures the next goal is to generate "acceptable" conditions upon which the people involved can voluntarily agree according to current scientific knowledge and under given sociological, technological, and organizational circumstances. Of course, the final goal is to generate "optimal" conditions which are so well adapted to human characteristics, capabilities, and desires that psychical, mental, and social well-being is achieved. Ergonomics is the application of scientific principles, methods, and data drawn from a variety of disciplines to the development of engineering systems in which people play a significant role.

Among the basic disciplines are psychology, cognitive science, physiology, biomechanics, applied physical anthropometry, and industrial systems engineering. A number of classic sciences provide fundamental knowledge about human behavior. The anthropological basis consists of anatomy, describing the building of the human body; orthopedics, concerned with the skeletal system; physiology, dealing with the functions and activities of the living body, including the physical and chemical processes involved; medicine, concerned with illness and their prevention and healing; psychology, the science of mind and behavior; and sociology, concerned with the development, structure, interaction, and behavior individuals and groups.

Of course, physics, chemistry, mathematics, and statistics also supply knowledge, approaches, and techniques. From these basic sciences, a group of more applied disciplines developed into the core of ergonomics. These include primarily anthropometry, the measuring, and description of the physical dimensions of the human body; biomechanics, describing the physical behavior of the body in mechanical terms; industrial hygiene, concerned with the control of occupational health hazards that arise as a result of doing work; industrial psychology, discussing people's attitude and behavior artwork; management, dealing with and coordinating the intentions of the employer and measuring techniques to the body at work. Of course, many other disciplinary areas have developed that also are part of ergonomics, or contribute to it, or partly overlap, such as labor relations.

Several distinct application areas use ergonomics as components of their knowledge base, or of their work procedures. Among these are industrial engineering, by definition concerned with the interactions among people, machinery, and energies; bioengineering, working to replace worn or damaged body parts; systems engineering, in which the human is an important component of the overall work unit; safety engineering and industrial hygiene, which focus on the well-being of the human; and military engineering, which relies on the human as soldier or operator. Naturally, other application areas are in urgent need of ergonomic information and data, such as computer-aided design, in which information about the human must be provided in the computerized form. Oceanographic, aeronautical, and astronautical engineering also rely intensively on ergonomic knowledge (Kroemer and Kroemer-Elbert 1994).

Wickens et al. (2004) define the goal of human factors as making the human interaction with systems one that

- Enhances performance.
- Increases safety.
- Increase user satisfaction.

The application of ergonomic principles in the workplace can result in the following (Fernandez et al. 2018): (i) Increased productivity, (ii) improved health and safety of workers, (iii) lower workers' compensation claims.

Ergonomics helps harmonize things that interact with people in terms of people's needs, abilities, and limitations (IEA 2018, p. 1).

Human factors involve the study of factors and the development of tools that facilitate the achievements of these goals. "Performance" is an all-encompassing term that may involve the reduction of errors or an increase in productivity (i.e., the speed of production). Hence, enhanced productivity may sometimes cause more operator errors, potentially compromising safety. Some companies may decide to cut corners on time-consuming safety procedures in order to meet productivity goals. Fortunately, however, these trade-offs are not inevitable. Human factor interventions often can satisfy both goals at once. For example, one company that improved its workstations design reduced worker's compensation losses in the first year after the improvement from $400000 to $940000. Workers were abler to continue work (increasing productivity), while greatly reducing the risk of injury.

Ergonomics (or human factors) is an applied discipline which draws on basic research in (behavioral) science and engineering, and on fieldwork and experience in industrial practice and many other domains, and of which the goal is to match the way in which people work, their environment, their tools and equipment, and the products they use, to human qualities and limits (Moray 2005a, b, p. 1).

The field of Human Factors Engineering (HFE) started in the 1940s as a joint effort between psychologists and engineers. Their overarching goal was to study the interactions that occur at the human–machine interface. They studied practical questions such as, "Why did a seemingly competent cockpit crew fly their aircraft into a mountain? How could the chemical tragedy in Bhopal, India, ever happen? Or perhaps more mundanely, why are people having such a hard time operating our software?" HFE concepts are applicable anywhere, and nearly everywhere. Although elaborate commercial systems such as power plants and aircraft offer many opportunities for human factors investigations and thus receive a lot of attention, sophisticated technologies are inherent in contemporary household appliances. Karwowski's (2000) definition logically applies to the entirety of the field: the design and engineering of human–machine systems for the purpose of enhancing human performance. Performance criteria include maximizing output, minimizing error, ensuring safety, and devising training programs to meet standards. These criteria are often interrelated. It is often possible to introduce a design idea that satisfies more than one objective. On the other hand, gains in speed might result in compromises in error rates or safety (Guastello 2006, p. 7).

Ergonomics promotes a holistic approach in which considerations of physical, cognitive, social, organizational, environmental and other relevant factors are taken into account (IEA 2018, p. 3). Ergonomics is concerned with the design of systems in which people carry out work. Its name comes from the Greek words *ergon* which means "work" and *nomos* which names "law". Ergonomics aims to ensure that human needs for safe and efficient working are met in the design of work systems.

The ability of people to do their jobs is influenced by both physical design and job content. A major goal of ergonomics is to describe both the physical and the psychological aspects of system design, which influence human performance and some of the ways knowledge of human characteristics can be used to optimize the design of systems.

The scope of ergonomics is extremely wide and is not limited to any particular industry or application. Ergonomics and Human Factors (E/HF) in Aviation is essential for the safety and efficiency of commercial airlines, passenger, cargo and military operations, and for the well-being of their passengers. However, it also extends beyond the aircraft to air traffic control and management, maintenance, regulatory bodies, and policy-makers (Stanton et al. 2019, p. 131).

In order to understand why accidents, errors, or any unexpected system behaviors occur, one must look beyond human behavior to the rest of the system. The important factors which need to be investigated are as follows:

1. Design of system components, particularly human–machine interfaces.
2. State of the system leading up to the incident (e.g., stable/unstable, quiet/busy, on course/off course).
3. Operator's mental and physical workload.
4. Work organization (e.g., shift system and during the shift, supervision, and the design of workgroups).
5. External factors (e.g., weather).

It is frequently the case that one or more of these factors increased the likelihood of "human error". Human error and inefficiency are often inadvertently programmed into systems by design deficiencies which do not take into account the characteristics and limitations of humans. Through its emphasis on the human element, ergonomics aims to design out deficiencies in existing systems and design in reliability and good performance into new systems so that good human performance leads to good system performance and so that system design does not degrade human performance or potential.

The purpose of ergonomics is to enable a work system to function better by improving the interactions between the human component and the other components. Better functioning can be defined more closely, for example, as more output from fewer inputs to the system (greater productivity) or increased reliability and efficacy (a lower probability of inappropriate interactions between the system components).

Ergonomics is a multidisciplinary subject which can be applied to the study and design of the human component of work systems. Its areas of application are not limited by the particular technology or by the scale of the system. Ergonomics provides a standardized approach to the analysis of work systems with an emphasis on the interactions between humans and machines. It has some areas of overlap with work study but is more scientific (and sometimes less quantitative) in approach. Its related disciplines are industrial medicine, industrial engineering, industrial psychology, and system design and analysis.

Ergonomics (or human factors) is the scientific discipline concerned with the understanding of interactions among humans and other elements of a system, and the profession that applies theory, principles, data, and methods to design in order to optimize human well-being and overall system performance (IEA 2018, p. 1). Historically, ergonomics can be seen to have arisen as a response to the need for the rapid design of complex systems. As technology becomes more complex and work systems operate under increasingly severe constraints, good ergonomic design becomes increasingly important. Thus "technology push" can be identified as one of the main factors influencing the direction and growth of the subject. The modern ergonomist has an important role to play as a source of scientific information about humans (a scarce commodity in many organizations), as a generator of knowledge about the human components of a working system, and as a member of a design team.

The field of ergonomics contains much scientific information which can be used to characterize the design issues which affect the health and productive capacity of workers. However, the classic ergonomic approach is really concerned with the integration of subsystems with machine subsystems—with respect to efficiency and occupational health. Little has been done to integrate the biological and psychological parts of ergonomics in such a way that they can be related directly to higher level aspects of system functioning. This has made it difficult to predict the outcomes and benefits of ergonomics to organizations.

One of the major challenges for ergonomics is to develop more integrated theories of human–machine systems, to explicate the relationships between lower level aspects of system functioning and higher level system outcomes, and to develop more formal procedures for designing the human parts of work system (Bridger 1995).

Ergonomics is a multidisciplinary research and development field that aims to reveal the basic laws of system efficiency and human–machine–environment adaptation in response to organic and psychosocial stresses (Erkan 2003; Dul and Weerdmeester 2007). Derived from the Greek ergon (work) and nomos (laws) to denote the science of work, ergonomics is a systems-oriented discipline which now extends across all aspects of human activity. Practicing ergonomists must have a broad understanding of the full scope of the discipline. That is, ergonomics promotes a holistic approach in which considerations of physical, cognitive, social, organizational, environmental, and other relevant factors are taken into account (IEA 2018, p. 2)

It is unthinkable that today's modern production systems, which are mostly devoted to machines for the purpose of increasing production, are economical and successful without regard to ergonomic principles. However, this increase is unlikely to be achieved without facilitating and enjoying human work. Technological development accelerates production by decreasing human physical work. However, in parallel with technological progress, the quality of human affairs is increasing, although the need for man seems to be diminishing. In other words, the people involved in production systems changing with technological developments must be more skilled and educated.

As the level of mechanization increases due to these relations, the system requires that human qualities be known more qualitatively and designed according to these qualities. Otherwise, on the one hand, a human who is hard-pressed over their abilities causes the increased chance of occupational illnesses and accidents, while at the same time, the expected job success of the system cannot be achieved (Sabancı and Sumer 2015).

The goal of ergonomics can be summarized as maintaining the health of a person working in a machine system, ensuring safety, and increasing the quantity and quality of work done. This multidisciplinary science is concerned with doctors in relation to human health, engineers in relation to machine design, and economists in the field of processing of the system (Sabancı et al. 2012).

Much of the emphasis of human factors (ergonomics) is on human capabilities and limitations and the need to design systems which take these into account. Although this is clearly necessary, it can be debated whether it is sufficient to optimize the design and performance of human–machine systems. Researchers state that a major problem with human factors is that it neglects to take account of a person's social and psychological needs. Human factors (ergonomic) solutions can remove barriers to effective productivity but cannot compel people to be productive (or to find work a satisfying experience). This is because productivity depends, to some extent at least, on the level of motivation and motivation depends on higher level factors such as work organization (Bridger 1995).

Productivity increases or falls depending on the proper use of the physical tools and the human resource that the work organization has. In other words, productivity depends on fitting jobs to employees. Optimal designing and arranging the tools with equipment used in the job to the characteristics of the employees and improving the physical working conditions will increase the productivity and quality of work by allowing employees to use their abilities fully.

Ergonomics is an important tool in adapting the job to the employee. Achieving productivity, which is a crucial part of organizations and their development, is also possible by giving importance to human resources as well as physical and financial production resources and using employees' capabilities optimally. It is now an undeniable fact that the most effective factor in the success of a production system is undoubtedly the human factor. A system that cannot optimally assess human capital is not expected to be economical in the long run.

The research and studies carried out to demonstrate that the increase in man—machine productivity is directly proportional to the knowledge of the physiological, psychological, and social characteristics of the human being during work and therefore, the increase in production may be possible under these conditions. It is important for these reasons that the purpose of the study is to improve corporate performance by analyzing the impact of employee engagement on job insecurity. In case the human being component of production is investigated in accordance with its own rules rather than according to the mechanical rules, the most suitable values will be available for the person working. The employee works with tools, machinery, and equipment while fulfilling their work.

These tools increase productivity by contributing to the natural power of the person. It is the human resource that organizes, regulates the usages and controls all kinds of equipment and energy sources given to the order of the employee in the industrial and business environment. At this point, it represents an important approach, to identify the human resource with biological properties, in order to provide optimum adaptation in human–machine–environment interaction, to protect the health of the worker, to increase the work security and to accelerate industrial development with work productivity.

Ergonomics provides a scientific approach to these aforementioned problems. The most important reason for the necessity of ergonomics is that it is the most important factor that increases productivity. One of the most important factors of productivity increase lies in recognizing the worker's contribution, providing work security to him and providing effective communication; so, briefly, it lies in developing the human resource. These basic factors are closely related to the studying field of ergonomics.

Ergonomics will be effective in the case of loses in productivity, quality, legal, societal, economic, and environmental in that it can help with reducing costs and expenses occurred due to time inefficiency time. To use corporate resources most effectively, an ergonomic-based perspective will be useful.

Inefficient work, time and expenditures can be reduced by ergonomic projects designed in such a way that will eliminate these problems. Improvements in the quality of working life of employees and the general social responsibility of the organization also require ergonomics. All responsibilities related to equal and fair labor regulation and production arising from attitudes and behaviors contrary to the specified safety standards are the essentials to be dealt with by the organization (Oge 2015, p. 189).

The goals of ergonomics are that the employee works productively. In this process:

- Examining problems related to job content, job environment, job charge, job cooperation, and job division, determining the rules;
- Providing freedom in accordance with the worker's job, improving their ability, acquiring new abilities;
- Presenting the possibility of developing a personality through mutual job division and communication with other employees;
- To make the employee happy in their job;
- Examining the job done by utilizing technological items such as workbench, tool, and hand tool;
- Investigating the conditions of the job done, the impact and consequences of employee, the changes in the employee attitude and performance of these results;
- Interrogating job evaluation and social problems related to the job;
- Analyzing the factors that affect job conditions humanizing the job; and,
- Ensuring harmless, workable, sustainable job conditions.

In all these studies, the common denominator is the harmony of human and job. There are two ways of ensuring this harmony:

- Job's adaptation to a human with job arrangements.
- Human's adaption to a job with his personality, history, memory, education, training, work practices, exercises, and experience (developed from Babalık 2016).

Human factors are all issues that influence our behavior as a human every day. Human factors are to be found in the way we perceive things (e.g., seeing and hearing), the way we make sense out of the world around us (e.g., situation awareness and decision-making), issues that influences our behavior (e.g., stress and fatigue), and the way we make errors and might be able to handle errors. Human factors are also about issues like design of equipment, interfaces between man and machine, training organization of work, and teamwork (JAA 2012).

A Look at Basic Background of Human Factors in Aviation

According to Flouris and Kucuk Yilmaz (2010, p. 25), the most important risk source for organizations is the human factor. Therefore, the management of human resources, which is a strategic element, is important in terms of ensuring the sustainability and competitive advantage of the operator, because managers are those who take strategic decisions and determine, control and interpret their implementation strategies of decisions thus directly affecting the achievement of organization objectives. In addition, it is a unique resource with human limits, qualifications, experience, and abilities, and it is not possible for the same source to be the same.

Therefore, the human is a strategic element. Flouris and Yilmaz (2010, p. 25) (Flouris and Yilmaz 2011, pp. 151–156) point out that management of risks in this context is also a decisive turning point for corporate success for an enterprise. Human factors are among the leading risk factors within the corporate management system and organization. Human-based risk factors have the potential to have a significant impact on corporate targets (financial results, operational performance) (Kucuk Yilmaz et al. 2018).

It is now universally acknowledged that human error is cited as the primary cause of about 70% of aircraft accidents. Might we, therefore, suppose that a similar proportion of the resources devoted to the maintenance and improvement of flight safety is expended upon the human elements involved? Training, for example, absorbs a large part of an airline's budget and is intimately concerned with the human contribution to safe operational practices.

Yet, in spite of such examples, there remains a conspicuous lack of balance between the vast numbers of aerodynamicists, engineers, and other hardware experts employed throughout the industry and the scarcity of specialists in matters relating to human performance. The question, therefore, remains: are sufficient resources being devoted to the ergonomics issues? Although some significant milestones in progress have been passed during the last few years, further advances are required before ergonomics is making its full contribution to safe and effective air transportation. Perhaps, it is time to review progress.

Fifty years ago, in the middle of the Second World War, ergonomists—although the name had not yet been devised—were hard at work attempting to understand the capabilities and limitations of human performance as applied to the piloting of aircraft. Between 1945 and 1950, the results of these pioneering studies appeared in print and established the basis of the literature of aviation ergonomics. It was at this time that such well-known design deficiencies as the three-pointer altimeter were clearly established, and the basic T-Layout of the primary flight instruments became an accepted standard. As early as 1940, the "70% human error" finding had first been published, although many people in the aviation industry were surprised to hear this figure several decades later. The 1950s saw the establishment of ergonomics as an independent technology, having outgrown its origins in applied psychology, physiology, engineering, medicine, and other disciplines.

The name ergonomics was adopted by the Ergonomics Research Society in the UK and later by other national societies and by the International Association. Rather, unfortunately, in the USA, the term human factors came into use and has remained to the present day although the term ergonomics has recently been incorporated into the name of the US-based professional society. While in the defense industries, ergonomics has played a long-standing role, its acceptance into civil aviation has been slow. It had been argued that a major contributory factor was the lack of appreciation of the nature and scope of the subject. For that reason, an annual introductory course was presented at a British university beginning more than 20 years ago. It must be admitted that, during the planning stage, the Royal Aeronautical Society was reluctant to offer encouragement, being unsure whether the time was yet ripe for "ergometrics" [sic]-in spite of the fact that degree courses in ergonomics had then been available in the UK for more than a decade!

Nonetheless, the course, entitled Human Factors in Transport Aircraft Operation, went ahead and was presented for ten years, attracting students from thirty different countries. Later, similar presentations were made at venues as far apart as Amsterdam and Melbourne. By 1992, the Society's misgiving had diminished sufficiently for it to sponsor a 1-week program along the same lines, and further courses have followed. Many national and international organizations—by no means the least of which are pilots' associations—have contributed to the development and dissemination of ergonomics ideas by means of conferences and publications. One particularly influential meeting was the 1975 ATA Technical Conference held in Istanbul.

At that time, several strands of ergonomics were becoming widely known and discussed. The importance of well-designed pilots' seats to provide proper support serves as an example. A second strand was that of instrument design and layout. (Interestingly, a quick poll at the meeting showed that some jet transport aircraft still used three-pointer altimeters nearly 30 years after the publication of the study on instrument reading errors.) A third, less well-defined, the notion was in the minds of many delegates who used words such as leadership, complacency, and communication to define an area felt to be in need of urgent attention.

Considerable effort was made by the organizers of the Istanbul conference to present ergonomics as a systematic and comprehensive technology rather than as a collection of anecdotes concerned with seats, altimeters and complacent crew members. To this end, use was made of what has become known as the SHEL model, which describes a system as an organized assembly comprising three types of resources interacting together and with their environment. The types of the resource include Hardware (e.g., engines, airframes, and instruments), Software (e.g., rules, standard operating procedures, and computer programs), and Liveware (e.g., pilots, air traffic controllers, and maintenance engineers). Within the framework provided by this model, ergonomics may be characterized as the technology concerned with the role of Liveware within the system. In the design phase, the emphasis falls upon the tailoring of all those interfaces with which human beings will be involved.

Thereafter, ergonomics contributes to the achievement of effective systems management, an area in which the many facets of communication and control play a critical part. The dissemination of such ideas does not occur instantaneously, and no overnight miracle took place following the 1975 meeting, but seeds were sown. Aircraft captains are systems managers; they themselves together with their fellow crew members are the principal "liveware" components within the system.

The aircraft, itself a complex assemblage of integrated subsystems, comprises the hardware. The concept of software embraces not only the programs and data stored within electronic equipment but also the rules, standard procedures and emergency drills that have been designed to facilitate safe and efficient operations. Their use may be enriched by the ingenuity, or airmanship, of crew members. These resources must be deployed within the constraints imposed by the environment. The task of the systems managers may be stated quite simply: it is to make the optimal use of the available resources in both routine and unexpected situations.

Numerous training schemes have evolved in an attempt to encourage people to understand the issues in these terms and to prepare crews to perform optimally in the face of unprogrammed situations. During the last 15 or 20 years, one of the principal topics under consideration has concerned matters subsumed under the heading of flight deck automation. Over a relatively short period the appearance of the flight deck has been transformed by the introduction of new generations of display and control devices.

Of even greater significance are the less conspicuous electronic computing devices that provide a range of support facilities for aircraft guidance and control. Properly enough, pilots have expressed some reservations about the acceptability of these automatic systems and the speed of their implementation. Undoubtedly, there have been highly successful technological innovations, of which the moving map display serves as an example, but there have also been—and indeed still remain—issues giving rise to lasting anxiety.

The term allocation of function has been employed in ergonomics since the issues of the division of tasks and responsibilities between men and machines were first treated systematically 40 years ago. Various sets of guidelines have been promulgated, although it must be stressed that while these provide a convenient framework, they cannot be expected to provide rule-of-thumb solutions to complex practical problems.

Questions of allocation of function (perhaps more aptly described as questions concerning the nature of the partnership between hardware, software and liveware) specifically related to civil aviation remain under active review within the ergonomics community. Analyses of questionnaires completed by pilots in the USA and later in the UK have shown that many of the problems arising from experience with sophisticated aircraft are those predicted in the mid-1970s. These were briefly reviewed in the report of a study carried out for the UK Civil Aviation Authority in 1976.

Ergonomics does not stop at the door of the flight deck. Safe and effective operations require attention to the design and management of the passenger cabin, to airline policies of recruitment, training, and operational management, and to maintenance. Work is under way in these areas in several parts of the world (Edwards 1995).

The term "human factors" has grown increasingly popular as the commercial aviation industry has realized that human error, rather than mechanical failure, underlies most aviation accidents and incidents. If interpreted narrowly, human factors are often considered synonymous with Crew Resource Management (CRM) or Maintenance Resource Management (MRM). However, it is much broader in both its knowledge base and scope.

Human factors involve gathering information about human abilities, limitations, and other characteristics and applying it to tools, machines, systems, tasks, jobs, and environments to produce safe, comfortable, and effective human use. In aviation, human factors are dedicated to better understanding of how humans can most safely and efficiently be integrated with technology. That understanding is then translated into design, training, policies, or procedures to help humans perform better.

Despite rapid gains in technology, humans are ultimately responsible for ensuring the success and safety of the aviation industry. They must continue to be knowledgeable, flexible, dedicated, and efficient while exercising good judgment. Meanwhile, the industry continues to make major investments in training, equipment, and systems that have long-term implications. Because technology continues to evolve faster than the ability to predict how humans will interact with it, the industry can no longer depend as much on experience and intuition to guide decisions related to human performance.

Instead, a sound scientific basis is necessary for assessing human performance implications in design, training, and procedures, just as developing a new wing requires sound aerodynamic engineering. Boeing has addressed this issue by employing human factors specialists, many of whom are also pilots or mechanics, since the 1960s. Initially focused on flight deck design, this group of about 30 experts now considers a much broader range of elements, such as cognitive psychology, human performance, physiology, visual perception, ergonomics, and human–computer interface design.

Applied collectively, their knowledge contributes to the design of Boeing airplanes and support products that help humans perform to the best of their capability while compensating for their natural limitations. Because improving human performance can help the industry reduce the commercial aviation accident rate, much of the focus is on designing human–airplane interfaces and developing procedures for both flight crews and maintenance technicians. Boeing also continues to examine human performance throughout the airplane to improve usability, maintainability, reliability, and comfort. In addition, human factors specialists participate in analyzing operational safety and developing methods and tools to help operators better manage human error. These responsibilities require the specialists to work closely with engineers, safety experts, test and training pilots, mechanics, and cabin crews to properly integrate human factors into the design of all Boeing airplanes. Their areas of responsibility include addressing human factors in (http://www.boeing.com/commercial/aeromagazine/aero_08/human_textonly.html)

- Flight deck design.
- Design for maintainability and in-service support.
- Error management.
- Passenger cabin design.

Aviation as a system is safe. Safety is made possible by people doing the work required diligently every day and occurs at the intersection of man (a human being), machine (an aircraft), and procedures. But safety is also made at the confluence of boundaries:

- The boundary of economic failure.
- The boundary of functionally acceptable performance.
- The boundary of unacceptable workload.

These three boundaries have been researched by Rasmussen. Within boundaries, people can safely do their work. Normal changes in local work conditions can lead to a situation where the boundaries are approached and when the boundaries are crossed, an error or accident may be the result.

It must be also seen from the point of view that what influences a human (the "human factors") also influence Crew Resource Management, CRM is described as CRM is the effective utilization of all available resources (e.g., crew members, airplane systems, supporting facilities, and persons) to achieve safe and efficient operation and to enhance the communication, human factors and management skills of the crew members concerned by The European Aviation Safety Agency—EASA. That is the reason for describing the basic human behavior as the use of senses and the way humans' process information, which all influence the end result: the way people work together.

The term "human factors" is used in many different ways in the aviation industry. The term is, perhaps, best known in the context of aircraft cockpit design and Crew Resource Management (CRM). However, those activities constitute only a small percentage of aviation-related human factors, as broadly speaking, it concerns any consideration of human involvement in aviation. The use of the term "human factors" in the context of aviation maintenance engineering is relatively new.

Aircraft accidents such as that of the Aloha aircraft in the USA in 1988 and the BAC 1-11 windscreen accident in the UK in June 1990, brought the need to address human factors issues in this environment into sharp focus. This does not imply that human factors issues were not present before these dates nor that human error did not contribute to other incidents; merely that it took an accident to draw attention to human factors problems and potential solutions.

"Human factors" refers to the study of human capabilities and limitations in the workplace. Human factors researchers study system performance; that is, they study the interaction of maintenance personnel, the equipment they use, the written and verbal procedures and rules they follow, and the environmental conditions of any system. The aim of human factors is to optimize the relationship between maintenance personnel and systems with a view to improving safety, efficiency, and well-being. In 1940, it was calculated that approximately 70% of all aircraft accidents were attributable to man's performance, that is to say, human error.

When the International Air Transport Association (IATA) reviewed the situation 35 years later, they found that there had been no reduction in the human error component of accident statistics (CAA-CAP 715 2002a). Human error is, by far, the most pervasive cause of accidents and incidents in technologically complex systems such as air transportation. One major database of worldwide jet transport accidents indicates that 65% of all such accidents have been attributed to flight crew error. It also indicates that for the approach and landing phase of flight, which accounts for 4% of total flight exposure time and 49% of all accidents, flight crew error is cited in 80% as a causal factor.

Other sources of human error, including maintenance, dispatch, and, importantly, air traffic control, account for another significant proportion of such accidents. Such studies indicate that between 80 and 90% of all aviation accidents are attributable to human error in one form or another.

Human Factors has come to be concerned with diverse elements in the aviation system. These include human behavior and performance; decision-making and other cognitive processes; the design of controls and displays; flight deck and cabin layout; communication and software aspects of computers; maps, charts, and documentation; as well as the refinement of staff selection and training. Each of these aspects demands skilled and effective human performance (CAA-CAP 720 2002c).

Traditionally, human factors endeavors have been directed toward flight crew performance and, to a lesser extent, toward the performance of air traffic controllers. Until recently, available literature showed little consideration of the Human Factors issues which could affect aircraft maintenance personnel who inspect and repair aircraft. This has been a serious oversight, since it is quite clear that human error in aircraft maintenance has indeed had as dramatic an effect upon the safety of flight operation as the errors of pilots and air traffic controllers.

Aircraft maintenance and inspection duty can be very complex and varied in an environment where opportunities for error abound. Maintenance personnel—at least in the most developed aviation systems—frequently work under considerable time pressures. Personnel at the maintenance base and at the flight line stations realize the importance of meeting scheduled departure times. Operators have increased aircraft utilization in order to counteract the economic problems that plague the industry. Aircraft maintenance technicians are also maintaining a fleet that is increasing in age (CAA-CAP 718 2002b).

After a series of accidents Transport Canada and the aviation industry identified 12 human factors which they then called "The Dirty Dozen". These human factors elements degrade people's ability to perform a task effectively and safely and could lead to maintenance errors. The Dirty Dozen are identified as lack of communication, complacency, lack of knowledge, distraction, lack of teamwork, fatigue, lack of resources, pressure, lack of assertiveness, stress, lack of awareness, and norms.

The infrastructure of studies for human factors in the aviation sector was established together with studies for equipment design and human performance, during World War II. These studies were primarily carried out in order to prevent accidents due to cockpit design and crew performance. In addition to the size, shape, and location of controls and displays, other psychological elements have also been noticed to influence human performance. As evidenced by the accidents, the human element is the most valuable and flexible one in aviation relations, and at the same time, it is the easiest incentive factor to affect performance in the opposite direction. Over the years, a large proportion of the accidents have occurred due to the inadequate use of optimum human performance, which is generally regarded as a "pilot error". Not only a pilot but, also the other elements that enable the flight are included in the human definition. It has been a necessity to examine at what phase of the flight, which group of people has either a direct or indirect influence on the flight. Most current flight systems' efficiency is constructed with the people who use them.

Undoubtedly, having more and accurate information about human behavior and fully benefitting from our knowledge, will be beneficial for the safe use of current systems. Almost no other area can state the relation between humans and machines and between humans and humans as clearly as modern aviation. In order to eliminate human error in the aviation sector and any mistakes that may be made at cockpit, it has been focused on automation, some accident prevention systems have been added to aircrafts which are already high-tech products themselves. However, similar systems have caused new pilot errors and have changed the dimension of the human factor's effect on pilot errors.

As a result of the development and automation at technology, the machines have taken the familiar tasks out of the hands of people, however, human's unique capabilities in solving unexpected and unusual problems have gained importance. In the sociotechnical systems such as aviation, aviation maintenance, air traffic control, space and aeronautics, nuclear power plants—where people and technology are heavily involved—the efforts of human factors engineers are increasingly required. The costs of the accidents that take place in today's new technological systems have increased considerably.

Consequently, the need to address the human factor has gained even more importance in two basic areas of efficiency and team health, including the system of safety and effectiveness, which are closely related to each other in many respects. In parallel with technological developments, the planes have nearly approached perfection, but the people who manage them have not changed much (Terzioğlu 2010).

Application of human factor principles in aviation spread beyond the technical arena of man–machine interface. The discipline has created a great impact on aircraft design, operations, and maintenance (Shanmugam and Robert 2015, p. 503). Human Performance in the working environment has become popularly referred to as Human Factors (HF). It underlies the focus of the applied science of ergonomics which is usually considered to cover the adaptation of work or working conditions to enhance the performance of the worker. Generally, and historically, the measure of such performance has been seen as efficiency or productivity and as an adaptive response rather than a core element of initial design. Of course, in the context of aviation and similar safety-critical activities where optimum human performance is equated specifically with operational safety standards rather than strictly with business efficiency, it is not surprising that the wider descriptive term HF has gained particular currency. Because of an early appreciation of the dual importance of both error reduction and error management, aviation has become one of the leading exponents of building HF into all aspects of human performance. Nowadays, there is a wide-ranging effort to make people aware of HF as well as a commitment to consider it in both new system design and the mitigation of unwanted effects of existing design which cannot be immediately substituted with improved alternatives.

Human Factors in its widest definition describes all the many aspects of human performance which interact with their (aviation) environment to influence the outcome of events. These may be related to either the physiological or psychological aspects of human capability, both of which are able to directly affect the way in which the human operator performs in different circumstances. Less than perfect human performance is cited as a causal factor in the majority of aircraft accidents and serious incidents.

If the accident rate is to be decreased, HF must be better understood, and the knowledge more broadly applied. Since front-line aviation personnel are rarely fulfilling their duties as isolated individuals, most effort to create training solutions which will deliver increased awareness of HF issues have gone into improved cooperation amongst coworkers.

Recent years have seen the widespread introduction by aircraft operators, by ATM and by aircraft maintenance organizations of Crew Resource Management and Line-Oriented Flight Training (LOFT) for pilots, Team Resource Management (TRM) for Air Traffic Control Officers (ATCOs) and Maintenance Resource Management (MRM) in aircraft maintenance. Particularly helpful in raising awareness of the importance of HF has been the trend to a Safety Culture in which people are increasingly willing to file safety reports about incidents, which might not otherwise have come to light an help establish how circumstances transpired to create the error chain which led to an incident so that the response to it can be effective.

The slowly increasing willingness for organizations to openly share useable levels of information on safety incidents and solutions has also begun to help improve understanding of just how important a comprehensive appreciation of HF is. Not very long ago, safety occurrence data appeared to show that technical faults were far more prevalent than human error, which was at serious variance with the findings of accident investigations. The breakthrough has come especially through seeing personal HF in the context of environmental or circumstantial HF (https://www.skybrary.aero/index.php/Human_Factors).

The number of pilots is far smaller than the number of drivers, and aircraft crashes are much less frequent than auto accidents. However, the number of people who fly as passengers in an aircraft is large enough, and the cost of a single air crash is sufficiently greater than that of a single-car crash, that the human factors issues of airline safety are as important as those involved with ground transportation. The human factors of transportation systems is a complex, global issue.

An individual's choice to fly, drive, or take ground transportation is influenced by complex forces related to risk perception, cost perception, and expediency. The consumer's choice for one influences human factor issues in the others. For example, if more people choose to fly, fewer automobiles will be on the road, and unless people drive faster as a result, highways will become safer.

However, the airspace will become more congested and its safety will be compromised. Air traffic controllers will be more challenged in their job. In the continuing quest for more expediency, demands will appear (as they have now appeared) for either greater levels of air traffic control automation or for more responsibility to be shifted from air traffic control to the pilots themselves for route selection and for maintaining separation from other traffic, in a concept known as "free flight."

Today "ergonomics" and "human factors" are different names for a single discipline (Moray 2005a, b, p. 1). Human factors are applied in aviation to manage human error. In order to reduce errors and mistakes a pilot may do, aviation human factors engineers are supposed to design the airplanes in a way that will be very clear to the pilot to avoid confusion that may lead to errors hence risking lives of many people (Kalim 2018, p. 4). Such global economic issues related to risk perception and consumer choice (itself a legitimate topic for human factors investigation) will impact the conditions in which vehicles travel and the very nature of those vehicles (levels of automation, etc.) in a manner that has direct human factors relevance to design (Wickens et al. 2004, p. 62).

Ergonomic is a vital and integral part of aviation business management and strategy since A modern commercial aviation maintenance operation is a complex sociotechnical system developed to ensure the availability of safe and airworthy aircraft at the lowest cost (Sogg 2002, pp. 1–4). Current economic conditions have emphasized the need for human factors in all aspects of commercial aviation maintenance operations. Increasing requirements to do more with less, as well as the projected shortage of trained and experienced maintenance personnel, have placed additional pressure on airline management to employ their workforce more efficiently. One of the most significant but often overlooked process tools for human factors design is the establishment of clear and concise design philosophies. In general, the design philosophies help dictate how the limitations and characteristics of the pilot are to be taken into account during the entire design needs evaluation process. There are three primary design philosophies of a crew-centered flight deck. First, fundamental human performance limitations must be accounted for in the design. This requires evaluating the full range of conditions that test human performance limits. For example, display format prototyping is usually carried out in a rather benign office lighting conditions. Knowing that the visual system reacts differently under the lighting extremes of the flight deck environment requires that format effectiveness or usability be tested under both bright and dark ambient lighting conditions. A second design philosophy requires that flight deck design accommodate individual differences in pilot performance capabilities. This means that the design should be tested for usability by a population with a wide variety of skills and backgrounds. One significant issue here is cultural differences among the pilot population. Another crew-centered design philosophy is that human error tolerance and avoidance techniques should be applied. A wide range of methods can be used to address this most difficult issue, in accordance with the degree of novelty in the crew interface and the associated risk of unexpected errors. These flight deck design philosophies serve not only to develop a design consistent with good human factors principles but also point to areas where the design needs to be tested and evaluated. These principles also serve high-level criteria for this testing (Jacobsen et al. 2002). Finally, human factors in aviation play a big role in avoiding fatigue. Air transport enables traveling very long distances without resting for pilots. Therefore, pilots need to use airplanes that are human-centered designed, i.e., do not add more unnecessary, tiresome tasks (Kalim 2018, p. 3).

Conclusion

Value-based enterprise risk management helps the organization both to create organizational value and to maintain it by enabling the management of uncertainty and the risks and opportunities involved in that. Enterprise risk management is the holistic process of identifying, evaluating, prioritizing, risk mapping and handling corporate risks and opportunities. By applying different risk management models within the management system, the achievement of targets is supported. Risk management is also adding value to the organization.

The principles of risk management are well-established across large businesses, which clearly recognize that they need to manage uncertainty in order to meet their strategic objectives. This has never been more so than at present. Increasing industry convergence, accelerating technological disruption, and ever-higher ethical and social standards add further degrees of complexity to the mix (Baes et al. 2016a, b, p. 28).

There may be disruptions in the very well-designed CRM system applications. At this point, the value-based approach would be useful as "optimum working culture" in minimizing disruptions.

As a strategic discipline, ERM supports the identification, assessment, and management of risks, uncertainties, and opportunities that may affect an organization's strategy, economic position, or operating performance. A comprehensive and sustainable ERM addresses all the major categories of risk exposure, including environmental, competitive, strategic, financial, regulatory, and operational risk, as well as the risk associated with technology and an organization's reputation (Tuten 2018, p. 4).

Value-based Risk Management (VBRM) is a balanced approach to risk management that is more effective in managing these challenges than either the "Accountant" or "Assurance" approaches. VBRM is all about responding to change and dynamically focusing risk management efforts where they deliver the most value to the business (Baes et al. 2016a, b, p. 28)

In several domains, the outcome of research on Human Factors has already led to the introduction of standardized methods in design and development processes, in safety assessment and training methods, as well as in regulation. In some cases, e.g., in automotive transport, the number of accidents is still too high, while in other cases, e.g., in civil aviation, the low rates of accidental events have reached a plateau value. These two domains represent opposite stereotypical situations that demand additional effort and improvement.

Yazgan and Kucuk Yılmaz (2019) state that airline business management is set on airworthy strategy. Airline sustainability depends on corporate-based strategy on airworthiness since airworthiness is a fundamental element to any airline's business management and strategy. The airline may achieve their aims about corporate sustainability if it has an airworthiness strategy and risk management. A fundamental condition of survival in the airline business given the key importance that safety plays in the industry, is the ability to maintain an airworthy fleet (Yazgan and Kucuk Yilmaz).

The Aircraft Maintenance Technician (AMT) has a dual role in aircraft maintenance system as the source of failure in maintenance process via his volatility and unmanageable qualifications and second as a source of management responsible for maintaining the airworthiness of the aircrafts in the airline. Situational awareness of managers about both limitations and qualifications of human factors is a vital determinant to the decision-making process in aviation.

Although continuously improving in related literature, one of the biggest weaknesses of current methods of AMT error or performance, the ability to model the reciprocal effects of the factors affecting the fault is limited. For this reason, an Analytic Network Process (ANP) model is developed that takes into account the effects of mutual dependences among factors in this study.

The results of this study show that time pressure, organization's culture, and safety culture and supervision are the most important criteria that contributed to AMT error. Their weights are 0.207, 0.172, 0.102, and 0.094, respectively. The researchers emphasized that there are many difficulties and limitations in measuring the factors that have an influence on AMT error. For this reason, the weights of criteria and sub-criteria necessary are determined by using ANP and in this way, it is possible to make better decisions in this process as ANP is a multi-criteria decision-making technique that takes into consideration qualitative factors in decision-making problems. Finally, they implied that the factors taxonomy determined as a result of the expert opinions and the extensive literature and the ANP model developed taking into account the dependencies between the factors will contribute to the literature in their study (Yazgan and Kucuk Yılmaz, In press process).

Kucuk Yılmaz and Yazgan (2018) explained that human resource is the most strategic element of corporate resources. In today's business management critical risk is a human factor which has both source side and risk side in their study. This research presents a strategic way of managing human resource risk in aircraft maintenance center at Anadolu University. Owing to this project, the dependency of an aircraft maintenance technician to external organizations is decreased to a considerable level. This means that the organization may do resource saving and gain strategic advantages beside increasing corporate performance (Kucuk Yilmaz and Yazgan 2018, p. 17)

The failures in basic organizational processes, such as allocation of resources, planning, budgeting, financing, establishing goals, and so forth, are the causes behind the symptoms observed at flight decks, in air traffic control rooms, at ramps, and at maintenance hangars. While it is important to address symptoms while longer-term strategies aimed at the causes take place, it would be regrettable if all energies continue to be devoted to myopic attempts to address symptoms exclusively.

While accident investigation must be recognized for its historical contribution to aviation safety, the industry cannot afford to use up meager resources in reactive endeavors. It cannot afford—neither ethically nor financially—to wait for accidents to learn safety lessons. More importantly, it need not wait. At the heart of this paper is the contention that, through the application of human factors knowledge to prevention strategies, there exists the possibility of proactively anticipating those flaws which already exist in the system and which will eventually lead to accidents. It is possible to apply techniques to identify latent unsafe conditions within the system, before they combine with failures in operational contexts to provoke accidents.

However, the shift in the safety paradigm and prevention strategies will not be possible unless air safety investigators acknowledge the value of applied human factors knowledge. Human factors knowledge has been incorporated into some countries' accident investigation protocols. Benchmark reports have been produced over the past years, attenuating by their sound and broad approach the reactive nature of the accident investigation process. By addressing the collective rather than the individual, these reports have offered the potential for significant improvement in safety and operational efficiency. This potential, by the way, can only be realized if the recommendations in these reports are acknowledged by decision-makers both in industry and government. However, make no mistake about it: most accident investigation agencies pay only lip service to human factors.

Within these organizations, the change implicated by the investigation of the broader human factors issues conflicts with conservatism and convention and is dodged by reasons of convenience. There are reasons for concern as to what the future might hold for a contemporary safety paradigm unless greater numbers of air safety investigators acknowledge that human factors are a core discipline.

This is an exceedingly important point because aviation has yet to arrive at the point at which existing barriers are demolished and proactive auditing schemes become fully accepted and implemented. Until then, the accident investigation process will remain the workhorse of safety for the immediate future, and the vehicle to fortify the architecture of the aviation system. If the accident investigation process does not generate a meaningful product, there is no way to receive feedback and, most important, feedforward prevention strategies.

As long as accident investigations consider human error without consideration of contexts and as the cause rather than the symptom, as long as it does not dig into the deeper layers of the processes surrounding the events under scrutiny, their only accomplishment will be to put losses behind and to reassert trust and faith in the system, that is to say, to fulfill political purposes. Only if accident investigations consider human error as a symptom and look for causes in the context, might aviation have a chance to learn about system vulnerability and to develop strategies for change, thus improving system reliability. Within the aviation industry, human factors are not an end in itself, an opportunity to generate research, nor the last frontier of aviation safety or a frontier of any kind.

The incorporation of human factors knowledge into aviation operations and practices presents another opportunity to contribute to the aviation system's production goals: the safe and efficient transportation of people and goods. If human factors knowledge is expected to be effective against systemic flaws and failures, its application must be predicated upon an understanding of systemic safety and a safety paradigm that are relevant to contemporary civil aviation. Some encouraging progress has been made, but there is a need for improvement. This work suggests one possible way to move forward. At its foundation, it carries the belief that the integration of human factors knowledge into aviation operations represents a cost-effective approach to anticipate human error rather than continue regretting its consequences (Maurino 2000, p. 43).

References

AIRMIC, ALARM, IRM. 2010. A structured approach to enterprise risk management (ERM) and the requirements of ISO 31000. [Online] Available at: https://www.theirm.org/media/886062/ISO3100_doc.pdf. Accessed 24 Ekim 2016.

Aven, T. 2008. *Risk analysis—Assessing uncertainties beyond expected values and probabilities*. Chichester, UK: Wiley.

Babalık, F. 2016. *Mühendislik İçin Ergonomi (İşbilim)*, 5th ed. Bursa: Dora Yayınları.

Baes, K., et al. 2016a. Embracing complexity with value-based risk management. PRISM (1): 28 (Arthur DLittle Global).

Baes, K., et al. 2016b. Embracing complexity with value-based risk management. PRISM 1(1): 27–41, 32.

Bagis, A. 2013. Ergonomi Ders Notları, 11. [Online] Available at http://www.abdullahdemir.net/wp-content/uploads/2013/12/Ergonomi-Ders-Notlari_Dr.-A.-Bagis.pdf. Accessed 18 Aug 2019.

Bailey, R. 1982. *Human performance engineering: A guide for system designers*. Englewood Cliffs, NJ: Prentice Hall.

Bilegt, E. 2012. *ÖRGÜT KÜLTÜRÜ İLE ÇALIŞAN MOTİVASYONU ARASINDAKİ İLİŞKİ VE BİR ARAŞTIRMA*. İstanbul: İstanbul Üniversitesi/ Sosyal Bilimler Enstitüsü/ İşletme Anabilim Dalı/ İşletme Yönetimi ve Organizasyon Bilim Dal.

BOEING. 2008. http://www.boeing.com/commercial/aeromagazine/aero_08/human_textonly.html. [Online] Available at: http://www.boeing.com/commercial/aeromagazine/aero_08/human_textonly.html. Accessed 23 Feb 2018.

Bozoglan. 2010. The effect of organizational culture on performance criteria and TESCO KIPA Aplication. http://hdl.handle.net/20.500.12397/10707

Bridger, R. 1995. *Introduction to ergonomics*. New York: McGraw-Hill.

BSI. 2016. ISO 31000 Kurumsal Risk Yönetimi. [Online] Available at: http://www.bsigroup.com/tr-TR/ISO-31000-Kurumsal-Risk-Yonetimi/. Accessed 25 Ekim 2016.

Bukvič, V. 2014. *Value based management with a practical example*, 195–205. Portoroz, Slovenia.

CAA. 2002a. CAP 715: An introduction to aircraft maintenance engineering human factors for JAR 66. [Online] Available at: https://publicapps.caa.co.uk/docs/33/CAP715.PDF. Accessed 23 Feb 2018.

CAA. 2002b. CAP 718: Human factors in aircraft maintenance and inspection. [Online] Available at: https://publicapps.caa.co.uk/docs/33/CAP718.PDF. Accessed 23 Feb 2018.

CAA, Civil Aviation Authority. 2002c. CAP 720: Flight crew training: Cockpit resource management (CRM) and line-oriented flight training (LOFT). [Online] Available at: https://www.skybrary.aero/bookshelf/books/890.pdf. Accessed 23 Feb 2018.

COSO. 2004. COSO enterprise risk management—Integrated framework (executive summary). [Online] Available at: http://www.coso.org/documents/coso_erm_executivesummary.pdf. Accessed 20 Ekim 2016.

COSO. 2018. https://www.coso.org/documents/ERM-FAQs.pdf. [Online] Available at: https://www.coso.org/documents/ERM-FAQs.pdf.

Curran, K.M. 2006. Value-based risk management. *Cost Engineering* 48(2), 15–22.

Deloach, J. 2015. *A value-based approach to risk management*. [Online] Available at: https://www.corporatecomplianceinsights.com/a-value-based-approach-to-risk-management/. Accessed 17 Aug 2019.

Demir, T. 2013. A research on the effect of personnel empowerment on internal entrepreneurship and the role of organizational culture in this relation, Istanbul, 2013.

Derici, O., Z. Tüysüz, and A. Sarı. 2007. Kurumsal Risk Yönetimi ve Sayıştay Uygulaması. [Online] Available at: http://dergi.sayistay.gov.tr/Default.asp?sayfa=3&id=521. Accessed 25 Ekim 2016.
Dul, J., and B. Weerdmeester. 2007. *Ergonomi: Ne, Neden, Nasıl?* Ankara: Seçkin.
Edwards, E. 1995. Aviation ergonomics: Whence and whither? *Ergonomics* 38 (3): 565–569.
Emhan, A. 2009. Risk management process and techniques used in risk management. Retrieved October 22, 2016, from Atatürk University Journal of Economic and Administrative Sciences: http://e-dergi.atauni.edu.tr/atauniiibd/article/viewFile/1025002889/1025002785. Accessed 22 Ekim 2016.
Erdem, E. 2014. Employee risk perception in enterprise risk management: A case study of a development agency. Retrieved November 01, 2016.
Erkan, N. 2003. *Ergonomi*, no. 373. Ankara: MPM Yayınları, Yayın.
FERMA. 2011. Risk management standards. Retrieved at October 22, 2016, from http://www.ferma.eu/app/uploads/2011/11/a-risk-management-standard-turkish-version.pdf.
Fernandez, J.E., M. Goodman, E.H. Group, and V.A. Alexandria. 2018. SOFOS Database on sustainable waste management. [Online] Available at: http://www.seas.columbia.edu/earth/wtert/sofos/nawtec/nawtec08/nawtec08-0019.pdf.
Flouris, T.G., and A.K. Yilmaz. 2010. Managing corporate sustainability: Risk management process based perspective. *African Journal of Business Management.*
Flouris, T.G., and A.K. Yilmaz. 2011. *Risk Management and Corporate Sustainability in Aviation.* Aldershot: Ashgate.
Fraser, J., and B.J. Simkins. 2009. *Enterprise risk management.* [Online] Available at: https://books.google.com.tr/books?hl=tr&lr=&id=kSrYCwAAQBAJ&oi=fnd&pg=PT22&dq=enterprise+risk+management&ots=d93teeUuKG&sig=r7VcrTrkJv_tCEa7puQTjGj8gQc&redir_esc=y#v=onepage&q=what%20is%20enterprise%20risk%20management&f=false. Accessed 19 Ekim 2016.
GleiBner, W. 2005. Value based corporate risk management. In: *Risk management: Challenge and opportunity*, 479–494, 480. Berlin: Springer. https://doi.org/10.1007/3-540-26993-2_24.
Guastello, S. 2006. *Human factors engineering and ergonomics: A system approach.* Mahwah, NJ: Lawrence Erlbaum Associates.
Güneş, Ş. 2009. A Study on Enterprise Risk Management and Awareness in Turkey. Retrieved October 22, 2016, from https://tez.yok.gov.tr/NationalTezCenter/. Accessed 22 Ekim 2016.
IEA. 2018. What is ergonomics? [Online] Available at: https://www.iea.cc/whats/index.html.
Improved from BOZOĞLAN, İ.T. 2010. *ÖRGÜT KÜLTÜRÜNÜN PERFORMANS KRİTERLERİNE ETKİSİ VE TESCO KİPA UYGULAMASI.*
ISO. 2016. ISO 31000—Risk management. [Online] Available at: http://www.iso.org/iso/home/standards/iso31000.htm. Accessed 24 Ekim 2016.
JAA. 2012. *Human factors/CRM in aviation training course book.* Hoofddorp: Joint Aviation Authority.
Jacobsen, A.R., B.D. Kelly, D.L. Hilby, and R.J. Mumaw. 2002. Human factors testing and evaluation in commercial airplane flight deck development. In *Handbook of human factors testing and evaluation*, 2nd ed., ed. Samuel G. Charlton and Thomas G. O'Brien. Mahwah, NJ.: Lawrence Erlbaum Associates.
Kalim, M. 2018. Human factors and ergonomics in aviation. [Online] Available at: https://sites.tufts.edu/maureenenp61/2018/02/13/human-factors-and-ergonomics-in-aviation/.
KIWA. 2016. KIWA. [Online] Available at: http://hizmetler.kiwa.com.tr/sistem-belgelendirme/risk-yonetimi. Accessed 25 Ekim 2016.
Kızılboğa, R. 2012a. Transition from traditional risk management to enterprise risk management system. Retrieved October 12, 2016, from http://e-dergi.atauni.edu.tr/ataunisosbil/article/view/1020009163.
Kızılboğa, R. 2012b. Risk Yönetimi ve Ülke Uygulamalarında Risk Yönetim Modelleri. [Online] Available at: http://www.academia.edu/7589977/R%C4%B0SK_Y%C3%96NET%C4%B0M%C4%B0_VE_%C3%9CLKE_UYGULAMALARINDA_R%C4%B0SK_Y%C3%96NET%C4%B0M_MODELLER%C4%B0. Accessed 23 Ekim 2016.

Kızılboğa, R. 2012c. Kurumsal Risk Yönetimi Odaklı İç Denetim veİstanbul Büyükşehir Belediyesi İçin Bir Model Önerisi. [Online].

Kizilboga, R. 2012. *KURUMSAL RİSK YÖNETİMİ ODAKLI İÇ DENETĠM VE İSTANBUL BÜYÜKŞEHİR BELEDİYESİ İÇİN BİR MODEL ÖNERİSİ*. İSTANBUL.

Kızılboğa, R. 2014. Risk Yönetimi ve Ülke Uygulamalarında Risk Yönetim Modelleri. *Akademik Araştırmalar ve Çalışmalar Dergisi*. (7): 83.

Koller, T. 1994. https://www.mckinsey.com/business-functions/strategy-and-corporate-finance/our-insights/what-is-value-based-management. [Online] Available at: https://www.mckinsey.com/business-functions/strategy-and-corporate-finance/our-insights/what-is-value-based-management.

Kroemer, K.K., and K. Kroemer-Elbert. 1994. *Ergonomics: How to design for ease and efficiency*. Englewood Cliffs, NJ: Prentice Hall.

Kucuk Yilmaz, A., and E. Yazgan. 2018. Corporate performance management: Process of organizational-tailored flow chart. *AEAT* 90 (9): 23. https://doi.org/10.1108/AEAT-09-2017-0201.

Kucuk Yilmaz, A., E. Yazgan, K. Malagas, and N. Nikitakos. 2018. Risk Matrix Approach to Human Factors in Aircraft Maintenance Organization, ATINER's Conference Paper Series MGT2018-2560, 16th Annual International Conference on Management & Marketing, 2–5 July 2018, Athens, Greece (Organized by the Management Unit and Marketing Unit of ATINER; Sponsored by the Athens Journal of Business & Economics).

Kucuk Yılmaz, A., and E. Yazgan. In press process. Corporate performance management: Process of organizational—Tailored flow chart. *Aircraft Engineering and Aerospace Technology*.

Leveson, N. 2015. A systems approach to RISK Management through leading safety indicators. *Reliability Engineering & System Safety* 136: 17–34.

Maurino, D.E. 2000. Human factors and aviation safety: What the industry has, what the industry needs. *Ergonomics* 43 (7): 952–959.

Moody, M.J. 2009. ERM: The big picture. *Rough Notes* [Online] 152 (1): 74. *Rough Notes Magazine*.

Moray, N. 2005a. *Ergonomics: The history and scope of human factors*, 1. London and New York: Taylor & Francis.

Moray, N. 2005b. *Ergonomics: Major writings*, vols. 1–4. London: Taylor & Francis, Routledge.

Müller, R., A. Wittmer, and C. Drax. 2014. *Aviation risk and safety management methods and Applications in aviation organizations*. London: Springer.

Oge, H. 2015. *Örgütsel Etkinlik için Ergonomi*, 189. Konya: Çizgi Kitabevi.

Olson, D.L., and D.D. Wu. 2008. *Enterprise risk management*. [Online] Available at: https://books.google.com.tr/books?hl=tr&lr=&id=iRL0TCMJEZsC&oi=fnd&pg=PR5&dq=enterprise+risk+management&ots=Ji9Uanynv2&sig=ii6sHwTSkWcnajgbHxOTiIFqG_k&redir_esc=y#v=onepage&q=enterprise%20risk%20management&f=false. Accessed 15 Ekim 2016.

Opgenorth, K. 2017. KnowlwdgerBlog, 1. [Online] Available at: https://info.knowledgeleader.com/bid/163293/what-is-the-coso-enterprise-risk-management-framework.

Ozturk, Z., and Ü. Arslan. 2016. HASTANE PERSONELİNİN DURUMSALLIK YAKLAŞIMINA GÖRE ORGANİZASYONEL KONUMLANDIRMA ALGISI. *Gazi Üniversitesi İktisadi ve İdari Bilimler Fakültesi Dergisi* 18 (1): 128–152.

Pehlivanlı, D. 2008. Enterprise risk management applications based internal audit and turkey. Retrieved from https://tez.yok.gov.tr/NationalTezCenter/.

Sabancı, A., and S. Sumer. 2015. *Ergonomi*, 3rd ed., 472. Ankara: Nobel Yayınevi.

Sabancı, A., S.K. Sümer, and S.M. Say. 2012. *Endüstriyel Ergonomi*, 3rd ed. Ankara: Nobel Yayınevi.

Şahin, A. 2010, p. 22. Örgüt Kültürü-Yönetim İlişkisi ve Yönetsel Etkinlik. [Online] Available at: http://dergiler.sgb.gov.tr/calismalar/maliye_dergisi/yayinlar/md/159/Ali, http://dergiler.sgb.gov.tr/calismalar/maliye_dergisi/yayinlar/md/159/AliŞAHİN.pdf. Accessed 01 Kasım 2016.

Saka, T., and A. Uğural. 2015. Enterprise risk management. Retrieved October 25, 2016, from TÜSİAD: http://tusiad.org/tr/faaliyet-raporlari/item/download/7447_ee46d69c7085eaf0f975bcad252b9afd.

Segal, S. 2005. *Value–based enterprise risk management*. [Online] Available at: https://www.soa.org/Library/Newsletters/The-Actuary-Magazine/2005/June/val2005june.pdf. Accessed 18 Nov 2018.

Segal, S., 2011. *Corporate value of enterprise RISK management*. [Online] Available at: http://www.wiley.com/WileyCDA/WileyTitle/productCd-0470882549.html. Accessed 15 Ekim 2016.

Shanmugam, A., and T. P. Robert. 2015. Human factors engineering in aircraft maintenance: A review. *Journal of Quality in Maintenance Engineering* 21 (4): 478–505, 503.

Shaw, M. 2008. *Enterprise risk management*. [Online] Available at: http://citebm.business.illinois.edu/TWC%20Class/Project_reports_Fall2008/Project%20and%20Risk%20Management/Marcel%20Hasan/Marc%20Heneghan%20559%20ERM%20Final.pdf. Accessed 15 Ekim 2016.

SkyBrary. 2018. *Human factor*. [Online] Available at: https://www.skybrary.aero/index.php/Human_Factors. Accessed 23 Feb 2018.

Sogg, S. 2002. An integrated systems approach to human factors in commercial aviation maintenance system. [Online] Available at: https://pdfs.semanticscholar.org/efa3/95eb6f0f1d4c881c482170ec4d040dfb9718.pdf.

Stanton, N.A., W.-C. Li, and D. Harri. 2019. Human factors in aviation. *Ergonomics* 62: 2, 131–137, 131. https://doi.org/10.1080/00140139.2019.1564589.

TAV Airports Holding. 2018. Management philosophy. [Online] Available at: http://www.tavhavalimanlari.com.tr/en-EN/Pages/ManagementPhilosophy.aspx.

Terzioğlu, M. 2010. *Ekip Kaynak Yönetimi*. İstanbul: Cinius Yayınları.

Topçu, B. 2013. *İşletmelerde Kurumsal Risk Yönetimi*. İstanbul: Kadir Has Üniversitesi.

TÜSİAD. (2008, Şubat). Enterprise Risk Management. Retrieved October 24, 2016, from http://tusiad.org/tr/component/k2/item/download/2466_aff40c11210dd71986e25302c58160ca. Accessed 24 Ekim 2016.

Tuten, P. 2018. Enterprise risk management. Retrieved October 24, 2016, from http://tusiad.org/tr/component/k2/item/download/2466_aff40c11210dd71986e25302c58160ca.

Wickens, C.D., et al. 2004. *An introduction to human factors in engineering*, 2nd ed. Upper Saddle River, NJ: Pearson Prentice Hall.

Yazgan, E., and Ayşe Kucuk Yilmaz. 2019. Prioritisation of factors contributing to human error for airworthiness management strategy with ANP. *Aircraft Engineering and Aerospace Technology*. 91 (1): 78–93. https://doi.org/10.1108/AEAT-11-2017-0245.

Yazgan, E., and A. Kucuk Yılmaz. In press process. Prioritization of factors that contributed to aircraft maintenance technician error with analytic network process. *Aircraft Engineering and Aerospace Technology*.

Chapter 3
Introduction: Risks of the Multi-cultural Business Environment in Aviation Business

Situation Awareness: The Ability to Maintain the Big Picture.
Air University (2013)

Contents

Introduction: Aviation Business in a Multi-cultural Environment

Aviation is a multi-cultural business environment in both its operational and management aspects. Managing aviation requires a high awareness of organizational behavior related topics.

Decision-making is a routine but also a vital part of managers' responsibilities. Especially in aviation, the decision may create considerable results owing to industry-related qualifications with high operational costs. Decisions pertaining to risk management should be made both carefully and thoughtfully. To manage risk holistically and to support sustainability, managers in aviation must optimize situational awareness in their decision-making process.

Situational Awareness (SA) is not only vital to operational side of aviation such as Pilotage, Air Traffic Control (ATC), Aircraft Maintenance, AMT, Ground handling, Airports, Airport Terminals, but also it has considerable critical importance to managers. To manage in both a systematic and holistic way, managers have to

A. Kucuk Yilmaz and T. G. Flouris, *Values, Ergonomics and Risk Management in Aviation Business Strategy*, https://doi.org/10.1007/978-981-15-1006-9_3

catch optimization in their SA process with decision-making integration. Situational Awareness should be considered as one of the required qualifications of managers in business and strategy.

Situational Awareness has a considerable impact on decision-making in both a timely and rightly manner. Situational awareness is, therefore, directly related to the ability to make the right decisions within the context of management and strategy. For this reason, situational awareness is one of the key managerial concepts in aviation. This chapter deals with the main issues in aviation management and strategy. Decision-making as presented is linked with the situational awareness concept. This chapter aims to improve the awareness of the holistic view in aviation management.

We assume that managers may achieve both their corporate strategies and also realized their corporate aims if they consider risk management and organizational behavior in their decision-making process. Here, situational awareness is a key factor in the decision-making process. This chapter is an important part that completes the other parts of the book. Because if there is no awareness, there can be no clear understanding, no proper decision-making, and no effective management. In order to keep situational awareness at the highest level, the factors that influence the level of situational awareness (positive and negative) are both well defined and well managed in a supportive direction.

Situational Awareness is based on the principle that in the face of technical skills and complex structures in aviation, pilots can understand the situation technically and make the right decisions so that the technical maintenance team can make the right decisions to manage the situation and operations. Situational awareness should not only be understood at the technical level but must be integrated with social, environmental, and psychological factors. In this respect, it is foreseen that awareness risk management which is compatible with the mentalities of multi-criteria decision-making problem-solving should be applied. It is assumed that good SA leads to good decision-making, which is then expected to result in a good outcome (Stanners and French 2005, p. 2).

Much can be said about the importance of attention on SA. How people direct their attention has a fundamental impact on which portions of the environment are incorporated into their SA. In this light, both the perceptual salience of environmental cues (i.e., the degree to which they draw attention) and the meaningful direction of attention of the individual are important. Numerous factors will dictate how people direct their attention in acquiring information including learned scan patterns and information sampling strategies, goals, expectations, and other information already processed (Endsley 2000a, b, c). According to Lichacz (2001), situational awareness represents an expanded view of the psychological processes that underlie situational awareness and are rooted in the information processing paradigm (Lichacz 2001). The human factor is the main risk element in aviation. The human has a dual role in aviation as both the source and manager of risks. Human Factors (HF) are all issues that influence our behavior as humans every day and are also about issues like design of equipment, interfaces between man and machine, training, organization of work and teamwork (Joint Aviation Authorities 2012).

Human factors science, or human factors technologies, is a multidisciplinary field incorporating contributions from psychology, engineering, industrial design, statistics, operations research, and anthropometry (FAA 2016, p. 3). It is a term that covers the science of understanding the properties of human capability, the application of this understanding to the design, development, and deployment of systems and services, and the art of ensuring successful application of human factor principles into all aspects of aviation to include pilots, ATC, and aviation maintenance. Wickens et al. (2004) defined the goal of human factors as making the human interaction with systems one that (see figure in 5.1).

a. Enhances performance,
b. Increases safety, and
c. Increases user satisfaction (Wickens et al. 2004) (Fig. 3.1).

SA is the ability to build and maintain the big picture, which supports both corporate and individual ability to make sound warning decisions. There are several controllable factors, such as workload, which can support one's ability to have good SA. Developing the ability to have good SA in the warning phase of a possible occurrence is dependent on understanding how these controllable factors together (Air University 2013, p. 1).

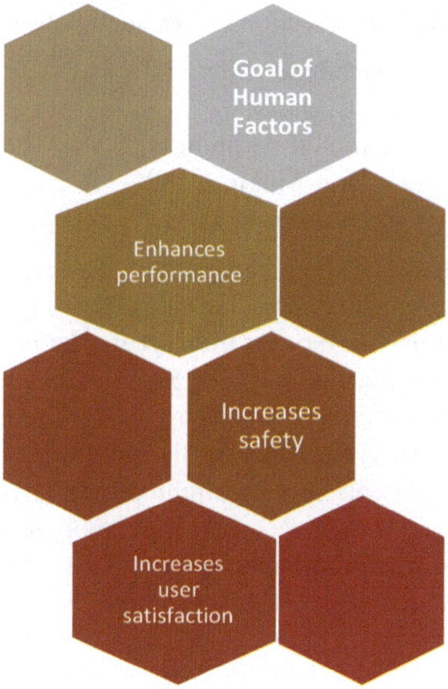

Fig. 3.1 Goal of human factors as making human interaction with systems. Developed from (Wickens et al. 2004)

Decision-Making in Aviation: As Fundamental Risk of Management and Strategy

> To see, to hear means nothing. To recognize (or not to recognize) means everything.
> Andre Breton (Air University 2013)[1]

The present-day world of aviation is quite different from 25 years ago; almost just one national culture and one national language were present in the cockpit. Nowadays, it is common to meet different cultures in the cockpit, in the cabin, and around an aircraft. Different cultures could be difficult to mix (Joint Aviation Authorities 2012, p. 1). Decision-making is based on situational awareness (Crew Resource Management 2018); managers must either identify or create the best options to make a decision. The decision is more than simply choosing: it is also about balancing all available information (Joint Aviation Authorities 2012, p. 2). Naturalistic decision-making is characterized by dynamic and continually changing conditions. Since conditions are dynamic, various goals and subgoals are likely to need to be redefined as new information is received, and priorities of goals and subgoals are likely to change as a situation redefines itself (Randel and LAUREN PUGH 1996, s. 579).

The human factor is a leading element in aviation like in all businesses. In aviation management, by using crew resource management (CRM) skills, a corporate climates can be created where with all respect for other persons involved in operation, freedom exists to question issues such below: (Joint Aviation Authorities 2012, p. 1):

- Leadership,
- Assertiveness,
- Situational Awareness,
- Decision-Making, and
- Communication.

It should be clearly noted, however, that technological systems do not provide SA in and of themselves. It takes a human operator to perceive information to make it useful. Nor do they create the need for SA. No matter how a person does his or her job, the need for SA has always existed, even in what would not normally be considered heavily cognitive or technological fields. In sports, such as football or hockey, for instance, the importance of SA in selecting and running plays is readily apparent. The highlighted emphasis on SA in current system design has occurred because (a) we can now do more to help provide good SA through decision aids and system interfaces, and (b) we are far more able to actually hinder SA through these same efforts if, as designers, we fail in adequately addressing the SA needs of the operator (Endsley 2000a, b, c, s. 6). Decision-making is a mental process and is a core issue in safety-related professions. Decisions are related to the objectives of, e.g., flight and the goals of an organization (Joint Aviation Authorities 2012) (see Fig. 3.2).

---

[1] Air University, Advanced Warning Operations Course IC Core 2 Lesson 2: Individual SA Warning Decision Training Branch http://www.au.af.mil/au/awc/awcgate/noaa/indiv_situation_awareness.pdf.

Fig. 3.2 Samples to goals of aviation organizations. Developed from (Joint Aviation Authorities 2012)

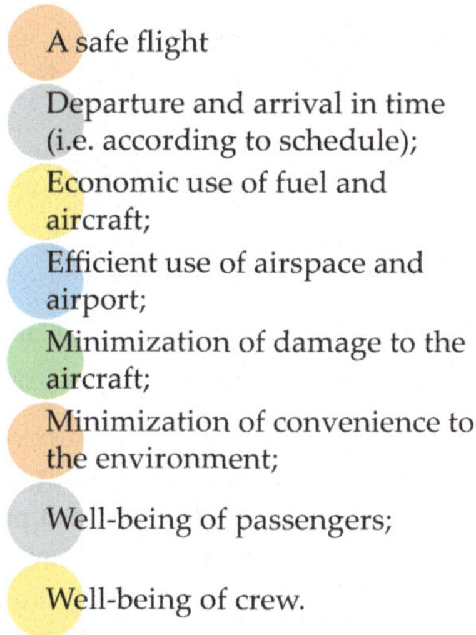

Decision-making can generally be represented by three phases, each of which itself can be elaborated into subphases: (i) acquiring and perceiving information or cues relevant for the decision; (ii) generating and selecting hypotheses or situation assessments about what the cues mean, regarding the current and future state relevant to the decision; (iii) planning and selection choices to take, on the basis of the inferred state, and the costs and values of different outcomes. The three stages often cycle and iterate in a single decision (Wickens et al. 2004, p. 73). In goal-driven processing, attention is directed across the environment in accordance with active goals. The operator actively seeks information needed for goal attainment and the goals simultaneously act as a filter in interpreting the information that is perceived. In data-driven processing, perceived environmental cues may indicate new goals that need to be active. Dynamic switching between these two processing modes is important for successful performance in many environments (Endsley 2000a, b, c, pp. 2–4)

Steps for good decision-making are (FAA 2016, pp. 2, 3)

I. Identifying personal attitudes hazardous to safe flight;
II. Learning behavior modification techniques;
III. Learning how to recognize and cope with stress;
IV. Developing risk assessment skills;
V. Using all resources;
VI. Evaluating the effectiveness of one's "Aeronautical Decision-Making" (ADM) skills.

An issue of discussion has centered on whether or not people acting with automaticity really need to have a high level of conscious SA. The example would be a person driving over a familiar route without really thinking about it, turning and stopping where appropriate yet unable to consciously remember the past few minutes of the

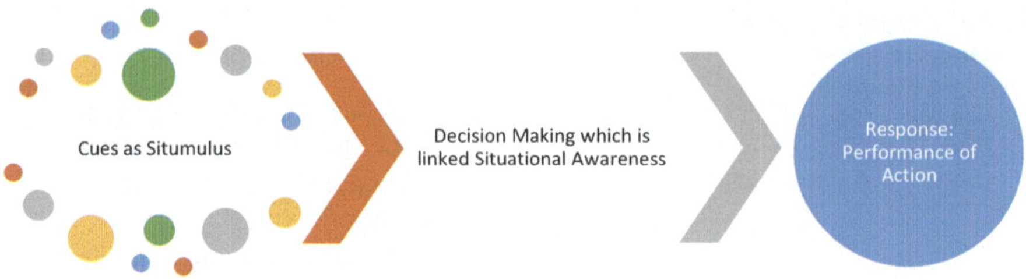

Fig. 3.3 Developed from Automaticity in cognitive processes (Endsley 2000)

trip. As opposed to the view of performance presented here, where environmental cues are interpreted to form SA, produce decisions, and then actions, automaticity would be seen to short-circuit that process. A more direct stimulus/response pairing would be elicited, and conscious awareness and decision- making would thus be very low. While the advantage of automaticity is the low level of attention required by the task, it also has significant hazards for SA and performance. Namely, such direct stimulus–response pairing (a) does not allow for novel integration of information; (b) people under automaticity tend to be non-receptive to novel events; and (c) errors tend to occur when there must be a change in the learned pattern (Endsley 2000a, b, c). The following figure has been developed from the Endsley model (Model) as Automaticity in cognitive processes (Fig. 3.3).

People frequently have to make decisions under conditions of uncertainty (Bridger 1995). Managers make problem-solving decisions under three different conditions: certainty, risk, and uncertainty. All managers make decisions under each condition, but risk and uncertainty are common to the more complex and unstructured problems faced by top managers. Decisions are made under the condition of certainty when the manager has perfect knowledge of all the information needed to make a decision. This condition is ideal for problem-solving. The challenge is simply to study the alternatives and choose the best solution (Harcourt 2016, p. 1). Uncertainty includes risks. While human decision-makers are good at making a judgment under uncertainty, they are not good at integrating them (Bridger 1995, p. 529). When new and unfamiliar problems arise, non-programmed decisions are specifically tailored to the situations at hand. The information requirements for defining and resolving nonroutine problems are typically high. Although computer support may assist in information processing, the decision will most likely involve human judgment. Most problems faced by higher level managers demand non-programmed decisions. This fact explains why the demands on a manager's conceptual skills increase as he or she moves into higher levels of managerial responsibility (Harcourt 2016, p. 2).

Decision-making, in a simple form, can be seen as an information step process (Joint Aviation Authorities 2012) as follows:

- Cue seeking: monitoring the environment where the human works and looks for cues to obtain near-perfect situation awareness or, in cases of deviations from the norm, what the deviation is and where it comes from;
- Situation assessment: use of cues interpreted to construct a mental model or a diagnosis of the situation, set against the knowledge and experience found in the Long-Term Memory (LTM);
- Options: what are the possible actions and alternatives that can be taken, i.e., problem-solving and thinking solutions;
- Assessing benefits, costs, and risks of possible solutions: the different options can have different advantages and disadvantages, set against the goals of the flight or organization;
- Choice: the actual decision-making with, as an end result, the outcome that best fits the situation at hand;
- Decision implementation: the effectuation of the decision, preferably not taken on impulse.

During each flight, the single pilot makes many decisions under hazardous conditions. To fly safely, the pilot needs to assess the degree of risk and determine the best course of action to mitigate the risk (FAA 2016).

The decision-making process normally consists of several steps before a pilot chooses a course of action. A variety of structured frameworks for decision-making provide assistance in organizing the decision process. These models include but are not limited to the 5P (Plan, Plane, Pilot, Passengers, Programming), the OODA Loop (Observation, Orientation, Decision, Action), and the DECIDE (Detect, Estimate, Choose, Identify, Do, and Evaluate) models (FAA 2014).

In order to keep situational awareness at the highest level, the factors that influence the level of situational awareness (positive and negative) are both well defined and well managed in a supportive direction. Situational awareness is, therefore, directly related to the ability to make the right decisions within the context of management and strategy.

Correct decision-making is one of the most critical elements supporting the success of the corporate strategy. Also, individual situational awareness is necessary for success. Situational awareness must also be shared in such teamwork as it is necessary to work for effective corporate success. In line with the goal of the team, individuals should be able to manage shared situational awareness well.

During each flight, decisions must be made regarding events that involve interactions between the four risk elements—the pilot in command (PIC), the aircraft, the environment, and the operation. The decision-making process involves an evaluation of each of these risk elements to achieve an accurate perception of the flight situation. To maintain situational awareness, an accurate perception must be attained of how the pilot, helicopter, environment, and operation combine to affect the flight (FAA 2014).

This mechanism provides good performance with a very low level of attention demand in certain well-understood environments. In this sense, automaticity can positively affect situation awareness by reducing demands on limited attention resources, particularly for demanding physical tasks. Situation awareness can be negatively impacted by the automaticity of cognitive processes, however, due to a reduction in responsiveness to novel stimuli. Information that is outside the routinized sequence may not be attended to. Thus, situation awareness may suffer when that information is important (Endsley 2000a, b, c, s. 15).

Once a pilot identifies the risks of a flight, he or she needs to decide whether the risk or combination of risks, can be managed safely and successfully. If not, make the decision to cancel the flight. If the pilot decides to continue with the flight, he or she should develop strategies to mitigate the risks. One way a pilot can control the risks is to set personal minimums for items in each risk category. These are limits unique to that individual pilot's current level of experience and proficiency (FAA 2016).

The factors supporting organizational success heavily depend on some factors in the field of both organizational behavior and management and strategy. We assume that the factors supporting organizational success may be similar to prioritized risks of the human factor in aviation (Kucuk Yilmaz 2019, p. 12) as follows:

i. Individual perspective, reason, results, references, inferences, and accountability,
ii. Complacency,
iii. Safety culture,
iv. Motivation (rewards, penalty, etc.),
v. Peer pressure,
vi. Ethical (integrity, honesty),
vii. Norms (most AMTs do not follow procedure, commonly acceptable practice of working routine jobs without manual, etc.),
viii. Social responsibility culture in the business environment,
ix. Philanthropic behavior of an individual,
x. Corporate change/restructuring (layoffs, reorganizations, pay cuts, etc.),
xi. Teamwork,
xii. Cultural differences,
xiii. Lack of management support,
xiv. Man hour planning/Manpower,
xv. Corporate change/restructuring (layoffs, reorganizations, pay cuts, etc.),
xvi. Mental or physical workload(overload/underload),
xvii. Sensory and perceptual limitations,
xviii. Cognitive abilities (memory, attention, etc.),
xix. Intelligence (Emotional Intelligence),

xx. The campaigner, volunteer and activist instinct in the individual that picks-up and supports issues affecting society,
xxi. Time pressure, and
xxii. Dissemination of information.

The results of the aviation industry are consistent with our list. After a series of accidents, Transport Canada and the aviation industry identified 12 human factors which they then called "The Dirty Dozen" (Joint Aviation Authorities 2012).

During the late 1980s and early 1990s, there was a spate of maintenance related to aviation incidents in Canada. These incidents spurred Transport Canada to launch an initiative that would aid aviation companies in their fight to prevent unnecessary accidents. Gordon Dupont, who was a Special Program Coordinator at Transport Canada at the time, was credited with the introduction of "The Dirty Dozen" which was the identification of 12 human factor elements highly likely to "degrade people's ability to perform effectively and safely, leading to maintenance errors". Today, the ubiquity of this term, in both the flying and maintenance communities is a testament to the success of the campaign. The RSAF adopted the Dirty Dozen concept in 1998 to complement the Human Error Accident Reduction Training (HEART) and Human Error Analysis Tool (HEAT) for our operations and logistics communities respectively. The Dirty Dozen consists of 12 identified human factors (RSAF 2012). They are (RSAF 2012)

i. Lack of Communication: A Lack of clear direct statements and good, active listening skills;
ii. Complacency: Self-satisfaction accompanied by loss of awareness of the potential dangers;
iii. Lack of Knowledge: Lack of experience or training for the task at hand;
iv. Distraction: Drawing one's attention away from a task;
v. Lack of Teamwork: Lack of working together to achieve a common goal;
vi. Fatigue: Weariness from labor or exertion, nervous exhaustion or the temporary loss of power to respond;
vii. Lack of Resources: Failure to use or acquire the appropriate tools, equipment, information and procedures for the task at hand;
viii. Pressure: Pushing for something in spite of opposing odds, creating a sense of urgency or hassle;
ix. Lack of Assertiveness: A lack of positive communication of one's ideas, wants and needs;
x. Stress: Mental, emotional, or physical tension, strain, or distress;
xi. Lack of Awareness: Failure to be alert or vigilant in observing;
xii. Norms: Commonly accepted practices where assumptions are made that the course of action or procedure is correct based on history without revalidating or verifying the current procedures.

The Dirty Dozen tends to focus on the maintenance technicians but can also be used to examine the organization in which the action is occurring. Discussions on the Dirty Dozen increase awareness of the factors and the hope is that will translate into a reduction in error and enhanced safety culture. It's also important to remember that the Dirty Dozen, by themselves, do not make up a human factors program. However, they're a good place to build from and a solid element in a robust Safety Management System (SMS) (Grenier 2016, p. 4).

Over the years, different areas of aviation have found that the Dirty Dozen offers a useful introduction to open discussions into human errors in the workplaces and organizations. The list has been adopted for pilots, ramp workers, air traffic controllers, and cabin crews (MA and Grover 2016, p. 5). For this reason, the dirty dozen may be considered in both risk management and organizational behavior related research in aviation.

Situational awareness is the accurate perception and understanding of all the factors and conditions within the five fundamental risk elements (flight, pilot, aircraft, environment, and type of operation that comprise any given aviation situation) that affect safety before, during, and after the flight. Monitoring radio communications for traffic, weather discussion, and ATC communication can enhance situational awareness by helping the pilot develop a mental picture of what is happening (FAA 2016).

However, measurement of decision-making is notably difficult to perform, as valid reproducible conclusions depend on both process and outcome measures, and assessment of process often depends on the user's limited ability to consistently define and report their own cognition (Wolf and Kuber 2018, p. 56). Situation awareness (SA) theory, design, training, and measurement have formed a substantive portion of the human factors research field over the past 25 years (Endsley 2015, pp. 8–10). The theories of situational awareness are strongly associated with the definitions that have given rise to the concept and the methods of assessing situational awareness in the world. Three main theoretical approaches dominate: the information processing approach, the activity approach, and the ecological approach (Stanton et al. 2001a, b, pp. 189–204).

Situational awareness can be broadly defined as the gathering of information about the external environment via observation, the identification of the present situation by comparison with the information generated by the aerator systems or previously generated information, and the estimation of how the future will be in the future by following changes in the environment (Sekerli 2006, pp. 60–62). Situation awareness (SA) is a relatively new concept that has captured the imagination of human factors professionals and others who are interested in the role of humans in complex systems (Flach 1995, p. 149).

SA is being aware of what is happening around you and understanding what that information means to you now and in the future. This awareness is usually defined in terms of what information is important for a particular job or goal. The concept of SA is usually applied to operational situations, where people must have SA for a specific reason, for example, in order to drive a car, treat a patient, or separate traffic as an air traffic controller (Endsley and Jones 2011, p. 13)

Most simply put, SA is knowing what is going on around you. Inherent in this definition is a notion of what is important. SA is most frequently defined in operational terms. While someone not engaged in a task or objective might have awareness (e.g., someone sitting under a tree ideally enjoying nature), this class of individuals has been largely outside the scope of human factors design efforts. Rather, we have been concerned mostly with people who need SA for specific reasons. For a given operator, therefore, SA is defined in terms of the goals and decision tasks for that job. The pilot does not need to know everything (e.g., the copilot's shoe size and spouse's name), but does need to know a great deal of information related to the goal of safely flying the aircraft (Endsley 2000a, b, c, pp. 2–5). The interest in SA grew quickly from its initial start in aviation to many disparate fields including air traffic control, military operations, transportation, power systems, law enforcement, emergency management, health care, space, transportation, education, mining, and oil and gas operations (Endsley 2015, p. 4).

Individual situational awareness is necessary for success. Situational awareness must also be shared in such teamwork as it is necessary to work for effective corporate success. In line with the goal of the team, individuals should be able to manage shared situational awareness well. Naturalistic decision-making is characterized by dynamic and continually changing conditions. Since conditions are dynamic, various goals and subgoals are likely to need to be redefined as new information is received, and priorities of goals and subgoals are likely to change as a situation redefines itself (Randel and LAUREN PUGH 1996, s. 579).

Situation awareness (SA) is a term that emerged from aviation psychology to describe the component of tactical flight operations that involve the pilot‘s understanding. Expanding SA to an operator's comprehension of a complex system has extended SA research to other domains in which the environment is dynamically changing and in which the operator is responsible for maintaining or achieving particular states or goals (Bhatt and Güsgen 2012, p. 127)

The terms situation (al) awareness, situation (al) assessment and situation (al) measurement are rife in the literature. For simplicity's sake, the term "situational" has been adopted in this paper as the terms appear interchangeable. Researchers and practitioners in this field have attempted to clear up the ambiguities in the definition of situational awareness (often abbreviated to SA in the literature) (Karwowski 2006, p. 892)

SA is widely recognized by operators and practitioners across aviation, power systems, emergency management, military, medical, and many other domains as being critical to effective decision-making and performance. It is incumbent on the human factors profession to respond to this need with improved systems and approaches for enhancing SA in the difficult and complex worlds where it is so essential.

In their work Jones and Endsley (1996) stated that in the dynamic flight environment, effective aircrew decision-making is highly dependent on situation awareness (SA)—a constantly evolving picture of the state of the environment. In this point, situational awareness (SA) is a crucial factor in effective decision-making, especially in the dynamic flight environment. Consequently, an understanding of the types of SA errors that occur in this environment is beneficial (Jones and Endsley 1996, p. 508). While some of these incidents may represent failures in actual decision-making (action selection), a high percentage are actually errors in situation awareness. That is, the aircrew made the correct decision for their picture of the situation, but that picture was in error. This represents a fundamentally different category of problem than a decision error—in which the correct situation is comprehended, but a poor decision is made as to the course of action to take—and requires different types of remediation actions (Jones and Endsley 1996, p. 507). It is often assumed that SA is derived simply from people's senses or by direct observation from the world (Gonzales and Wimisberg 2007, p. 70).

Three main definitions dominate. The first of these centers around an information processing framework, the second emphasizes the reflective quality, and the third presents an embedded world view. Each definition will be presented in turn, followed by a brief analysis of the differences and an integration of the approaches taken (Stanton et al. 2001a, b, p. 2) The failures of human decision-making are frequently cited in investigations of error in a wide variety of systems (Jones and Endsley 1996, p. 510).

According to Stantan et al. (2001a, b), definitions of SA may integrate in view of its main elements as: the person (comprising three main subsystems: working memory, mental models (drawing on knowledge, skills, and experience), and reflection together with projection with the world (comprising many subsystems not mentioned here). This also indicates an interaction between the two main system elements (i.e., the person and the world) (Stanton et al. 2001a, b, p. 191). Situational Awareness (SA) is generally described as the perception of the elements in the environment within a volume of time and space, the comprehension of their meaning and the projection of their status in the near future. SA has emerged in military aviation for improving safety and preventing accidents. In the past decade, it was also used in user-focused areas like the civil aviation sector, air and sea traffic operations, nuclear plant facilities, offshore oil platforms, etc. This is critical proof of the importance of how SA works in sustainable aviation management. Situation awareness (SA), or people's understanding of what is happening around them and what could happen in the future, is a complex construct that plays a key role in the performance of dynamic tasks, such as flying an airplane, driving an automobile, and conducting military operations (Gonzales and Wimisberg 2007, p. 56).

According to Stanton et al. (2001a, b), improvement of situational awareness seems to focus on two main strategies, either the design of the system interface to encourage better sampling and reduce the cognitive workload or training in situational awareness at the individual and team levels. Also, currently, some researchers have incorporated situational awareness training into crew resource management programs in where strategies for improving timely sampling of appropriate displays, dynamic workload distribution, communication and feedback, and tactics in emergency scenarios are included (Stanton et al. 2001a, b, p. 189). With their research Jones and Endsley (1996) provide good evidence that problems with situation awareness are indeed a primary factor underlying aviation accidents (Stanton et al. 2001a, b, p. 56).

Interest in SA within the operational world has been so strong because people know what they are struggling with and that modern systems have let them down. The average layman does not always know why this is or how to fix the problem. That is why they seek our help. There are plenty of companies selling more sensors or software or automation claiming they can fill the gap with technology, but which unfortunately do not address the real challenges for SA in these systems, and often which suffer from the exact same shortcomings. It is incumbent on the human factors profession to more fully understand the challenges that lead to poor SA, and the mechanisms that lead to high levels of SA in even difficult operational environments. The theoretical debate hinges on whether situational awareness is a process or a product. The three-level model and interactive subsystems emphasize product (i.e., the resultant state of situational awareness in the mind of the human operator) whereas the perceptual cycle emphasizes process (i.e., the acts of acquiring situational awareness by the human operator (Stanton et al. 2001a, b, p. 56)

Although the concept of situational awareness has not been a subject of much interest for researchers until the late 1980s, the latter has become a popular research topic. we have been concerned mostly with people who need SA for specific reasons. For a given operator, therefore, SA is defined in terms of the goals and decision tasks for that job. The pilot does not need to know everything (e.g., the copilot's shoe size and spouse's name) but does need to know a great deal of information related to the goal of safely flying the aircraft (Endsley 2000a, b, c, 2001). The factors that affect the level of situational awareness negatively with the increase of automation in aviation are as follows (Durso and Sethumadhavan 2008, p. 284):

- Understanding and Complexity: Increasing the number of systems used in conjunction with automation has increased complexity and has increased the workload of pilots, affecting intelligibility in the negative direction.
- Non-loop Performance: It has been found that system operators working with automation are less able to detect system faults and then manually perform tasks in the face of automation failures relative to manual performance on the same tasks.
- Decision to Combine Man and Machine in Almada: If the system recommendation is ambiguous or incorrect, it is much more likely that the system will reduce human decision quality and speed.

Conceptually, situation awareness is divided into three levels—perception (level 1), understanding of the situation (level 2), and anticipation of future events (level 3).

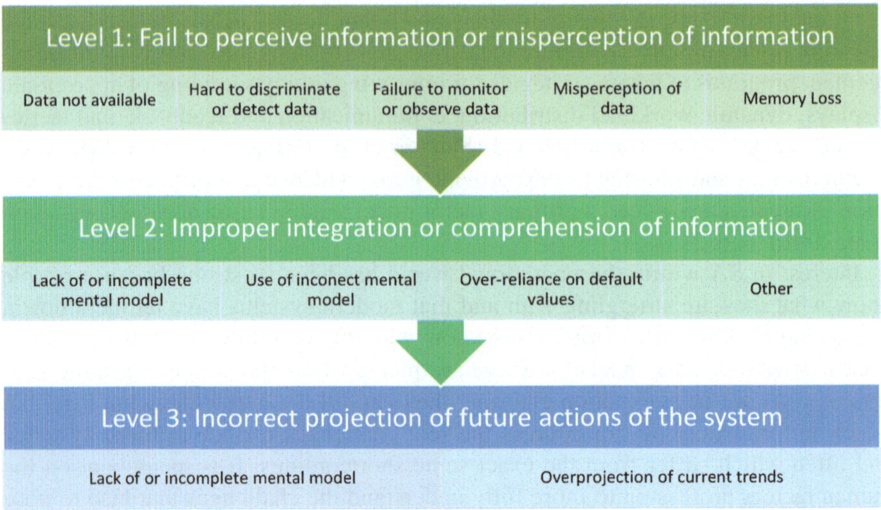

Fig. 3.4 Taxonomy of levels of situation awareness

To sum up, situation awareness plays a major role in domains where humans operate complex systems, general aviation being one of them. A high percentage of aviation accidents and incidents that are based on human factors can be traced back to errors in situation awareness. Causes of many kinds can favor these mistakes (Muehlethaler and Knecht 2016, p. 69) (Fig. 3.4).

In her model, Endsley presents that information proceeds directly from sensory memory to long-term memory, which is necessary for pattern-recognition and coding. Those portions of the environment that are salient remain in working memory as a highlighted subset of long-term memory through either localized attention or automatic activation. In this way, information from the environment may be processed and stored in terms of the activated mental model or schema (i.e., it provides the current situation values of these more abstract models). Thus, once activated, these schemas provide a rich source of data for bringing to bear on the situation including mechanisms for processing the data (i.e., forming Level 2 and Level 3 SA) (Endsley a, b, c) and default values for filling in missing information (e.g., a Cessna is probably going about a certain speed).

It encompasses not only an awareness of specific key elements in the situation (Level 1 SA) but also a gestalt comprehension and integration of that information in light of operational goals (Level 2 SA), along with the ability to project future states of the system (Level 3 SA). These higher levels of SA (Levels 2 and 3) are particularly critical to effective functioning in complex environments such as the cockpit (Jones and Endsley 1996, p. 510). The three-level model seems to be the most developed approach, in terms of measures and interventions, although there is some controversy about the ideas underpinning it. Practical measures have been developed that can assess both the process of acquiring situational awareness and the product of situational awareness. Improvement of situational awareness seems to focus on two main strategies, either the design of the system interface to encourage better sampling and reduce the cognitive workload or training in situational awareness at the individual and team levels (Stanton et al. 2001a, b).

Situation Awareness is a term that emerged from aviation psychology to describe the component of tactical flight operations that involve the pilot‘s understanding. Expanding SA to an operator's comprehension of a complex system has extended SA research to other domains in which the environment is dynamically changing and in which the operator is responsible for maintaining or achieving particular states or goals (Durso and Sethumadhavan 2008, p. 290). According to Muehlethaler and Knecht (2016), simulation-based training seems appropriate for the training of situation awareness for general pilots. To further guarantee transfer, the existing training clearly needs to be incorporated in a structured design which allows immediate feedback on performance (e.g., by using eye-tracking glasses) and that is based on practice-based exercises that are accompanied by theoretical information on situation awareness and scanning techniques (Muehlethaler and Knecht 2016, pp. 66–71). The theoretical debate hinges on whether situational awareness is a process or a product. The three-level model and interactive subsystems emphasize product (i.e., the resultant state of situational awareness in the mind of the human operator) whereas the perceptual cycle emphasizes process (i.e., the acts of acquiring situational awareness by the human operator) (Stanton et al. 2001a, b, p. 4).

Situation Awareness can be enhanced if the domain is designed to support human attention, which is a limited resource. Attention manages the multiple data streams, as well as their relative priority. Attention must also function to screen out information that is not relevant, such as audio and video noise. It is important that the domain (systems and people) does not overly tax human attention (Air University 2013, p. 1); appropriate design can support attention (Air University 2013, p. 1). An overall essential problem when it comes to errors in situation awareness is associated with the limited mental capacity of humans. And mental capacity is affected by factors like a distraction, mental fatigue, or stress (Muehlethaler and Knecht 2016, pp. 66–71). The human operator has conscious choice in making the decision to implement the linked recognition-primed decision action plan or to devise a new one. This behavior can be seen in combat tasks, for instance, where people often wish to be unpredictable. In the many instances where no action plan is readily linked to the recognized situation, a separate decision as to what to do must take place. Just as easily as SA and decision-making can be linked in practice, they can also be unlinked. While this distinction may be purely theoretical, it is made here for the purpose of clarity of discussion. SA is not decision-making and decision-making is not SA. This distinction has implications for the measurement of SA (Endsley 2000a, b, c, p. 1).

An example of how an operator anticipates could be a pilot, who is taking off in a strong crosswind and who will be ready to apply control surface corrections to counter the wind as soon as the landing gear leaves the ground (Muehlethaler and Knecht 2016, p. 67). Examining the relationships between performance-shaping factors such as stress and fatigue and work SA (WSA) may identify their relative contribution to accident involvement (Sneddon et al. 2013, p. 86). Several factors will influence the accuracy and completeness of situation awareness that individual operators derive from their environment. First, humans are limited by working memory and attention. The way in which attention is employed in a complex environment with multiple competing cues is essential in determining which aspects of the situation will be processed to form situation awareness.

Once taken in, information must be integrated with other information, compared to goal states and projected into the future—all heavily demanding on working memory (Endsley 2000a, b, c). Difficult to define, but easy to recognize, situation awareness if tested that can be used to determine if the cognitive theory can "scale-up". It can be used by cognitive psychologists to determine if the mechanisms induced from our controlled laboratory experiments, and held out as fundamental, are in fact important constituents of a complex process—a cognitive process so evident, despite its complexity, that it was identified by the pilots and operators who rely on it (Durso and Sethumadhavan 2008, p. 305).

It should be noted that the elements defined for a given domain and operational role take into account the full range of the aspects of the situation that are relevant to the decision-maker—the technical system, the outside environment (e.g., weather, terrain), the state of other actors (e.g., location of other aircraft, actions of enemies and civilians in a military action), and the state and status of teammate activities (e.g., the level of workload and abilities of one's copilot, the location and plans of other team members). It is not constrained to any one subset of this information (Endsley 2015, p. 12).

The SA construct evolved in real-world environments, where pilots struggled to keep up with the rapidly changing information provided by a myriad of sensors, displays, and new technologies and the complexity and challenges of the flight environment and has spread to a wide variety of domains that struggle with many of the same challenges. Initial questions about SA have been largely laid to rest, and substantive research has been conducted in the intervening years (Endsley 2000a, b, c, p. 4)

Situational Awarenes s provides greater comprehension (insight) of the problem. Situational Awareness is the appreciation of *what* is happening, but not necessarily *why* it is happening. Judgments based on this comprehension provide an understanding of the problem (foresight) (Lovering 2014, p. 52). The pilot does not need to know everything (e.g., the copilot's shoe size and spouse's name), but does need to know a great deal of information related to the goal of safely flying the aircraft (Endsley 2015, p. 12).

Decision-Making and Situational Aware-Ness in Aviation Management

Human capacity is limited, which means that the original, primary task cannot be processed anymore. Interruptions or distractions can have a major influence on the mental model of a person (Muehlethaler and Knecht 2016). Since human error is a major contributor to aviation incidents and accidents, human factors must be an important focus of any aviation safety strategy. Whether for off-line safety analysis or within real-time operations, there is always a need to improve understanding of human performance in an operational context. Human factors provide a universal basis to tie all the ingredients of risk management together into a meaningful whole (Skybrary 2010).

Why are human conditions, such as fatigue, complacency, and stress, so important in aviation? These conditions, along with many others, are called human factors. Human factors directly cause or contribute to many aviation accidents and have been documented as a primary contributor to more than 70% of aircraft accidents. Typically, human factor incidents/accidents are associated with flight operations but recently have also become a major concern in aviation maintenance and air traffic management as well (FAA 2016).

Situational awareness is the continuous extraction of environmental information, its integration with previous knowledge to form a coherent mental picture, and the use of that picture in anticipating future events. Situational Awareness is the ability to identify, process, and comprehend the critical elements of information about what is happening (Livnat et al. 2005, p. 1). Situational Awareness is not just a theoretical notion. It is pertinent to most accidents or incidents, it is real, and its absence causes accidents. Research from The Australian Transportation Safety Board (ATSB) indicates that human factors are a contributing cause in around 70% of all incidents and accidents. Approximately 85% of incident reports include a mention of the loss of situational awareness. Degraded situational awareness can lead to inadequate decision-making and mistakes (Flight Safety Foundation 2016). Situational awareness is more than just perception—it is understanding the meaning of what you perceive, how it might change in the future, and the implications (Crew Resource Management 2018).

The enhancement of operator SA has become a major design goal for those developing operator interfaces, automation concepts, and training programs in a wide variety of fields including aircraft, air traffic control, power plants, and advanced manufacturing systems. This dramatic growth in interest in SA, beginning in the mid-1980s and accelerating through the 1990s, was spurred on by many factors, chief among them the challenges of a new class of technology (Endsley 2000a, b, c).

Good automation requires an understanding of the operator, the task requirements, and environment training in complex environments to take place in context. This allows the novice operator to begin to acquire the experiential repertoires and mental models to support recognition-primed decision-making. The accumulation of this aggregation of repertoires and mental models can be facilitated by focused training of particular cognitive and behavioral task components. Once the operator has sufficient experience and has achieved a level of expertise, the goal of training shifts to helping the operator remains a critical evaluator of the evolving situation, appropriately considering conflicting observations—in other words, strategies for maintaining their SA (Durso and Sethumadhavan 2008, p. 446). This shows relation SA with the automation concept.

Research shows that a significant part of the aviation accidents in which human error plays a role is related to situational awareness. The inability of the cockpit team to develop adequate situational awareness, and the failure to correctly determine the aero-state, causes collisions with ground shapes and other aircraft. On the other hand, it is reported that the cockpit team cannot develop an effective situational awareness in accident and crime reports published by many different aviation authorities every year, resulting in a wrong airport or wrong landing. The effectiveness of decision-making and evaluation processes depends on the situational awareness process. The low situational awareness of the individual causes an error in the decision-making process. An accurate situational awareness development of the team depends on effective teamwork and communication.

Physical and psychological stress, intense attention, heavy workload and such situations commonly encountered in the flight environment can cause loss of ability to perceive. Problems in these perception skills have many definitions of situation reasoning, which express the ability to perceive what is happening around. Situational reasoning is defined as "the ability to synthesize the correct and up-to-date mental state of a person's environment and situation, and to use this synthesis so that future possible situations can be predicted (Karal 2012, p. 58)." General aviation pilots should receive the opportunity to acquire information on scanning techniques in-flight as well as feedback on their practiced behavior from an experienced flight instructor. The combination of practice-based exercises with eye-tracking data promises a reasonable way to enhance awareness and visualize human behavior in a training setting.

In aviation, the decision-making process normally consists of several steps before a pilot chooses a course of action. A variety of structured frameworks for decision-making provide assistance in organizing the decision process. These models include but are not limited to the 5P (Plan, Plane, Pilot, Passengers, Programming), the OODA Loop (Observation, Orientation, Decision, Action), and the DECIDE (Detect, Estimate, Choose, Identify, Do, and Evaluate) models (FAA 2016). From the point of view of air transport, it is the systematic evaluation of the changes that occur during the decision-making flight operation and how these changes affect flight safety.

Furthermore, the link between human decision-making and overall performance is indirect in many environments. A desired action may be mis-executed due to physical error, other workloads, inadequate training or system problems. The system's capabilities may limit overall performance. In some environments, such as the tactical aircraft domain, the action of external agents (e.g., enemy aircraft) may also create poor performance outcomes from essentially good decisions (and vice versa). Therefore, SA, decision-making and performance can be seen for theoretical purposes to be distinct stages that can each affect the other in a circular ongoing cycle, yet which can be decoupled through various other factors (Endsley 2000a, b, c, p. 19).

Jones and Endsley (1996) conclude that by far the largest proportion of errors result from the failure of the flight crew or air traffic controllers to observe or monitor data. It is possible that these errors might be reduced by better means of displaying the data in the first place and improved training in situational assessment strategies (Stanton et al. 2001a, b). Situational awareness is needed by the individual him/herself alone or as a member of a team in order to perform the needed tasks. The individual needs to have an adequate level of awareness of the processes and information requirements and after these the necessary level of awareness of the devices that support the actual information sharing (Koskinen-Kannisto 2013, p. 5). In this sense, comprehensive pre-flight preparation and planning are crucial for decisions to be made in flight. However, it is not right to say that this is sufficient on its own. Preflight planning by team members will ensure the most effective participation of the other team members in decisions about the flight. Therefore, as the flight progresses, it is important for the flight crew to have good situational reasoning that informs the captain pilot about the changes made to the flight plan to be made to the flight team regularly (Sekerli 2006, p. 181).

General aviation pilots should receive the opportunity to acquire information on scanning techniques in-flight as well as feedback on their practiced behavior from an experienced flight instructor. The combination of practice-based exercises with eye-tracking data promises a reasonable way to enhance awareness and visualize human behavior in a training setting (Muehlethaler and Knecht 2016). With the advent of the machine age, our emphasis shifted to creating a new class of tools to help people perform tasks, largely those physical in nature. The Computer Age and now the Information Age have followed rapidly on the heels of basic mechanization. The tools provided are no longer simple; they are amazingly complex, focused on not just physical tasks, but elaborate perceptual and cognitive tasks as well. The pilot of today's aircraft, the air traffic controller, the power plant operator, the anesthesiologist: all must perceive and comprehend a dazzling array of data which is often changing very rapidly. This challenge could be termed "information gap" (Endsley 2000a, b, c)

Conceptually, situation awareness is divided into three levels—perception (level 1), understanding of the situation (level 2), and anticipation of future events (level 3). To sum up, situation awareness plays a major role in domains where humans operate complex systems, general aviation being one of them. A high percentage of aviation accidents and incidents that are based on human factors can be traced back to errors in situation awareness. Causes of many kinds can favor these mistakes. The first level of situation awareness—involving the perception of the elements of the environment—requires an awareness of the condition and state of all relevant elements one is surrounded by.

Simply put, SA knows what is going on around you. Inherent in this definition is a notion of what is important. SA is most frequently defined in operational terms. While someone not engaged in a task or objective might have awareness (e.g., someone sitting under a tree ideally enjoying nature), this class of individuals has been largely outside the scope of human factors design efforts. Rather, we have been concerned mostly with people who need SA for specific reasons. For a given operator, therefore, SA is defined in terms of the goals and decision tasks for that job.

The pilot does not need to know everything (e.g., the copilot's shoe size and spouse's name) but does need to know a great deal of information related to the goal of safely flying the aircraft. A surgeon has just as great a need for situation awareness;

however, the things she needs to know about will be quite different, dependent on a different set of goals and decision tasks (Endsley 2000a, b, c)

First, remarks on flight training implied that theoretical background (learned in flight schools) on scanning behavior and situation awareness varies strongly among all participants. Furthermore, it seems evident that there do not exist any specific and uniform theories on situation awareness or scanning behavior which are taught in flight schools for private pilots. Second, the planned simulation-based training on situation awareness seems to be as interesting for licensed pilots as well as for flight cadets, although routine in aircraft handling (due to flight experience) is essential for the improvement of situation awareness skills. Third, the use of an eye tracker as a biofeedback tool and as an instrument for flight instructors to assess their pilots' scan paths is essential to visualize and display subjective processes on perception and comprehension during flights. Fourth, workload and stress (e.g., in emergency situations) are cited as important influencing factors that would need to be incorporated into the training of situation awareness (e.g., by involving flight schedules that provoke workload).

Conclusion

Situational awareness is not performance. In other words, SA should not be understood as performance. During the analysis of corporate performance, managers should not use the level of SA to evaluate both their managerial and individual performance. But improved situational awareness of managers may support corporate performance and for this reason, SA has an important place in decision-making. But also, a high level of situational awareness cannot give absolute assurance to high performance in both ergonomics and management.

Looking is different from seeing. Seeing is not the same as looking. Generally, Situational Awareness may be considered as the ability to holistic decision-making, which is vital to both perceive instant data and get direct decisions. Especially in critical times both individual and environmental awareness is required to make a decision. It is important to look at it but to understand what it looks like is also of utmost importance. So, to be aware of what's going on.

There are three general stages of situational awareness:

I. awaiting of critical information,
II. understanding of information's meaning,
III. drawing out the results to the future situation.

Decision-making is critical in management. And in this process, SA may provide both a holistic and systematic structure for management, ergonomics,, and strategy in contemporary business environment.

References

Air University. 2013. Situation awareness and decision making in a warning environment. Advanced Warning Operations Course IC Core 2 Lesson 2: Individual SA warning decision training branch. [Online] Available at http://www.au.af.mil/au/awc/awcgate/noaa/indiv_situation_awareness.pdf. Accessed 20 Feb 2018.

Bhatt, M., and H.W. Güsgen. 2012. *Situational awareness for assistive technologies*, 127. Amsterdam, the Netherlands: IOS Press.

Bolstad, C., M. Endsley, A. Costello, and C. Howell. 2010. Evaluation of computer-based situation awareness training for general aviation pilots. *The International Journal of Aviation Psychology*, 269–294.

Bridger, R.B. 1995. *Introduction to ergonomics*. Singapore: McGraw-Hill.

Crew Resource Management. 2018. Module 4—Situational awareness. [Online] Available at: https://www.crewresourcemanagement.net/situational-awareness. Accessed 20 Feb 2018.

Durso, F.T., and A. Sethumadhavan. 2008. Situation awareness: Understanding dynamic environments. *Human Factors* 50 (3): 442–448. https://doi.org/10.1518/001872008x288448.

Endsley, M.R. 1997. *Supporting situation awareness in aviation systems*. Atlanta, Georgia: SA Technologies.

Endsley, M.R. 1999. Situation awareness in aviation systems. In D.J. Garland, J.A. Wise, & V.D. Hopkin (eds.). *Human factors in transportation. Handbook of aviation human factors*, pp. 257–276. Mahwah, NJ, US: Lawrence Erlbaum Associates Publishers.

Endsley, M.R. 2000a. *Situation awareness*. Mahwah, NJ: Lawrence Erlbaum Associates.

Endsley, M.R. 2000b. Theoretical underpinnings of situation awareness: A critical review. In *Situation awareness analysis and measurement*, ed. Endsley and Garland. Mahwah, NJ: Lawrence Erlbaum Associates.

Endsley, M.R.S. 2000c. Theoretical underpinnings of situation awareness. In *Situation awareness analysis and measurement*, 1–25. Mahwah, NJ: Lawrence Erlbaum Associates.

Endsley, M.R., and M. Robertson. 2000. Situation awareness in aircraft maintenance teams. *International Journal of Industrial Ergonomics*, 301–325.

Endsley, M.R. 2001. Situational awareness and safety. *Safety Science* 39: 189–204.

Endsley, M.R. 2015. Situation awareness misconceptions and misunderstandings. *Journal of Cognitive Engineering and Decision Making Special Issue* 9 (1): 4–32.

Endsley, M.R., and D.G. Jones. 2011. *Designing for situation awareness: An approach to user-centered design*. Boca Raton, Florida, London: CRC Press.

FAA. 2014. Effective aeronautical decision-making. In: *Helicopter fliying handbook*, 14. Washington, DC: FAA Federal Avaition Administration.

FAA. 2016. Aeronautical decision-making (ADM). [Online] Available at: https://www.faa.gov/regulations_policies/handbooks_manuals/aviation/phak/media/04_phak_ch2.pdf.

Flach, J.M. 1995. Situation awareness: Proceed with caution. *Human Factors* 37 (1): 149–157.

Flight Safety Foundation. 2016. Operator's guide to human factors in aviation. In *Human performance and limitations*. [Online] Available at: https://www.skybrary.aero/index.php/Situational_Awareness_(OGHFA_BN. Accessed 20 Feb 2018.

Flin, R., K.M. Goeters, H.-J. Hormann, L. Martin. 1998. A generic structure of non-technical skills for training. In: 23'üncü Avrupa Havacilik Psikolojisi Birligi Konferansin'a Sunulan Bildiri, 9. Viyana.

Gonzales, C., and J. Wimisberg. 2007. Situation awareness in dynamic decision making: Effects of practice and working memory. *Journal of Cognitive Engineering and Decision Making*, 70.

Grenier, J. 2016. Everything old is new again: Revisiting "The Dirty Dozen". *Aviation MX Human Factors FAA*, 4.

Harcourt, H.M. 2016. Conditions that influence decision making. [Online] Available at https://www.cliffsnotes.com/study-guides/principles-of-management/decision-making-and-problem-solving/conditions-that-influence-decison-making. Accessed 18 Aug 2019.

Joint Aviation Authorities. 2012. *Human factors and crew resource management in aviation.* KC Hoofddorp Netherlands: GDC Cross MEdia Group.

Jones, D.G., and M.R. Endsley. 1996. Sources of situation awareness errors in aviation. *Aviation, Space and Environmental Medicine*, 507–512.

Karal, H. 2012. *Uçak Kazalarinda İnsan Kaynakli Risklerin Önlenmesine Yönelik Ekip Kaynaklari Yönetimi*, 58. İstanbul: Beykent Üniversitesi, Yüksek Lisans Tezi.

Karwowski, W. 2006. p. 892. *International encyclopedia of ergonomics and human factors*, vol. 3. New York: CRC Press, Taylor & Francis.

Koskinen-Kannisto, A. 2013. *Situational awareness concept in a multinational collaboration environment*, pp. 287. Helsinki: National Defence University Department of Military Technology. https://core.ac.uk/download/pdf/39956817.pdf, http://www.doria.fi/bitstream/handle/10024/89998/SituationalAwareness_netti.pdf.

Kucuk Yilmaz, A. 2019. Strategic approach to managing human factors risk in aircraft maintenance organization: risk mapping. *Aircraft Engineering and Aerospace Technology* 91 (4): 654–668. https://doi.org/10.1108/ AEAT-06

Li, W.-C. 2011. The casual factors of aviation accidents related to decision errors in the cockpit by system approach. *Journal of Aeronautics, Astronautics and Aviation*, 159–166.

Lichacz, F.M. 2001. The missing cognitive link in situation awareness research. In: *Engineering psychology and cognitive ergonomics volume five: Aerospace and transportation systems*, 307. Hants England: Ashgate Publishing.

Livnat, Y., J. Agutter, S. Moon, and S. Foresti. 2005. *Visual correlation for situational awareness.* Minneapolis, MN: IEEE Minneapolis. https://doi.org/10.1109/infvis.2005.1532134.

Lovering, T. 2014. Odin's ravens: From situational awareness to Understanding. *The Three Swords Magazine* 27 (2014): 50–52.

MA, M., and J. Grover. 2016. From "Dirty Dozen" to "Filthy Fifteen"—Professionalism in aircraft. *Aviation MX Human Factors*, 5.

Muehlethaler, C.M., and C.P. Knecht. 2016. Situation awareness training for general aviation pilots using eye tracking. *IFAC-PapersOnLine* 49–19: 66–071.

Plant, K.L., and N.A. Stanton. 2016. The development of the Schema-Action-World (SAW) taxonomy for understanding decision making in aeronautical critical incidents. *Safety Science*.

Randel, J.M and H. LAUREN PUGH. 1996. Differences in expert and novice situation awareness in naturalistic decision making. *International Journal of Human - Computer Studies* 45: 579–597.

RSAF. 2012. *FOCUS magazine The Dirty Dozen The beginning.* [Online] Available at: https://www.mindef.gov.sg/oms/content/dam/imindef_media_library/pdf/air_force/Focus70.pdf.

Sekerli, E.B. 2006. *Yüksek Lisans Tezi.* Eskişehir: Anadolu Üniversitesi.

Skybrary. 2010. Human factors strategy (OGHFA BN) operator's guide to human factors in aviation. [Online] Available at: https://www.skybrary.aero/index.php/Human_Factors_Strategy_(OGHFA_BN). Accessed 20 Feb 2018.

Sneddon, A., K. Mearns, and R. Flin. 2013. Stress, fatigue, situation awareness and safety in offshore drilling crews. *Safety Science* 56: 80–88.

Stanners, M., and H.T. French. 2005. *An empirical study of the relationship between situation awareness and decision making*. Edinburgh, South Australia: DSTO Systems Sciences Laboratory.

Stanton, N.A., P.R.G. Chambers, and J. Piggott. 2001a. Situational awareness and safety. *Safety Science*, 189–204.

Stanton, N.A., P.R.G. Chambers, and J. Piggott. 2001b. Situational awareness and safety. *Safety Science* 39: 189–204.

Wickens, C.D., J. Lee, Y. Liu, and S.G. Becker. 2004. *An introduction to human factors engineering*, 2nd ed. Upper Saddle River, NJ: Prentice-Hall.

Wolf, F., and R. Kuber. 2018. Developing a head-mounted tactile prototype to support situational awareness. *International Journal of Human-Computer Studies* 109 (2018): 54–67.

Yazgan, E., and D. EROL. 2016. SİVİL PİLOT ADAYLARI İÇİN SEÇİM KRİTERLERİNİN BELİRLENMESİ. *NĞÜ Müh. Bilim. Derg. / NGU Journal of Engineering Science*.

Chapter 4
Enterprise Risk Management in Aviation Management and Strategy

Contents

Introduction: ERM and Aviation

The gaps in the risk management implementations bring about the need for the development of a new type of management system. Enterprise Risk Management (ERM) is a popular system becoming popular in recent years. It was developed to make known the fact that the risks comprise not only the threats but also the opportunities. The businesses give importance to ERM not only to avoid the risks that can affect them adversely and react accordingly, but also to add value to the business.

A. Kucuk Yilmaz and T. G. Flouris, *Values, Ergonomics and Risk Management in Aviation Business Strategy*, https://doi.org/10.1007/978-981-15-1006-9_4

ERM stands in the center of the risk management system. While the classical risk management systems focus on specific risks, ERM is applied considering the fact that the risks are not independent; on the contrary, they are interrelated with each other. Thus, in ERM, the result that reacting a risk may affect the other risks as well shouldn't be neglected.

For ERM to be understood well, the perception of the risk management, development process, and its components must be reviewed well. Risk management is a type of management, starting from the 1930s continuing up to now, which is developed more every year as the deficiencies in management models are noticed. The businesses want to survive in their sector and get bigger while increasing their sources. That wish of the businesses makes the risk management perception obligatory for the businesses. The wish of a business to survive being indifferent to the risks while carrying out its activities is nothing but a dream.

Risk management methods can vary from business to business; an ideal method for a business, maybe useless for another. Thus, before the formation of the risk management of a business, the meaning of risk management, its concepts, and the general structure must be learned well by the business managers and employees. Also, the risk management subject must be evaluated especially by the decision-makers carefully. The risks that the businesses face must be identified and defined correctly, evaluated and assessed.

The Risk Management Process: Systematic Management Perception

Risk management is a systematic management perception that contains identifying, defining, assessing, and giving needed reaction to a risk (Preston and Guy 2002). According to another definition, risk management, "is a suitable transition from risk to return suitable for the business or is a process that leads to change and risk management is a basic function" (Yuzbasioglu 2003, p. 4). The businesses may not be alone in their sector when they want to increase their income. The existence of the rivalry may always be the case as a nature of the sector in which the businesses are active and their surroundings. For this reason, businesses must take necessary precautions to continue their existence and reach their strategical targets. Maybe at the top of these precautions comes the risk management application. The businesses, owing to many reasons such as providing a competitive advantage, attaining their strategic targets or wanting to exist in the business area where they are active and there are many dynamic factors, need an efficient risk management application that can comply with their concept of management.

Risk management applications occur in three steps. The first step is the detection stage of the risk. Both measurable and not measurable risks at every level are defined. The second step is the stage of the evaluation and assessment of the risks. For the assessment and evaluation process, various techniques and methods such as scenario analysis, simulation, and susceptibility analysis are used. The last step is the stage of risk management. At this stage, risks are responded to with transferring, ensuring, sharing, and reducing (Benton 2001).

For a risk management formation within a business, first it is necessary that the managers of top management support risk management. After that, the creation of a common language, high level of communication, good flow of information and efficient teamwork play an important role (Secretariat Treasury Board 1999, p. 22).

If an efficient application is expected in the management of uncertain risks, a risk management policy to be followed by the business must be defined. This policy must also include the content of the risk management. The content of the policy to be followed must be expected to include the following subjects (Gunes 2009, p. 7):

- The content of the risk management,
- The methods and means to measure the risks,
- The duties and responsibilities of the risk management team,
- The structure of the risk committee and their meeting frequency,
- The obligatory approvals and confirmations to be given in the face of various events,
- The type and methods of feedback,
- The measures used at the stage of monitoring and controlling,
- The risk appetite, risk tolerance and the risk capacity of the business.

Considering this information, the question that comes to mind is why businesses need risk management. Just like humans, the needs are the biggest factors that urge businesses to search. Needs may occur because of absence or shortage. Like all organisms, organizations look for ways to meet their needs to continue their existence. With technological advances, many businesses are active in the global arena nowadays. Thus, regardless of which sector they are active in, the businesses in touch with their surroundings will have an increase in the variety and quantity of their risks correspondingly. In the most general sense, if the needs of the businesses for risk management applications are to be stated:

- The desire of the businesses to continue their existence and operations,
- Their desire to minimize the surprises they might face,
- The possibility to face the crisis frequently,
- Variable environment conditions,
- Providing income stabilization,
- Minimizing the cost and loss,
- Their desire to make the growth and strategic targets real,
- The difficulties of the competitive environment,
- The obligation to comply with the legal regulations can be stated.

The reasons stated above are the universal reasons for all the businesses regardless of the sector they are active in (Uzun 2010, p.64).

The Evolution of Risk Management

It is possible to summarize the development of risk management under five phases. The first phase is the process that started in the 1930s and continued up to the 1970s (Haller 1999). Officially, the first applications of risk management were seen in the 1950s. In the 1970s, risk management was approached from the aspect of finance (Fraser and Simkins 2009). The concept that comes alive especially in the banking and insurance sector started to be mentioned a lot in this process. But, at this phase, risk management was just precautions taken to prevent losses. In the second phase that started in the 1970s, risk management focused especially on the insurance sector. In this period, with the establishment of many companies, risk management was in need especially in the management of the credits. As a nature of the insurance sector, the high profit margin makes it necessary to manage the risks efficiently. Also, in the development of risk management applications, this sector was the pioneer.

In the 1980s, financial risk management emerged. In this period, within the financial risk management, an extensive risk engineering coordinative with the finance of the risks and partly with the insurance coverage stood out. But in the late 1980s, some big-scale unlucky events in the insurance sector caused mistrust and revealed the need for more elaborative communication in risk management. In the 1990s, the phase in which risk management was approached from the operational aspect started. The way risk management works in the aviation sector focused on detecting and preventing the possible crises that may cause insecure conditions (Haller 1999). The terrorist attack to the United States of America (the USA) on September 9, 2001 added a different dimension to the risk management. After this terrorist attack, many businesses including the airline businesses were damaged financially. After this event, the businesses that apply the risk management efficiently saw the deficiencies in focusing on just specific risk factors and taking precautions only to prevent damage (Arslan 2008). On the other hand, the existing competitive conditions in the area where the businesses are active brought about more complicated and interrelated risks (Haller 1999).

Besides, globalization, liberalization, technological advances, e-commerce, the economic crises made the business area more complicated and made it obligatory to develop the risk management applications (Misiura 2015). Various legal regulations formed especially as a result of the financial and enterprise crises created the necessity to handle the risk management of businesses with an institutional point of view.

The insurance sector especially contributed a lot to the risk management application models. The crises experienced through the years are very effective in risk management taking its current form. In the past, in order to not lose money, the organizations used to want to manage the risks which, they think, affect certain parts of the business. But, nowadays, with the ERM application models, businesses are seen in a holistic manner, and the risks are evaluated at every level. Thus, the risks should be managed not just to abstain from money loss, but to gain value and have profits with good and efficient risk management.

In recent years, businesses look for ways to take advantage of the risks they face because of the environment they are active in instead of avoiding the uncertainty or perceiving the risks as a threat. While handling these risks, they evaluate the risk management with an integrated approach, handling the internal and external risk factors of the organization relevant to the risk management as a unity instead of evaluating them one by one (Muller and Drax 2014). Businesses want their operations to be uninterrupted. They must decrease the possible surprises for a continuous activity; otherwise, the possible surprises that they may face can create another cost.

On the other hand, the obligation to comply with the legal regulations is another factor. Because of all these reasons, businesses passed from the perception of traditional risk management to ERM—extensive enterprise risk management applications. The businesses that apply risk management efficiently, with the help of their ERM applications, not only respond to the risks that might cause money loss but also may give decisions that make a profit for the business.

The Risk Management Concept with Its Hypothesis & Principals

For risk management to be useful in businesses, the managers and the decision-makers must analyze the concepts of risk management, hypotheses, and the principals. The managers and the decision-makers must agree on the necessity of the risk management and its contributions to the business. For the creation of good risk management, the hypothesis and the principals of the risk management must be known by the employees. Before the creation of the risk management application, all the employees must be persuaded about the suitability of the risk management model and the benefits it will bring. If the concepts of the risk are assimilated by the decision-makers and analyzed well, the success of the risk management will not be a coincidence. In regard to risk management perception, concepts such as what the crisis is, the risk appetite of the business, the risk capacity, the risk tolerance, and the risk balance must be defined well. While giving decisions, the role of these concepts shouldn't be ignored.

The Risk Management Concept

When the literature is analyzed, various definitions of risk appear. According to one definition, risk appears as any kind of event that can hinder the business' targets (Arslan 2008). With this respect, risk is a vital event for businesses that may have negative results. The effects of risks on business might not be too great, but on the other hand, they might cause serious results that can give an end to the existence of the business as well. When risk is mentioned, the possibilities are the case. Therefore, for all organizations, risks have uncertainty. Thus, when risk is mentioned, one of the first concepts that comes to mind is uncertainty. Uncertainty is the situation that has both positive and negative results (Kucuk Yilmaz 2003). While the positive results add value to businesses, it is obvious that the negative results will cause financial loss.

There is a basic difference between risk and uncertainty. Uncertainty is a haphazard event whose probability distribution is unknown and that which cannot be controlled, while risk is a haphazard, uncontrolled event that can be measured with specific methods making use of current data and probability distribution (Fikirkoca 2003). But, as the uncertainty increases, so does the risk. Risk, if managed well, is a situation that has opportunities. The important thing is that the businesses be aware of which risks they can take to what extent. Besides, the businesses must define their obtainable strategic targets. Also, the businesses have to analyze the risk types that they face or will face with respect to their sustainability and respond to the risk types, respectively.

Businesses, to make proper decisions to attain their goals must know their power well, and must be aware of their risk appetite, risk capacity, and risk tolerance. Strategic decisions made without realizing their power and competence will do nothing but leave the business' future to chance.

If strategic targets are well defined, realistic and attainable results can be realized in time. Risk tolerance is a concept that shows the level of uncertainty that a business can easily overcome or the risk quantity that it can easily take to attain a target. Also, risk tolerance can differ according to age, income, and financial targets (investopedia.com).

Risk capacity is the measure of how much tolerance a business shows to negative events without creating greater negative effects on the attainment of important financial targets (Finametrica). Different from risk tolerance, risk capacity is the risk quantity that the business must take to attain its financial targets. On the other hand, in order for businesses to decide to what extent they can take risks, they should assess their income targets first (investopedia.com).

Risk appetite is the risk quantity and the risk type that the businesses are ready to take to attain their strategic goals about the future (http-5). According to another definition, risk appetite is the risk level that the businesses perceive as acceptable without needing to take any precaution (Arslan 2008, p. 42).

Businesses must understand and analyze the difference between risk capacities and risk tolerance in order to make the risks they face have positive results for the business. When the risk appetite of a business is more than its risk tolerance, the decisions that the business makes about these risks may have consequences that will put its future targets in danger (investopedia.com). Therefore, businesses must balance between risk tolerance and risk appetite. They must take this balance into consideration especially while giving strategic decisions. This balance is called risk tolerance.

The Hypothesis and Principals of Risk Management

Every business may face different risks depending on the nature of its environment. Businesses cannot escape the adverse effects of the potential risks sometimes owing to the lack of time, sometimes owing to not taking enough precautions. For businesses not to lose money or face negative consequences, the managers must be foresighted and must take care of the potential risks. In order to respond to these risks well, they must take strategic and operational precautions (Muller and Drax 2014). Especially during a crisis period, the strategic importance becomes clearer. Making the right predictions about risk management gives the business superiority over the rivalry in their surroundings. In order to get higher profits, businesses take many risks, respectively.

At this point, the important thing is that the managers make the proper decisions on which risks they can take for the business (Speckbacher et al. 2010). If the risks that the business faces due to the decisions of the manager are interpreted in a wrong manner, first the image of the business can be damaged, and its trademark value can decrease. This decrease follows the fall in income in parallel with the fall in the number of passengers. After that, the cost of risk coverage of the business increases. As a result of this situation, the business may face a financial shortage in the short or long term, it may even go bankrupt if it cannot overcome the crisis it faces (Nomura 2003).

Businesses that have risk management want to get the highest efficiency possible. For the formation of the efficient and fruitful risk management and its application, there are seven important principles that must be taken care of by the businesses:

- There must be a clear communication channel.
- Decisions must be made with respect to the future.
- The fact that the risk management is a continuous process shouldn't be ignored.
- The business must have a global perspective that is so important for the design and development of its activities and can give the business the chance to be informed of the potential opportunities.
- Shared product vision is another principal. For the vision of the business to be adopted is extremely important.
- Integrated management and risk management means, and methods must be synchronized with the structure and culture of the business
- For the risk management to be effective and successful, the effect of the teamwork shouldn't be neglected. The synergy created by the teamwork will contribute positively to the success of the risk management of the business (Kucuk Yilmaz 2003, p. 57).

The Organizational Culture, Climate, Norms, and Values of the Risk Management

Risk management applications are extremely important for the sustainability of a business. It is natural that a risk management application that has successful results in business may end up with a failure in another business active in the same sector. Although they are active in the same sectors as a result of some factors, the results may be different. We can categorize these factors that affect the results significantly under four headings:

Especially after the 1980s, with the new approaches of management, the concept of organizational culture came out. Before applying a management model and application to a business, whether the organization is ready for it must be evaluated well. The organizational culture that faces us as the unity of the values, norms, and the beliefs that define the operation of the organization, is a concept that emphasizes the importance of the belief system that forms their loyalty to the organization and effects the employees' behaviors (Wallace et al. 1996).

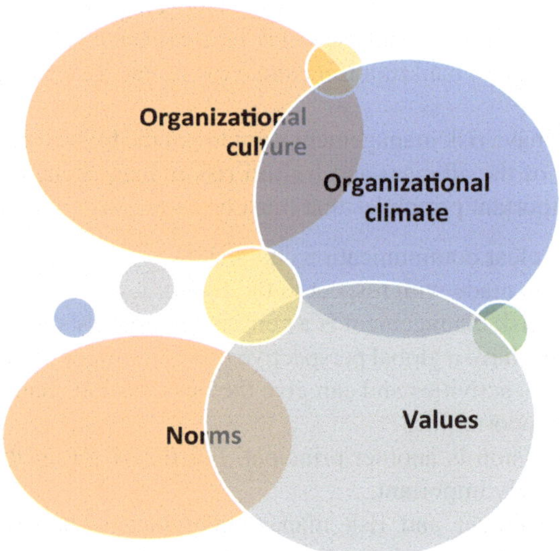

According to another definition, the organizational culture are the basic values that are composed of details such as the organizational stories that are created at the time of the employees' adaptation to the outer environment and their integration and those which must be taught to the new members—ceremonies, the common language, and even the current clothing model. The beliefs, values, norms, general customs, intrapersonal relationships that form the organizational culture affect the performance and the operation of the organization (Schein 1992). Culture is a feature that explains the organizational behavior of a business and separates it from other organizations. The managers must understand and analyze the organizational culture well. Because of the organizational differences, the possibility that the risk management application which has successful results for one business may lead another business to failure is not a surprise. The organizational culture takes shape with the wishes and needs of the employees, changes according to the environmental conditions but keeps its balance as well (Aydogan 2004).

Every organization wants to have its members' support to attain its goals. The individuals' integration of their surroundings is extremely important for the organization's efficiency and productivity. Therefore, the individuals that comply with the cultural features of the organization, are the individuals that contribute to the management's and organization's expectations for the organization to attain its goals. Thus, it is a desirable situation that the individuals comply with the organizational culture in a short time. The closer the cultural environment of the individual is to the organizational culture, the shorter the adaptation period of the individual to the organization will be (Kose et al. 2001).

Before starting a new risk management application, the top managers have important duties. Firsy, they must persuade their employees about the necessity of this perception of management. At this point, the concept of organizational climate comes out. The organizational climate has permanent features that separate an organization formed with the coordination of its employees than the others. It also contains the employees working in harmony, their ability to work together, their common perception that they developed in innovative and fair dimensions (Moran and Volkwein 1992). According to Wallace et al. (1996) six dimensions of the organizational climate can be stated:

- The support of management,
- The feeling of occupational and organizational unity,
- Mutual trust,
- Conflict and uncertainty,
- The collaboration of the working teams, and
- The importance of the work, its being different and attractive.

Taking this information into consideration, it is suitable to say that in the risk management model in which management believes, the employees of the business must believe as well. As is the nature of a human being, resistance to innovations is always the case. But, in the light of truth they believe, the mutual trust and coordination of the employees and the managers are important. Thus, the business will not face any great obstacle for success with respect to the results of the new risk management model complying with the organizational culture and climate.

It is possible to define norms as the rules, orders, and measures that the individuals with certain roles must obey (Erdogan 2007). Norms are sometimes implicit; sometimes they are composed of unwritten rules. Although they are implicit or unwritten, they are extremely effective in people's behaviors. For instance, the norms told or shared as "Don't argue with your superiors" or "Don't be the one who gives bad news" give clues as to how the behaviors in that organization should be (Sabuncuoglu and Tuz 1998). Cultural norms are composed of cultural values (Ozkalp and Kiral 2016).

Values form the invisible and the inner side of the culture. They show the acceptable way of solution of the organizational problems (Sisman 1994). These values limit the ways of the people to attain their goals. Also, they direct their behaviors defining which is wrong (Erdogan 2007). Therefore, norms and values play an effective role in the behaviors of the organization.

Basic Risk Categories

If we count the risk types, it is possible to state many risks such as market risk, competitive risk, supplanted risk, sales risk, stock risk, earthquake risk, terror risk—that every business can face. But, in order to make the subject clear, it is suitable to categorize the most accepted risks under certain headings. We can collect the risks in four groups. These are financial risks, operational risks, environmental risks, and strategic risks (TIBA 2008).

Financial risks are the type of risk that forms a basis for the perception of risk management to appear and develop. When the development dates of the risk management application are studied, in their beginning phases it is the risk type that many businesses take care of most to manage and that they give much importance to. Risks such as credit risk, interest rate risk, and cash risk are evaluated as financial risks.

Operational risk includes the risks that affect a business's activities. Within the scope of operational risks, the risks that come to mind such as sales, supplanted, product development, rivalry, the functionality of the equipment, the motivation and the performance of the employees, legal regulations, and brand management face us.

Strategic risks are the risks that can affect the targets of a business defined in short, medium, or long term. The risks such as market analysis, planning, work portfolio,, and work model can be evaluated as strategic risks.

Environmental risks are those that appear independently. Within the environmental risks, it is possible to count the risks such as natural disasters, terror threats, political developments between countries, legal regulations, and the customers' preference tendencies.

It will be extremely wrong to think these risk groups, ordered as four groups, independent from each other or separate them from each other with sharp lines. For example, credit risk belongs to the financial risks group in view of its results, it also belongs to operational risks group in view of its reasons (Saka 2008). The important thing is to have consciousness that these risk groups are related to each other directly or indirectly. So, while evaluating these risk groups, this relationship shouldn't be ignored.

Enterprise Risk Management as Enterprise Competence: Threats and Opportunities

ERM is an enterprise competence rather than an enterprise function. A business can follow two different ways while managing the risks. The first of these is to handle them one by one and manage each separately. The second is to manage the risks as a whole. The system in which the risks are handled as a whole is enterprise risk management.

In the literature many definitions for ERM show up. But the most extensive and accepted definition belongs to COSO (Committee of Sponsoring Organizations of the Treadway Commission). According to COSO, ERM "is a systematic process applied in a specific strategy and in the whole business comprising the inner control, affected by the business' board of directors, managers and all the other employees, created to provide reasonable assurance related to the suitability aims of the applicable laws and regulations, the reliability of the financial reporting, defining the potential events that can affect the existence of a business, managing the risks according to ERM profile of the business and attaining business' targets" (Adopted from COSO 2004). As can be understood from the definition, ERM is a process that concerns the people starting from top managers to all the employees of the enterprise. One of the most important points is that the enterprise must be managed in accordance with its risk taking profile. Thus, the businesses will avoid taking unnecessary risks besides providing cost optimization.

When ERM is mentioned, it is possible to talk about two events that come to mind:

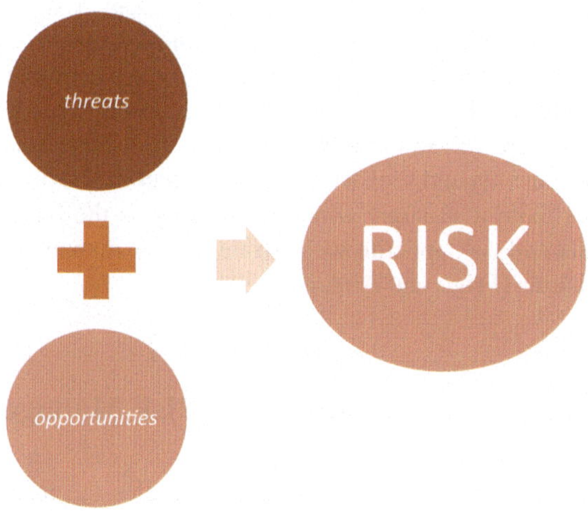

As the events may have positive or negative effects, they may have both positive and negative effects. If we evaluate the events that have negative effects as risks, risks are the events that can cause a loss in value or that hinders the increase in value. Opportunities face us as the events that contribute to the business' attainment of the goals and that provide an increase in value of the business contrary to the risks (Adopted from COSO 2004). ERM is a standard created for all levels of management and applied in the whole business. It comprises the standards created for risk controlling, relieving, or eliminating the adverse effects, taking advantage of the events that can have positive effects on the business.

The traditional risk management methods are the methods developed to prevent losses of the enterprise rather than add value to them. All the units in the businesses try to minimize the possible loss evaluating the risks in their area one by one and taking necessary precautions. Traditional risk management is a method used to dispose of the risks just the relevant unit faces. Thus, while in one of the subunits of a business risk management is managed well, in another subunit, it may be managed poorly. This condition may cause the business to lose value. But, ERM is composed of methods handling the business as a whole and aiming to add value the business and its shareholders. One of the most important duties that management must fulfill is to decide how much of the existing and possible risks can be accepted while adding value to the business and its shareholders (Arslan 2008).

ERM differs from the traditional risk management in view of the concept as focus, emphasizing, objective, measure, and application. While traditional risk management handles a business separating to its subunits, ERM handles it as a whole. Since traditional risk management is interested in the current capacities of the businesses, it doesn't focus on the benefits they may get in the future. One of the biggest reasons for transferring to ERM is that traditional risk management methods cannot prevent big losses in the businesses.

The emphasis of ERM is on the business' strategic targets. Thus, in ERM rather than decreasing the risks, managing them and creating a strategy for the management is of top priority. At this point, the concept of strategic risk management faces us. Strategic risk management, at any point in business strategy, can be defined as defining, evaluating, and managing the process of the crises in order to save the shareholders and their values. Also, strategic risk management forms a basis for ERM. In the way which a business follows to attain its goals, in order to understand well the internal and external events and scenarios that can affect the business, it is necessary to look at the risks from a strategic window. As long as the businesses define the tolerable risk levels and risk appetite well, strategic risk management will guide to give strategic decisions (Frigo and Anderson 2011).

The Benefits and Targets of Enterprise Risk Management

Since ERM, unlike traditional risk management, handles the business as a whole, the advantages are the values that concern the whole business. It is composed of the methods that not only give the necessary responses to the risks but also add value to its shareholders. If the benefits of the ERM are given:

- Businesses minimize income fluctuation besides increasing their profits.
- An increase in the collaboration of the unities and the communication ability is observed.
- Opportunities and threats are detected better.
- Value is created out of uncertainty and variability.
- Businesses create and use their sources more efficiently.
- Businesses increase their competitive power in their environment.
- Proactive management can be applied instead of reactive management.
- The performance measure is risk based.
- The continuity of the businesses' conformation with legal procedures and legislations will be provided (Saka 2008).
- The cost of risk management is at an optimum level.
- Businesses select the suitable form of ERM that applies to them by defining the response alternatives that can be given to the current or potential risks. This response alternatives must be as in the form of avoiding the risks, minimizing the risk, sharing and acceptance.
- Businesses by defining the potential risks and selecting the necessary responses will prevent possible surprises and the costs associated with them.
- Working in cooperation with each other, all the units of a business move in unity to add value to the shareholders and the business. When the risks that concern many subunits of the business are the case, the responses to be given to these risks will be at an optimum level and since they concern the whole business, they will be more efficient and productive.
- Management, with the use of ERM tools, by evaluating the business' strategic alternatives better, set goals about these alternatives. By developing necessary mechanisms to manage the risks related to these targets, they can give decisions about the business' risk capacity better (Arslan 2008).

ERM applications may differ according to the businesses' scales, the sectors they are active in and environmental conditions. Again, because of the same reasons, the prior targets of the businesses' ERM applications may differ. Although the order of priority is different, it may be thought that the possible targets of ERM are common. It is possible to count the expected targets of ERM as the following:

- Able to detect the possible surprises early,
- Efficient in the responses provided for the risks,
- Efficient reporting system to see the risks in all of the activities, and
- Supportive of business functions such as defining a strategy, business development, provide the source and performance follow-up (Pagach and Warr 2007).

Roles and Responsibilities in Enterprise Risk Management

No matter which sector they are active in, the authority and the responsibilities must be indicated clearly in the ERM applications for the businesses to meet their expectations from these applications, and for the efficiency of the ERM they apply. Since ERM is a process that concerns the whole business, all the employees must know their duties regarding risk management well and must fulfill their responsibilities with this consciousness.

The duties and responsibilities of each unit, stated in the structure of an ideal organization, are different from one another. For efficient application of ERM in the businesses, the board of directors, CEO, CRO (Chief Risk Officer), SBU (Strategic Business Unit), and the risk committees must fulfill their responsibilities.

The primary duties and responsibilities of the risk committee which is directly connected to the board of directors are

- Reviewing and approving the risk management policies, by defining its perception and standards throughout the business,
- Within the observation activities, following the risks seen as critical and the developments about these risks,
- Again, within the observation activities, following and evaluating the efficiency and the results of the risk management activities throughout the business.

The duties and responsibilities of the secondary risk committee that is directly connected to the CEO are

- Making sure that the system works efficiently by following the risk management activities closely,
- Following the risks of the business with the help of the risk reports prepared by the units responsible for the risk management at needed periods such as daily, weekly or monthly ones and the information that comes from the other channels.
- Making decisions on every kind of response needed for the risks of the business and applying them and conveying the situation to the primary committee when necessary.

The biggest responsibility in the businesses belongs to the managers. If we want to count the responsibilities of the managers:

- First of all, the managers must believe in the necessity of ERM. It will be an unrealistic approach to expect them to convince their employees of the necessity of the system they don't believe in and to achieve success.
- The managers must convey the business' risk extent and framework and the perception of the risk culture aimed with this respect to the employees and make them understood by the employees.
- The managers must adopt and integrate the risk management activities in their management activities.

- Every manager must understand the risks in their area, which are especially at critical levels, observe, and report. Also, they must give efficient risk management decisions related to these risks.
- They must always work in coordination with the unit responsible for the risk management. They must always contribute to the development and recovery of the risk management system.

The duties and responsibilities of the board of directors are to define the risk management policy and standards of the business and to review and approve the developments and risk management activities about especially the critical risks.

Top managers are those who are authorized and responsible for the risk management applications at top level (Duran 2013). The biggest duty and responsibility of a CEO in terms of ERM is to follow the risk management activities closely and to guarantee that the risk management system works efficiently. Besides, the top managers, with an efficient reporting structure, follow the risks of the business; they make the decisions applied by thinking that they are necessary for all the risk responses.

One of the most responsible people for the risk management is undoubtedly the CRO, in other words, chief risk officer. Responsibilities of the chief risk officer can be stated as the following:

- Developing the risk management culture of the business and taking precautions to make it prevalent,
- Providing the correct definition of the critical risks by the decision-makers and their efficient management,
- Providing the same understanding of the risks to all of the employees,
- Providing the position in which the balance between the expected income rates and the risks to be taken must be considered when decisions are given by the decision-makers at the business,
- Creating an efficient reporting and information flow system to manage the risks well,
- Providing the integration of ERM into the organizational culture,
- Making ERM a part of the strategic planning, operational planning and business planning.

Functional units are the units that work in coordination with the risk management teams and those which take risks. The general duties and responsibilities of the functional units for risk management are as follows:

- Detecting and analyzing the risks,
- Providing the situation in which the decisions on the necessary responses for the risks are given within the framework of risk policies formed in the business and are applied,
- Reporting the risk for SBU.
- All the employees of the business should adopt the risk management plan. Every employee is responsible for the ERM's application in the business (Duran 2013).

Risk management teams are one of the most active units of risk management. In order to increase the efficiency of ERM, they fulfill their responsibilities working in coordination with strategic business units. The main duties and responsibilities of the risk management teams include

- Contributing to the preparations of risk management policies,
- Providing the uninterrupted information flow for an efficient risk management,
- Observing the risk management functions,
- Supplying the necessary means and support for risk management,
- Providing the situation in which the risks are observed and reported to the board of directors after being gathered, and
- Working in coordination with the internal management unit continuously.

The activities of the internal management unit must be ensured with policies and the standards defined and approved by the primary risk management committee. Main duties and responsibilities of the internal management unit include

- Providing oversight of the controls done with respect to the risk management,
- Overseeing the activities of risk management objectively,
- Guaranteeing the management and executive management committee with respect to the risk reporting (Saka 2008), and
- Detecting whether the critical risks are neglected or not (Duran 2013).

ERM is a part of the employees' responsibilities to a certain extent. The employees must perceive the necessity of resisting the pressure of their superiors that can affect the ERM applications adversely and must prevent the process from getting harm by reporting it to the relevant units in a suitable way (Kucuk Yilmaz 2007). Being especially true for top management, all managers must believe in the necessity of this reporting system and support it. For such situations, they must form alternative communication channels.

In ERM, besides the employees inside business, the employees outside the business have important roles. For a successful ERM application, the support of the employees outside the enterprise is extremely important. Within ERM the employees outside the enterprise are third persons such as external supervisors, lawmakers, external source service suppliers, suppliers, business partners, and credit rating agencies (Gunes 2009).

Legal Regulations About Enterprise Risk Management

Preparing much legal legislation was needed for preventing the risk factors from damaging the businesses, assuring the standards in ERM applications and eliminating the deficiencies in risk management applications.

Civil Authorities and Legislations

There are some decisions and legislations prepared as a result of the studies made for increasing the efficiency and productivity of risk management applications in especially the banking and insurance areas and eliminating the gaps in the applications.

SOX (Sarbanes–Oxley) LAW

SOX law was signed by George W. Bush, while he was president, on July 30, 2002. It was developed by the SEC (Securities and Exchange Commission), the equivalent of the capital markets board. This law imposed serious responsibilities and reporting conditions on the management teams active in the capital markets (Karaca 2007).

Sox law is composed of 11 main headings that contain the following:

- Establishment of the accounting observation board and its operation.
- The independence of the oversight firm.
- The responsibility of the business.
- Increasing financial information.
- The conflicts of analysis and benefit.
- Commission sources and its authority.
- Studies and reports.
- The enterprise and criminal abuse responsibility.
- Increasing the punishment of the white-collar crimes.
- Enterprise tax refunds.
- Enterprise abuse and responsibility (SOX 2002).

With this law, detecting the risks of a businesses' financial reporting, turning the controlling of these detected risks into written form and evaluating them became an obligation. The managers became responsible for the efficiency of the controls. Heavy penal sanctions, which came with the law, caused all the beneficiaries besides business managers at the top to report finance and launch extensive projects to improve the inner controls.

The Objectives of the Sox Laws

Because the currently accepted accounting principles are inadequate in some situations, the standards of accounting have been reviewed in a continuous manner. Most recently, the Sox law which went into effect after oversight and accounting scandals occurred in the USA. The law aimed at increasing the transparency of businesses restoring their credibility to the public.

Other objectives of the Sox law were as follows:

- Operation of improved corporate governance,
- Providing the investor with right, timely, detailed, and apprehensible financial information,
- Providing a more efficient execution of the internal controls,
- Providing the independent mobility of the oversight committee responsible for the internal oversight and supported by the external oversight firms, and
- Establishing a Public Company Accounting Oversight Board, aiming at full implementation of sanctions (Ozeke 2004).

8th Directive of Eu (European Union)

The 8th directive with the number 84/253/ECC is about the responsibilities and occupational standards of the auditors, who make an audit on the accounting reports legally. Its objective is to meet the legal auditors' needs and make necessary regulations for oversight in the members of the EU. It was accepted on April 10, 1984. In this respect, the members of the EU were given time until 1988 to make necessary regulations. It came into force on February 1, 1990. This directive was composed of five parts as follows:

- Content,
- Rules related to the authorization,
- Occupational rules,
- Occupational honesty and independence, and
- Clearness and last provisions.

In this directive, the mentioned people that make an audit may be the oversight firms that are legal persons as well as being natural persons (Sevim et al. 2006).

Basel I

Basel I is an enterprise that was formed by the union of the countries' central banks. BIS (Bank of International Settlements), formed the Basel Committee in 1974. In 1988, the Basel Committee published the Basel I Standards that define the working conditions which banks have to obey (Yildirim 2015). This document went through various changes. In 1996, market risk was included. According to Basel I standards, CAR (Capital Adequacy Ratio) is defined as the ratio of the resource to the total risk-weighted assets. Total risk-weighted assets mean the total of the amount at credit risk basis and the amount at market risk basis (Aykut 2008).

But, in time, as a result of the experiences, the deficient sides of the Basel 1 standards appeared. The most important criticism of the Basel I is that it ignores the other risks except the credit and market risks while calculating the capital adequacy ratio. But in the banking sector, the risks such as interest rate risk, operational risks,, and liquidity risk started to gain importance. This situation caused a result that the capital adequacy ratio which is calculated with the current formula may not be a good sign of the financial situation of the bank.

Basel II

With the development of the financial markets in time, Basel II standards started to be inadequate. Following the publication of the first-term advices in 1999 for the review of the committee's capital adequacy regulation, an extensive study was launched in all of the member countries. In 2001 and 2003, additional advices were published for opinion and consultation. Regulation and its standards were found appropriate by the Central Bank Directors and the Chairmen of the Banking Regulation and Supervision Agency of the G-10 countries. A reviewed, extensive version of the document published under the name Basel II in 2004 was published in 2006 by BIS (Aykut 2008).

The Objectives of the Basel II

Basel I handled the market and credit risk. But, Basel II, in addition to the market risk, differentiated the calculation of the credit risk and handled operational risk besides the risk groups. In Basel II, the methods for calculating the risk sensitivity were changed. In Basel, it was foreseen that while the risk weight of the governments of the countries that were the members of OECD (Organisation for Economic Co-operation and Development) was zero, the risk weight of the countries that were not members of OECD was a 100%. But in Basel II, it was decided that the independent rating agencies should be appointed to calculate the risk weight. Also, in Basel II, it was decided that while foreseen risks should be responded, minimum capital should be spared for the unforeseen risks as well. The targets of Basel II focus primarily on banking supervision, strengthening risk management, reaching the standards of market discipline and credibility calculation (Serim 2006).

OECD Enterprise Management Principles

The Enterprise Management Principles Report prepared by OECD in 1999 and composed of four main factors—equity, transparency, responsibility, and accountability—was reviewed and arranged again in 2004. Enterprise management was defined as a system in which the companies are directed and controlled. According to the

Enterprise Management Principles Report, enterprise management contains the relationships of the company management, board of directors, shareholders, and other interest groups. Among the responsibilities of the board of directors are providing the reliability of the business' accounting and financial reporting system, providing the operability of the supervision, financial and operational controlling systems and supervision systems that supervise the conformity with the standards of laws. Also, the boards of directors are responsible for the risk policies, too (OECD 2004).

Turnbull Report

The Combined Code on Corporate Governance, known as the Turnbull report, is based on the three reports published before in England in 1998 and was revised in 2003. It is a guide report based on the "apply-if not, explain" principle that was prepared for the London markets by the private sector directors about the inner controls and risk management (Atamer 2006). The Combined Code report comprises the topics such as the independence of half of the board of directors, self-evaluation of the board of directors, accountability and supervision, and the relationships of the shareholders (Capital Market Board Department 2016). There is another version of this report under the heading of "The Guide For The Board of Directors To The Inner Control, Combined Rules" published by an institute called ICAEW (The Institute of Chartered Accountants in England-Wales) (Saltik 2007). ICAEW was founded in England in 1880. Its center is in London. Being an institute leading the foundation of the International Accounting Standards Committee in 1973, it has over 138000 members in 160 countries in the world. Having 7 departments such as financial reporting, supervision and guarantee, finance and management, financial services, tax, enterprise finance and information technology, ICAEW, is the only institute that is a member of the World Economic Forum (http-7).

Aviation Authorities

The aviation authorities such as FAA (Federal Aviation Administration), ICAO (International Civil Aviation Organization) and IATA (International Air Transport Association) prepared documents that contain legislations that advise various regulations to guide the aviation sector for the management of the risks that are faced because of the dynamic environment and variable parameters as a nature of the aviation sector, giving them needed responses with a right approach. With these regulations, efficient management of the risks in the aviation sector whose risk factor is high, giving suitable responses to the relevant risks was aimed.

Federal Aviation Administration

The FAA's duty is to follow every valid aeronautical legislation of the plane, flight, production, intervention, efficiency, and safety in the USA air zone, control its application and supply the air safety in the USA. It is a government institute established by the USA Congress in 1958 connected to the USA Ministry of Transportation (http-8).

The FAA has publications about the risk management as an advice for the applications such as fatigue risk management system (http-9). On the other hand, according to the Profit Management Policy of FAA, the risk management was defined as "management applied to the management process of its life cycle to define the risks of attaining the FAA goals and targets and to relieve them." According to this policy, all the businesses must organize the risk management process in four steps:

- Defining and evaluating the risk areas,
- Developing and applying the strategies to relieve or eliminate the risks,
- Following and valuing the relieving efforts, and
- Continuing the relieving applications until the risks are eliminated or until the results come to an acceptable level.

Risk management is a management applied in the activities at all the levels of FAA from the smallest scale projects to the biggest scale programs. Risk management is applied in especially the risk areas such as costs, technical issues, system safety, all the safety disciplines, human factors, operability, productivity, profitability, management, finance, satisfaction of the shareholders (http-10).

Besides, the FAA published the "Risk Management Guidebook" to define and manage the risks. This guidebook is a manual prepared especially for pilots that have to do different works at every phase of the flight. According to the data of NTSB (National Transformational Safety Board), 85% of the plane crashes experienced in the past 20 years were the result of a pilot error. The pilots, if they detect the risks of flight correctly by internalizing the techniques in this guidebook will be able to manage these risks successfully. Also, this guidebook is a book that defines the risk management personnel, studies the human behaviors, aims to define the risks, and minimize their adverse effects and that contains the necessary principles for right and healthy decision making by valuing the risks (http-11).

International Civil Aviation Organization

ICAO, the center of which is in Montreal, is an organization founded in 1944, connected to the United Nations, leading the important and permanent developments in civil aviation at a global scale. ICAO gathers once every 3 years with all the members of its board of directors present. It is possible to summarize the aim and goals of the ICAO as the following:

- Providing the secure and regular development of civil aviation at a global scale;
- Developing flight safety.
- Contributing to flight and airport safety.
- Supporting the production and operation of aircrafts.
- Meeting the global needs of safe, regular, and economical air transportation.
- Providing the equality of opportunity in international airline management and not discriminating against biased countries.
- Making efforts for the development and innovation of all the subjects that concern international civil aviation (http-12).

On the other hand, ICAO gave importance to the fatigue risk management within the framework of risk management in order to contribute to the civil aviation development. According to ICAO, for the fulfillment of their duty and responsibilities efficiently, within the framework of fatigue risk management, the flight crew should rest sufficiently. The businesses must implement fatigue risk management within the framework of the Safety Management System (SMS), its processes and procedures.

Both the Safety Management System and the Fatigue Risk Management System are based on an efficient safety reporting culture. Employees must report any possibly dangerous factors in their working area to the necessary units within the framework of the Safety Management System.

Business directors must separate the intentional human faults from the unintentional ones and must take encouraging precautions for this system to proceed (http-13).

On the other hand, SARPs (Standards and Recommended Practices) published by the ICAO is applied and supervised by the international aviation authorities (Misiura 2015). Thus, the airline business cannot go off the advice of the national aviation authorities and consequently of the ICAO. They must comply with the SARPs about the risk management published by ICAO.

International Air Transportation Association

IATA is an association composed of 265 airline businesses forming the 83% of the total air traffic. IATA operates to supply safe and profitable airline transportation (http-14).

While the airline transportation keeps its place as the safest transportation method, there are some points that the airline businesses must pay attention to as the maximum flight hours, the resting time of the flight crew. IATA, in order to attract attention to this case, published the FRMS (Fatigue Risk Management System), which is prepared based on the ICAO standards for airline businesses. This document is or should be of the cornerstone for airline business directors (http-14).

IATA gives education on evaluating the risks correctly in the Safety Risk Management, developing the responses to be given to the possible risks that may be dangerous and their applications. At the end of this education, providing the businesses' learning to realize the safety system vulnerability, dangers, and risks, to apply the safety management principles and to define the safety risk evaluation criteria lie in the targets aimed at (http-15).

On the other hand, IATA published the "Integrated Risk Management Guidebook" as a guide for the practical application of ERM. The Integrated Risk Management Guidebook is an extremely beneficial document for the airline businesses with respect to detecting the maturity levels of ERM in the businesses, getting competitive superiority by managing the risks faced in a better way, the application's compliance with the legal necessities (http-16).

The Stages of Enterprise Risk Management: Transition and Application Process

It is possible to define the ERM applications at two stages within the standards of risk management:

- ERM Transition Process
- ERM Application Process

Before the establishment of ERM in a business, the relevant business must build a subsystem for the risk management application. The establishment of this subsystem consists of various stages. All of these stages form the transition process of ERM. After the transition process is formed successfully, the process of the application of ERM is launched. In a business prepared for an application process, following the successful transition process, ERM applications will have productive results.

The ERM Transition Process

Before the transition to ERM, the businesses have to make necessary preparations by making the preparations they consider necessary. These preparations must contain many topics ranging from the education of the personnel to the operational changes (Topcu 2013). Because ERM is a perception that the businesses handle and manage the risks they face as a whole in contrary to the traditional risk management applications. In recent years, the businesses that define their strategies with traditional risk management transferred to the ERM applications realizing the deficiencies in the risk management applications. ERM provides efficient management of the risks. Also, it leads to a rise in the value of the business' current assets besides helping it to avoid loss (Saka 2008).

At the stage of a subsystem establishment for ERM, the concept of risk culture faces us. For the businesses, the risk culture results from the business' risk philosophy and risk appetite (Topcu 2013). The departments of the business may have different risk cultures, and consequently, cause different attitudes in decision making. For instance, while some directors are prepared to take more risks, some directors may be more cautious and conservative in taking risks. Shortly, the formation of risk management culture is especially related to the formation of behavioral changes in the way the decisions are given (Holiwell 1998). A motivating and encouraging atmosphere for risk taking must be created in a business.

At this point, the dimension of the risks will change proportionally depending upon the decision making level (Topcu 2013). In this period, the businesses carry out ERM without integrating their applications into their own management understandings as in the following ways:

a. Target accusation,
b. Situation analysis,
c. Identifying the most suitable structure,
d. Planning of the difference analysis, and
e. Application of the risk management transition process (Saka 2008).

Target Accusation

Primarily, the main goal of all businesses is to create value for its shareholders (Matheson and Matheson 1998). In order to attain this goal, businesses must have logical and attainable targets. At the target acquisition stage, the businesses must determine their general strategic targets clearly and in detail. The policies to follow on how to attain the strategic targets the business determined must be clear enough to be understood by all the employees. As well as general strategic targets, enterprise risk taking profile is extremely important at this stage. The businesses, by forming their enterprise risk-taking profiles, must be aware to what extent they can take risks with respect to their general strategic targets (Saka 2008). At the stage where a business must decide on its risk profile level, the enterprise policy that shows the business' general current position, its targets and which strategies to follow to attain these targets has great importance (Arslan 2008).

While defining the targets, the businesses must give decisions on whether to use a result-focused or process-focused approach in the ERM standard they will apply. COSO and similar standards handle the process process-based. Within the process, inputs are identified, operations are defined and the output is taken. The advantage of the process-based approach is easy acquisition of the possible risks. But, focusing on the details and facing the possibility of missing the whole picture can be a disadvantage of the process-based approach. The decision-makers are interested not in the details but only in the risks at critical levels and just critical risks of the sub levels. Therefore, in the decision making stage, for the business to have a result-focused approach in risk management will provide more benefits. Besides, a result-focused approach in ERM is important in providing the separation of the inner management and risk management areas (Topcu 2013).

Current Situation Analysis

In current situation analysis, for an effective risk management application, there are some points that must be paid attention to. The first is the acquisition of the risk management strategy and arranging a working area in accordance with it. Risk management strategy contains the business' understanding of the risk management, its main principles, its risk appetite, the importance it gives to the risk management, acceptable risk levels, and duties and responsibilities in the risk management application. Another important point is the extent to which the business fulfills its risk management activities. For an efficient risk management application, access to the related units to the information they need at a needed extent and time must be ensured. Therefore, information sharing and communication levels must be defined at the stage of current situation analysis (Arslan 2008). Shortly, at this stage, businesses must analyze the current risk management subsystem in detail. Current situation analysis is the answer to the question "Where are we?" (Duran 2013). The businesses pay attention to these headings while making this analysis:

- Current risk management environment; it should be analyzed with questions such as: Is there a risk management policy or guide explaining the risk management expectations at the business? Is the current risk management policy compatible with the culture, climate, norm, and values of the business? Are the risk appetite and risk tolerance of the business clear?
- Risk management application; it should be analyzed with the questions as: Do the current risk management applications meet the steps of risk acquisition, evaluation and responding appropriately?
- Control; whether the risk management policies and the controls are guaranteed or not should be analyzed.
- Information and communication; whether there is information flow within the business, whether the problems are reported or not, whether there is a healthy communication ability within the units should be analyzed.

Goal Structure Determination

The stage, after which the analysis of the current situation is made, is the stage where the acquisition of the Goal and aims structure aimed after the improvements is executed (Arslan 2008). In the acquisition of the goal structure, some criteria, stated below, must be taken into consideration and analyzed carefully:

- The strategies and goals of the institution,
- Enterprise risk taking profile,
- Sectors in service,
- The geographical distribution of the activities,
- The complexity level of the activities,

- Size of the institution,
- Organizational culture,
- Sector applications,
- Legal regulations,
- Human resources;
- The phase like development, recession and shrinking in which the institution exists.

Difference Analysis and Planning

It is a stage which contains the detection of the difference between the current and aimed structures by comparing them and the preparation of the course of actions needed to eliminate this difference (Saka 2008). In the course of actions, the cost–benefit analysis must take part. Along with the plan, duties and responsibilities must be defined and standards, guides, and application documents must be created. With which method the risks will be defined, measured, and what kind of responses will be given to the risks must be detected. Also, the education activities that can increase the employees‘ information and ability levels to the needed levels must take place in this plan (Arslan 2008).

The structure that defines the way between the business' current position and aimed structure is strategic planning. Strategic planning is long-term planning and has a prudential point of view (T.R. Prime Ministry State Planning Organization (PMSPO) 2006). The strategic planning process helps a business to respond to four basic questions (Duran 2013):

- Where are we?
- Where do we want to reach?
- How can we reach our destination?
- What should we do to continue and evaluate our success?

Two of the four questions above, that a business must ask itself, are the questions necessary for the difference analysis. The rest of the questions, which are the questions about strategic planning, comprise the planning of the future. The business, while searching an answer to the question "Where are we?" must make an extensive analysis of the internal and external surroundings it is active in. While searching for an answer to the question "Where do we want to reach?" two important concepts face us. These are: "mission" that shortly explains the reason for the business' existence and "vision" which is a conceptual and brief expression of the aimed future (Duran 2013). The business must define its mission and vision correctly and realistically and set reasonable and logical goals for itself.

In a business, whether the observation activities performed in relation to the risk management and the business' risk management activities are in coordination with the business' mission and vision or not is evaluated. According to the results obtained at the end of the evaluation, what can be done to develop the mentioned activities is detected.

The Application of the Transition Process

Standards, risk policy guides, and application documents must be created. The authority and responsibilities of the members of the business from the top manager to the employee working at the lowest level must be stated clearly. All the employees must be aware of their responsibilities (Saka 2008). About the risk policy defined by the top manager of the business, risk committees connected to the board of directors and the general director must be formed. Risk management departments must create a working area where they can work in coordination with the other departments with strategic planning and internal supervision at the top within the framework of the risk policies prepared by the risk committees. To get the maximum benefit from the risk management, it is extremely important that the risk management applications work in coordination with strategic planning. Internal supervision is the unit that will supervise the operability and efficiency of the process (Topcu 2013).

Revisions for the Continuous Development

The process must be controlled and observed continually. Needed changes must be made in needed situations, the continuous development of the system must be ensured. For this, previous stages must be operated healthily. An uninterrupted communication and information flow is extremely important. Getting the needed information at the desired time is important for the improvement of the malfunction of the system straight away (Saka 2008). In a business, the existence of the units that are not in communication with each other within the risk management means that ERM is not applied according to its purpose in that business.

Enterprise Risk Management Application Process

Following the formation of the base for ERM application and the successful execution of the transition process, comes the stage of risk management application. The risk management application process is process composed of various stages as:

1. Risk identification and categorization;
2. Evaluation of the risks: Analyzing and measuring the risks;
3. Prioritizing the risks;
4. Defining and applying the best responses for the risks.

Risk Identification and Categorization

After the first stage of risk management in which the needed base is formed, the second stage, risk identification of the business' activities and its categorization, comes. At this stage, the market in which the business is active, and the internal and external environments must be analyzed carefully, the risks that may affect the business' activities must be defined clearly. No matter how successful the risk management team is, in order to control the risk, what the risk is must be defined clearly (Allen 2003).

The following questions that can be asked to define the risks will be a guide at the stage of risk detection:

- What are the potential events that can hinder the business' growth?
- In which area does it make the biggest effort for control?
- In which area are most of the business resources used?
- Which areas are exposed to important management reports?
- What are the subjects and events that the employees complain about?

If the risk management of a business is formed for the first time, all the risks that the business is exposed to are defined (Gunes 2009). But, if there is a valid risk management system, the concept of risk record comes out. At the risk management process, observing the fluctuations of the risks, the risk record must be updated continuously by taking the events off the risk record if they are no longer considered as risks or recording the new events that has risks depending upon the developments in the sector they are active (Derici et al. 2007).

Analyzing and Measuring the Risks

Before deciding on how the expected risks should be managed, presenting the dimension of the risks and showing the business' potential effects on its profitability, digitizing the risks is necessary. After that, the businesses should take risk capital quantity and risk appetite into consideration. The businesses decide on which response such as acceptance, transfer, and evasion to give to the risks and on the risk capital quantity which is the business capital spared for the possible loss caused by these risks. The businesses should spare the risk capital at an amount they consider adequate for the worst scenarios. But, the point that must be paid attention to is that the risk capital spared more than needed will be in vain and will decrease the profitability; the inadequate risk capital will cause the inability to pay the business debts (Berk 2005).

In their evaluation and analysis, both the effects and the possibilities of occurrence of the risks must be taken into consideration. Many techniques are used in risk analysis and evaluation (Kucuk Yilmaz 2007). Risk evaluation and analysis methods and techniques that are used widely are as follows (Fig. 4.1).

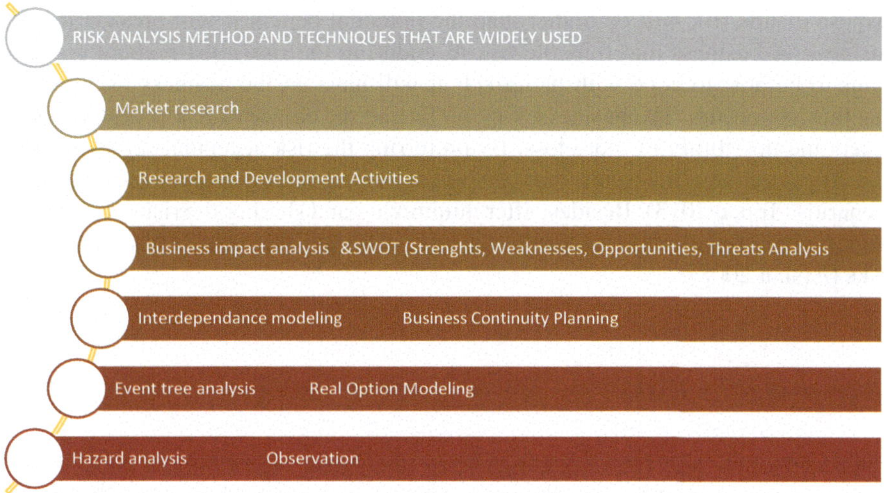

Fig. 4.1 Widely used risk analysis methods and techniques (Adopted from COSO2004)

Detecting the Suitable Responses and Their Application

If the scaling of the risks is at a satisfactory level for the business, the next question is how the business will control these risks (Allen 2003). This stage contains the detection of alternatives for risk management actions, deciding on the most appropriate one of these alternatives, preparing and applying an action plan for the responses. So, the stage of giving and applying suitable responses to the risks contains the detection of risk management strategies. The aim of giving a response to the risks is to provide benefits for the business by limiting the threats for turning the uncertainty situation of the business to its benefit. Risks can be responded to in various ways. These can be accepting, decreasing, sharing, and avoiding. Besides, the businesses must always observe the opportunities.

The businesses, with respect to risk management, manage the risks they face applying one or some of the strategies. At the decision making stage, a careful selection must be made by taking the potential benefits and probable hazards it will cause the business at the end of this selection into consideration. It is useful to explain the risk management and the options of risk management.

Accepting the Risks

A business accepting the risk as a risk response is a decision of the business' being in favor of taking risks and giving reactions to the situations the risk causes by doing nothing but observing passively (Tchankova 2002). In brief, it means that the risk faced is acceptable or if it is not acceptable, the fact that the cost of the action to dispose of this risk will be higher than the potential benefit it will provide for the business. A business that runs the risk of enduring the risk must prepare urgency plans to be able to cope with the effects it will have on the business in the event that this risk occurs. The businesses, by preferring the choice of risk acceptance will accept the possibility of more loss. By preferring the risk acceptance, they believe that they can control the results they can face as a result of the risk and write optimistic scenarios (Topcu 2013). Besides, after minimizing and sharing the risks, some risks are left. The businesses must accept the risks left after they give a response to the risks (Arslan 2008).

Decreasing the Risks

The business' choice of the risk reduction strategy means reducing the risk's dimensions and potential effects on the business to a reasonable level by reducing the possibility and effect of the risk to the lowest level (Meulbroek 2002). In fact, this strategy is like putting the eggs in small quantities in separate baskets rather than putting all the eggs in only one basket. The aim of this strategy is to ensure that, in a possible situation of negative effects of the risk on the business, not all of the sources and actions of the business are affected, only its certain parts are affected by this (Topcu 2013).

At the risk reduction strategy choice, the business can adopt two basic strategies. First is, with the help of the suitable controlling mechanisms, to decrease the accrual possibilities of the events that are potential to cause the business to have loss. Second is forming and operating the controlling mechanisms to reduce the business' loss by decreasing the dimension of the negative effects that can cause risk for the business.

The point that a business must pay attention to is, as long as the controlling activities operate in the way as they have to, risks will be reduced (Akcakanat 2012).

Sharing the Risk

Risk sharing also means transferring the risk. When the risk is shared, for the risk not to happen, the business transfers some actions to the experts. For instance, the business may have given a decision to assign some of the production processes to the outer institutes. In that case, some risks, which can happen in a business, can be disposed of before they happen. Also, getting some actions done by the expert institutions and organizations out of the business by agreements will decrease the possibility of making a mistake owing to the existence of an expert in the business with which an agreement has been made (Topcu 2013). Shortly, it is possible that some or all of the risk is undertaken by the others in the event of risk sharing or transferring. But, it must not be forgotten that risk transferring, if not managed by the sides transferred appropriately will bring about new risks.

In the method known as alternative risk transfer, transferring and sharing the credit risks and activity risks is the case. With this respect, risk transfer is the controlling means which ensures that another institution rather than the business that got damaged undertakes the damage (Rejda 1992). Similarly, a method that provides the transferring of every risk to the other side by the business' risk directors, with some credit derivatives, banks or various organizations transferring the credit risks to financial markets is frequently used. Sharing the activities that cause risks with business partners or transferring them to the insurance companies can be given as examples for the mentioned technique (Topcu 2013).

Avoiding the Risk

Not starting the activities which cause the risk to happen or cause its possibility and/or effects to increase, or ending the related activity is risk avoidance choice (TIBA 2008). In other words, if the businesses don't want to accept the possible results of the risk, they protect the business from risk by not taking part in the activities and situations that have risk. But, while making this decision, they must be careful. It must be ensured that an opportunity that is for the benefit of the business is not missed. If the risk avoidance choice is preferred, missing a big opportunity may be possible. On the other hand, the possibility that the importance of the other risks may increase shouldn't be ignored (Rejda 1992).

In risk management, the businesses must analyze the balance between the benefit and cost well (Berk 1992). When the choice of not taking the risk is preferred, the opportunity that can be missed must be realized. Taking the cost of the relevant risk into consideration, a response to that risk must be given. If the cost is more than the benefit that it is expected to provide, risk avoidance will be the right choice.

The Continuous Observation and Revision of the Process

For efficient operation of the risk management system, the risk management process must be observed continuously. With various control mechanisms, the process must be reviewed continuously. Basic parameters such as observation and evaluation of the risk management process' efficiency, conveying the measuring results to the relevant units, giving feedback to the decision mechanisms and improvements of the processes that are considered inefficient in risk management must be reported (Fikirkoca 2003).

Reports are arranged by the persons responsible for the risk at the business at certain periods for the updating of the risk record. The risk observation and evaluation stage is the stage that comprises reporting the changes in risks and the developments of the controlling activities, renewing the related units even, if needed, the whole process, reviewing the risk management process, and measuring its activity (Derici et al. 2007). The observation process provides that the controls are used according to the organization's activities. At the same time, the observation and revision processes, with the controls applied, aim to detect whether the business can attain the results it defined before, whether enough data was gathered to make an evaluation and whether the current procedures are suitable or not. At this point, numeric and non-numeric performance measuring techniques must be defined. Also, the performance of the risk management applications must be observed continuously. By evaluating the results with methods adapted to the risk, to what extent the results of the risk management applications reflect on the results of the business must be detected (TIBA 2008). Thus, the observation and revision stage are extremely important.

One of the most important stages that define the efficiency of the risk management process is the communication and consultation stage. Instead of the decision-makers‘ one-sided monolog informing of their shareholders, establishing a reciprocal dialogue will be useful for the risk management. Reciprocal communication and interaction are extremely important at every step of the risk management process. At the risk detection stage, getting all the directors' opinions who are in communication with each other interrelatedly, at the risk analysis stage, transferring different experiences and at the risk evaluation stage, giving place to different opinions, with no doubt, will be extremely important for the efficiency of the risk management process applied in the business (http-17 tarih yok). An approach open to communication will provide that the risk management is understood, adopted, and supported better by the directors and the decision-makers (TIBA 2008).

Risk Management at the Airline Businesses

Since the airline businesses are an open system, they are in a form that is affected by the environmental changes fast. Therefore, the directors must take many factors into consideration in the risk management applications. Besides, the risk factors based on their own structure, there also risks that they are exposed to as a result of the geography and conditions in which they are active.

The Key Points of the Airline Risk Management

In order to understand the risk the airline businesses are exposed to, their accrual possibilities and their potential effects on the businesses, it is necessary to understand the key focus points of the airline risk management programs. It is possible to study the key focus points under four headings:

- Safety risk management,
- Airline Insurance Policies,
- Crisis Management and Possibility of Planning, and
- Financial Risk Management.

Safety Management

The airline business is an extensive subject that contains the operational safety risks and safety threats (Brooker 2006). Providing land and air safety and carrying out the operations safely are the basic concerns of the airline risk management programs. Airline businesses must carry out their activities in coordination with a series of developed safety policies, guides, and applications. Airline businesses focus on the safety management not only because of the policies and legislation, but also because they may pay a big price at the end of an event based on an unsafe situation. A possible plane crash may not reflect on an airline business just as must as the cost of the plane that crashed. At the same time, the compensation to be paid for the victims' relatives at the end of the event, a sudden depreciation of the relevant business' trademark value, can bring about the problems such as having financial troubles in the future. With this respect, it may be inevitable for many businesses to undertake many negative results. Insurance, in this context, while important in mitigating financial exposure, is not adequate in protecting image and perception.

When we study the development of the safety risk management, it is realized that from the 1950s to 1970s, by giving importance to the technique factors, technological faults were focused to be eliminated. During this period, it is obvious that human factors are focused, human–machine relationship and human-driven faults are the primary reasons for the plane crashes. Since the 1990s, it has been considered that human actions are affected by the organization's structure. Aviation events and accidents have been approached with a systematic point of view. In the last 20 years, the factors that cause accidents related to aviation safety have been detected. Taking the relationship of the human-organization structure into consideration, protective models related to the safety risk management have been developed and new precautions were started to be taken (ICAO 2013a, b).

On the other hand, the terrorist attack that happened in the USA on September 11, 2001 created a different dimension for safety in aviation. Since the attack was a surprise, the aviation authorities began again to discuss safety and security regulations. Until this terrorist attack, all the risks considered about safety took place in the most predictable external risks focus (Bazerman and Watkins 2005). After the event, especially in America, many new precautions were taken, strict security measures were applied. After this experience, the airline businesses began to give more importance to the safety management with respect to the risk management.

Airline Insurance Policies

In order to relieve or eliminate the negative effects of the risks, one of the most applied methods is insurance policies. Airlines take insurance out on events like a plane crash whose accrual possibility is low, but if it happens it can cause very big negative results for the business. Insurance policies, since they lay the burden of the risks' financial results on the third parties, take the stress of the risks whose accrual possibility is low but the cost of which may be high (Lane 2005).

With no doubt, airline businesses cannot respond to all their risks with insurance policies. While some risks' effects can be eliminated by managing them well, negative effects of some risks on the business will be at a reasonable level. The business will prefer accepting these negative effects. On the other hand, the fact that many risks are interrelated with each other is inevitable. The insuring operations made for certain risks may not involve the other risks related to these risks. In that case, the insurance policy will be inefficient by itself.

Crisis Management and Planning the Possibility

Airline businesses are active in a dynamic environment under many risks. The risks in the geography where the businesses are active can change in a short time, sometimes it can change into a crisis rapidly. The businesses may have to cancel or retard their flights owing to the meteorological events such as the cancelation of the flights owing to the meteorology, the ash cloud, which the volcanic eruption causes, closing the air space for some time. In such cases, the businesses must be prepared for crisis situations in order not to let the crisis get bigger and must urge caution by giving importance to the less possible risks. The unsuccessful management of the risk may put the businesses into trouble not only in an economic but also in a commercial sense. Therefore, the businesses must give enough importance to the crisis and crisis management, must evaluate all the possibilities.

Financial Risk Management

Airline businesses are exposed to very big financial risks as a nature of their activities. A shrink in their cash flow or fluctuations in the exchange rate can yield results as getting the airline businesses into trouble financially or even dragging them into a crisis. Therefore, the businesses must also give importance to the financial risk management. The businesses, within the financial risk management, make various agreements over fixed prices by applying a method called "hedging" in order to protect themselves from price movements.

Operational Risk Management in Airline Businesses

Planning the operations in an uncertain environment and its safety are among the subjects to which the airline businesses pay attention most. For taking the capacity to an adequate level, the optimization of the route, flight network, hub and code sharing, the adaptation of the airline operations to the changing environment must be performed regularly (Ahmed and Poojari 2008). Although the operational risks have a broad range like income and stock management, improvement of the products and the service, limiting the cost, human resources policies, the topics related to the security constitute the basis of the risk management for the airline businesses. When we look at the content of airline operational risk management programs, it can be seen that preventing plane crashes or serious events are among the biggest targets. Besides, the fact that the dangers cannot be disposed of totally is accepted. In accordance with this hypothesis, security was explained as "a situation where the possibility of the human's and property's getting damaged is reduced, the danger is defined at an acceptable level and the safety risk management process is maintained" (ICAO 2013a, b).

Contrary to many sectors, in the aviation sector, risks of airline safety were arranged seriously. ICAO, IATA, and EASA European Aviation Safety Agency (EASA) published important advice on especially maintenance, land services, flight and cabin operations or personnel certifications.

Safety risk management has an important place in operational risk management. When the first years of the civil airline transportation are studied, it is seen that accident risk is considered as an inheritance. But, with the development of operational risk management and safety risk management in parallel, the accident risk is no more an inheritance (Netjasov and Janic 2008). With this respect, while the technical factors stand out in the 1950s, in the 1970s the human factor, and since the 1990s the organizational factors have stood out.

In the 1950s, since the safety management programs focused on preventing technological failures, an important decline in aviation accidents was recorded. Afterward, the scope of the operational risk management was extended. Since the 1970s the focus of operational risk management has been the human factor. In aviation accidents, the human–machine relationship, human faults were defined as the repeated events in the plane crashes and plane events. Since 1990, with the human-driven errors getting more complicated, organizational factors became more efficient in operational risk management.

With the aviation events and accidents being perceived as a systematic perspective, organizational culture started to be explored in regards the efficiency of the safety risk management system of a company. Gathering information about the safety events and accidents and analyzing it by using a reactive method was completed by detecting the safety threats with a proactive method. As the safety accidents and events that the human-driven and organizational factors cause are defined, many models were developed to prevent many accidents. These models were primarily focused on the human–technology interaction the people's behaviors in the organization.

Reason (1997) claims in the "Swiss Cheese" model that aviation safety events, incidents, and accidents are not caused by just one safety system error, but by many problems such as technological problems, human errors and organizational problems. This model, at the same time, defends that operational safety accidents are a product of implicit and explicit events. Also, it highlights the fact that as certain errors are focused to boost the safety systems' performance, the hidden events that can affect

Fig. 4.2 ICAO's safety management system framework Adapted from by Misiura (2015) from ICAO (2013, pp. 5–2)

aviation safety must be revealed by observing the organizational processes (Reason 1997). In aviation, a result of the improvements of safety, safety management system that the aviation authorities advise strongly was developed.

Aviation authorities defend that the System Safety concept must be used for managing many risks of the safety. Safety Management System (SMS) obligatory for the airline business made by ICAO is defined as a systematic approach of safety management that comprises the important organizational structures, policy, and procedures. SMS, which ICAO defines, is composed of 4 main components and 12 elements as shown in Fig. 4.2 (ICAO 2013a, b).

Risk Factors That Effect the Flight Operations

Airline businesses, like all the other businesses, want to carry out their activities without trouble. Airline transportation, by nature, is a sector that has a burden of stress because of the low-profit margin and high costs. Therefore, the airline businesses have many risk factors that can affect the airline businesses.

In the aviation sector, the rules of which were written in blood, flight safety comes first. For the airline businesses, the passengers' satisfaction, their wish for safe travel even in bad weather conditions take place in the first place of importance. Flight safety doesn't start with take-off. The flight team's getting enough rest, being healthy, having high spirits and motivation are the factors that affect flight safety directly. On the other hand, the flight team's excessive self-confidence caused bad experiences in the past. Flight indiscipline caused by awkwardness and excessive self-confidence can cause high costs for airline businesses.

The flight team's education being regular and complete is extremely important for the flight safety too. The ability of the pilots to carry out the checklist items they have to do in case of an emergency, knowing which trouble must be treated in which way is of high importance for flight safety. When we consider the case with respect to the cabin team since the first aid team is out of the cabin team in case of trouble with one of the passengers, the knowledge of the cabin team must be kept fresh, their education must be regular and must be freshened.

Apart from the flight safety, the passengers want to get a good service from the airline business where they bought their tickets in return for the price they paid. Feeling valued with a smiling and helpful approach is extremely important for a passenger while choosing an airline business for his travel. Also, the passengers want to travel with an understanding of a smiling service since the time they check-in. They want to get professional service when they face a problem before, during, and after flight. Therefore, it must be a wanted feature for the business managers that the personnel working in the airline businesses are successful in social relationships besides their occupational educations.

Maintenance is another factor that affects the flight safety directly. Maintaining the planes completely and in full, the examination of some failure, which is considered exceptional to the plane, by the flight team, is a deciding factor whether the airplane will be accepted to flight or not carefully are of high importance for the flight safety. The plane crashes based on maintenance are rarely encountered in aviation history. The airline managers must follow the hourly and scheduled maintenance of the airplanes in their fleet carefully and take needed precautions in time.

Natural disasters such as flood, earthquake, and volcanic eruption and meteorological events such as heavy snowfall, or low vision owing to fog are the events that can affect flight operations. The weather forecast must be followed closely, and situations that can hinder flight operations must be analyzed carefully. A possible retard or cancelation of the flight hour must be reported to the passengers in a short time and the passengers shouldn't be aggrieved as much as possible. While an airline canceling the flight or landing in another area by taking any risks can be safer for flight safety, under the same weather conditions, another airline continuing the flight by taking risks at a reasonable level may be evaluated differently by the passengers. The balance between the levels of risks to be taken and the flight safety must be evaluated well and analyzed carefully.

As the ash cloud, caused by the volcanic eruption in Iceland in April 2010, caused the airline flights of the Europe air scope to close for 6 days, the airline businesses must define their policy in case of a possible natural event. In case of a natural disaster similar to the mentioned event, a reasonable policy must be determined to compare the possible loss the flight in the area might cause and the cost it might bring about with the benefits the passengers in the area may provide for the business. But, in this event, many businesses canceled their flight and had a financial loss.

Political relationships of countries can affect the collaboration between two countries in many areas. At the top of these areas comes the tourism sector. The political relationship of the two countries being tense can affect tourism between the two countries negatively. Tourism's getting affected negatively means that the airline transportation is affected negatively, too. The decline in the number of passengers the airline businesses carry between the two countries will cause some flights to be canceled. Therefore, the international political relationship is a risk factor that affects the airline transportation positively or negatively.

The terror threat is an important threat that sabotages the tourism. The sabotage of tourism means that airline transportation is affected negatively, too. Even if it is one of the most attractive places in the world, the existence of terror threat can cause the people who plan a travel to the relevant area to get into panic or cancel their travel by changing their plans. The tourism' s getting affected negatively can cause a decline in the number of the tourists that can come to the relevant area, and therefore in the number of the passengers to be carried by airline. On the other hand, airline businesses that plan an overnight stay in the area where there is a terror threat must take necessary safety precautions. Also, it is obligatory for the airline businesses to detect the areas they operate carefully, to take necessary safety precautions taking the terror threat and, if any, the flight team's safety into consideration.

The Way of the Airline Risk Management Applications and Researches

When the academic studies carried out in the past 20 years are studied, topics such as airline management, airports and substructure, passenger demands and price flexibility, environmental factors such as pollution and carbon emission, airline transportation safety, airline alliance, airline management, and safety stand out. Out of these popular studies, in the airline management and safety category, the airline risk management applications have an extensive place. Within this scope, among the most searched topics, financial, operational and safety risks take place. On the other hand, the research conducted in recent years are on the inadequate regulations and policies, weak sectoral structure, inconsistent strategies in airline transportation.

But, in the airline business, studies on ERM are extremely limited. ERM concept is a quite new concept for the nonfinancial sectors. A research was carried out by Airline Business Journal in which 51 airline businesses in the top 200 with respect to their income joined. Two-thirds of the airline businesses that joined in the research pointed out that they have risk management strategies which they have prepared taking the strategic risks within the organization into consideration. Seventy-five percent of the participant airline businesses pointed out that risk management responsibility is handled at the top management level, even 45% of CEOs take the strategic risks into consideration while comparing the management strategies (Jenner 2007, pp. 74–76).

Airline businesses notify their annual reports through enterprise internet websites and other external communication channels. Hence, airline businesses must adopt an extensive risk management understanding. Airline businesses such as Air France, KLM, Air Canada, Malaysia Airlines, Air Mauritius, and many others reported that they adopt ERM by defining their risk management structure and process (Misiura 2015).

References

Adopted from COSO, 2004. COSO. *Eterprise risk management-integrated framework.* Committee of Sponsoring Organizations of the Treadway Commission (COSO).

Ahmed, A.H., and C.A. Poojari. 2008. An overview of the issues in the airline industry and the role of optimization models and algorithms. *The Journal of the Operational Research Society* 59 (3): 267–277.

AIRMIC, The Association of Insurance and Risk Managers and ALARM, The National Forum for Risk Management in the Public Sector, A Risk Management Standard. http://www.ferma.eu/. IRM, The Institute of Risk Management,. n.d. http://www.ferma.eu/app/uploads/2011/11/a-risk-management-standard-english-version.pdf. Accessed 15 Apr 2017.

Akcakanat, O. 2012. Kurumsal Risk Yönetimi ve Kurumsal Risk Yönetim Süreci. *Süleyman Demirel Üniversitesi Vizyoner Dergisi* 4(7).

Allen, S. 2003. *Financial risk management: A practictioner's guide to managing market and credit risk.* Hoboken, NJ: Wiley.

Arslan, I. 2008. *Kurumsal Risk Yönetimi.* Ankara: Ministry of Finance Strategy Development Presidency.

Atamer, M. 2006. *Halka Açık Anonim Şirketlerde Kurumsal Yönetim ve Doğrudan Yabancı Yatırımlar Açısından Değerlendirilmesi.* Ankara: Treasury Undersecretary Publishing.

Aydogan, Z.F. 2004. Örgüt Kültürü ve İklimi. *Gazi University Journal of Trade and Tourism Education*, 203–215.

Aykut, C. 2008. Basel II Standartları. *Journal of Economic Issues*, 30.

Baydar, C. 2006. Operasyonel Risk Yönetiminde Seçilen Risk Modelinin Önemi. *Journal Of Aylık Finansal Risk Yönetimi.*

Bazerman, M.H., and M. Watkins. 2005. Airline security, the failure of 9/11, and predictable surprises. *International Public Management Journal* 8 (3): 365–377.

Benton, A.B. 2001. Step by step enterprise risk management. *Risk Management* 48 (9): 41–50.

Berk, A.B. 1992. *Sigortacılıkta Risk Yönetimi.* Istanbul: Turkish Insurance Institute Foundation.

Berk, N. 2005. *Finansal Yönetim.* Istanbul: Turkmen Publishing.

Brooker, P. 2006. Air traffic management accident risk, Part 1: The limits of realistic modelling. *Safety Science* 44: 419–450.

Capital Market Board Department. 2016. Kurumsal Yönetim Uyum ve Raporlama. http://www.spk.gov.tr/displayfile.aspx?action=displayfile&pageid=63&fn=63.pdf#31. Accessed 10 Sept 2016.

Ceylan, H., and V.S. Bashelvaci. 2011. Risk Değerlendirme Tablosu Yöntemi İle Risk Analizi: Bir Uygulama. *International Journal of Engineering Research and Development* 3(2): 27.

Charette, R.N. 2010. Enterprise risk management. In P. Simon, (ed.). *The next wave of technologies: opportunities from chaos.* Hoboken, NJ: John Wiley & Sons.

Derici, O., Z. Tuysuz, and A. Sari. 2007. Kurumsal Risk Yönetimi ve Sayıştay Uygulaması. *Journal of Sayistay*, 65.

Duran, E. 2013. Kamu İdarelerinde Kurumsal Risk Yönetimi Uygulamaları, 92. Financial Services Expertise Research Report, Turkish Republic Ministry of Environment and Urban Planning Strategy Development Department, Ankara.

Erdogan, I. 2007. *İşletmelerde Davranış*. Istanbul: Miad Publishing.

Fatigue Risk Management Sysytems. n.d. https://www.iata.org/publications/Documents/FRMS%20Implementation%20Guide%20for%20Operators%201st%20Edition-%20English.pdf. Accessed 25 Oct 2015.

Fikirkoca, M. 2003. *Bütünsel Risk Yönetimi*. Istanbul: Pozitif Imprint.

Finametrica. https://riskprofiling.com/riskprofiling/assessing/risk_capacity. Accessed 3 May 2016.

Fraser, J., and B.J. Simkins. 2009. *Enterprise risk management: An introduction and overview, in enterprise risk management*. Hoboken, NJ: Wiley.

Frigo, M.L., and R.J. Anderson. 2011. Strategic risk management: A foundation for improving enterprise risk management and governance. *The Journal of Corporate Accounting & Finance* 22 (3): 81–88.

Greenberg, M., and K. Lowrie. 2010. From the editors. *Risk Analysis* 30 (12): 873–874.

Gunes, S. 2009. *Kurumsal Risk Yönetimi ve Türkiye'de Farkındalığına İlişkin Bir Uygulama*. Istanbul: Istanbul Technical University of Science, Unpublished Master's Thesis.

Gupta, P.P., and J.C. Thomson. 2006. Use of COSO 1992 in management reporting on internal control. *Strategic Finance* 10: 28.

Güneş, S. 2009. Kurumsal Risk Yönetimi ve Türkiye'de Farkındalığına İlişkin Bir Uygulama. Yayımlanmamış Yüksek Lisans Tezi. İstanbul: İstanbul Teknik Üniversitesi, Fen Bilimleri Enstitüsü. p. 7.

Haller, M. 1999. *The global development of risks-consequences for integrated risk management*. St. Gallen: Risk Management Foundation, I-VW HSG.

HKICPA. 2005. *Internal control and risk management basic framework*. Hong Kong: Hong Kong Institute of Certified Public Accountents.

Holiwell, J. 1998. Risk enough rope to hang the business? In *Mastering finance: The definitive guide to the foundations and frontiers of finance*. London: Financial Times Pitman Publishing.

http-5. n.d. https://www.theirm.org/knowledge-and-resources/thought-leadership/risk-appetite-and-tolerance/. Accessed 3 May 2016.

http-6. n.d. Accessed 13 Oct 2016.

http-7. n.d. http://www.isikun.edu.tr/sem/p542. Accessed 13 Oct 2016.

http-8. n.d. https://tr.wikipedia.org/wiki/Federal_Havac%C4%B1l%C4%B1k_Kurulu. Accessed 8 Jan 2017.

http-9. 2013. https://www.faa.gov/regulations_policies/advisory_circulars/index.cfm/go/document.list?omni=ACs&q=risk&display=current&parentTopicID=0&documentNumber= Accessed 4 Jan 2017.

http-10. http://fast.faa.gov/. 2016. Acquisition http://fast.faa.gov/EMP_Risk_Management.cfm. Accessed 3 Jan 2017.

http-11. n.d. http://www.faa.gov/regulations_policies/handbooks_manuals/aviation/media/faa-h-8083-2.pdf. Accessed 25 Oct 2015.

http-12. n.d. http://www.mfa.gov.tr/uluslararasi-sivil-havacilik-orgutu-_icao_.tr.mfa. Accessed 8 Jan 2017.

http-14. n.d. Accessed 8 Jan 2017.

(IATA), International air transport association. Fatigue risk management sytems. 2015. https://www.iata.org/publications/Documents/FRMS%20Implementation%20Guide%20for%20Operators%201st%20Edition-%20English.pdf. Accessed 25 Oct 2015.

ICAO. Safety Management Manual (SMM) . Vers. 3. 2013. http://www.skybrary.aero/bookshelf/books/644.pdf. Accessed 1 Aug 2017.

investopedia.com. 2016. investopedia.com. http://www.investopedia.com/ask/answers/08/difference-between-risk-tolerance-and-risk-capacity.asp. Accessed 19 Aug 2019.

ICAO. 2013a. FRMS fatigue risk management systems manual for regulators. http://www.icao.int/safety/fatiguemanagement/frms%20tools/doc%209966%20-%20frms%20manual%20for%20regulators.pdf. Accessed 25 Oct 2015.

ICAO. 2013b. Safety Management Manual (SMM). Vers. 3. http://www.skybrary.aero/bookshelf/books/644.pdf. Accessed 8 Jan 2017.

Integrated Risk Management Guidance. 2016. http://www.iata.org/publications/store/Pages/integrated-risk-management-guidance.aspx. Accessed 3 Jan 2016.

Jenner, G. 2007. Premium rate. *Airline Business* 23 (6): 74–76.

Karaca, I. 2007. *Unilever ve İç Kontrol, TIDE XI.* Turkey Internal Audit Congress.

Kizildag, D. 2011. *Yönetsel Açıdan Risk Yönetimine Bir Bakış: ISO 31000 Risk Yönetimi.* Ankara: Seckin Imprint.

Kose, S., S. Tetik, and C. Ercan. 2001. Örgüt Kültürünü Oluşturan Faktörler. *Celal Bayar University Journal of Yonetim ve Ekonomi* 7(1).

Kucuk Yilmaz, A. 2003. Risk Management in view of Safety at Aviation: Sample Practices from Aviaiton Organizations Havacılıkta Emniyet Açısından Risk Yönetimi ve Havacılık Örgütlerinden Uygulama Örnekleri. Eskisehir: Anadolu University Social Science Institute, Unpublished Doctoral Thesis, 2003, p.57.

Kucuk Yilmaz, A. 2007. Havaalanlarında Kurumsal Risk Yönetimi: Atatürk Havalimanı Teminalleri İşletmesi İçin Kurumsal Risk Yönetimi Model Önerisi. Unpublished Doctoral Thesis, Anadolu University Institute of Social Sciences, Eskisehir.

Lane, M.N. 2005. Pricing issues in aviation insurance and reinsurance. *The Journal of Risk Finance* 6 (3): 192–207.

Matheson, D., and J. Matheson. 1998. *The smart organization.* Boston: Harward Business School Press.

Meulbroek, L. 2002. The promise se and challenge of integrated risk management. *Risk Management & Insurance Review* 5: 9.

Misiura, A. 2015. Enterprise risk management in the airline industry—Risk management structures and practices, Unpublished Doctoral Thesis, Brunel University Brunel Business School, London.

Moeller, R.R. 2014. *Executive's guide to COSO internal controls: Understanding and implementing the new framework.* Hoboken NJ: Wiley.

Moran, E.T., and J.F. Volkwein. 1992. The cultural approach to the formation of organization climate. *Human Relations* 45 (1): 19–47.

Morris, P., and J.K. Pinto. 2010. *The Wiley guide to project control.* Hoboken: Wiley.

Muller, R., and C. Drax. 2014. *Aviation risk and safety management, management for professionals.* Switzerland: Springer.

Netjasov, F., and M. Janic. 2008. A review of research on risk and safety modelling in civil aviation. *Journal of Air Transport Management* 14 (4): 213–220.

Nomura, K. 2003. Managing risks in airline industry. *Japan and World Economy*, 469–479.

OECD. *OECD Principle of Corporate Governance.* 2004. OECD principle of Corporate Governance. http://www.oecd.org/corporate/2004revisionoftheoecdprinciplesofcorporategovernance.htm. Accessed 18 Dec 2016.

Oktay, N. 2006. "http-2." *Stratejik Amaçlar.* Turkey Industrial Management Institute. 2006. http://www.tepav.org.tr/upload/files/haber/1255436676r4646.5._Sunum_Stratejik_Amaclar.pdf. Accessed 5 Mar 2016.

Ozeke, H.B. 2004. *Kurumsal Yönetim Bağlamında Yönetim Kurulu Üyelerinin Sorumluluklarının Hukuksal Çerçevesinin İrdelenmesi.* Istanbul: Corporate Governance Association.

Ozkalp, E., and C. Kiral. 2016. *Örgütsel Davranış.* Bursa: Ekin Publishing.

Pagach, D., and R. Warr. 2007. *An empirical investigation of the characteristics of firms adopting enterprise risk management*, 8. College of Management North Carolina State University.

Preston, G.S., and M. Guy. 2002. *Proactive risk management controlling, uncertainty, in product development.* New York: Productivity Press.

Reason, J. 1997. *Managing the risks of organizational accidents.* Ashgate: Ashgate Publishing Limited.

Rejda, G. 1992. *Principles of risk management and insurance*, vol. 4. Harper Collins Publisher.

Risk Management, Standards Australia/Standards New Zealand, Australian New Zealand Standard. AS/NZS 4360:2004. Joint Technical Committee OB-007. 2004. http://broadleaf.com.au/old/pdfs/trng_tuts/tut.standard.pdf. Accessed 12 Mar 2017.

Sabuncuoglu, Z., and M. Tuz. 1998. *Örgütsel Psikoloji*. Bursa: Alfa Aktuel Publishing.

Saka, T. 2008. *Kurumsal Risk Yönetimi ve 2008 Yılı Risk Öngörüleri*. TIBA.

Saltik, N. 2007. *İç Kontrol Merkezi Uyumlaştırma Dairesi İç Kontrol Standartları*. Ankara: Ministry of Finance General Directorate of Budget and Financial Control Publishing.

Schein, E. 1992. *Organizational culture and leadership*, 2nd ed. San Francisco: Jossey Bass.

Secretariat Treasury Board. 1999. Best practice in risk management: *Private and public sectors internationally*. Ottawa, Ontario: KPMG.

Serim, A. 2006. 10 Soruda Ekonomide kurumlar, Derecelendirme ve Basel. www.radikal.com.tr. 10 Soruda Ekonomide kurumlar, Derecelendirme ve Basel II. Radikal Gazetesi, 1 Aralık. http://www.radikal.com.tr/yorum/10-soruda-ekonomide-kurumlar-derecelendirme-ve-basel-ii-799070/. Accessed 7 Apr 2016.

Sevim, S., T. Cetinoglu, and N. Kurnaz. 2006. Avrupa Birliği Müzakereleri Sürecinde AB 8. Yönergesi Kapsamında Türkiye'de Denetim ve Denetçilik Mesleğinin Durumu: AB Müzakereleri Gelişim İçin Bir Fırsat Mıdır? *Journal of Financial Solution* 74: 45–75.

Sisman, M. 1994. *Örgüt Kültürü*. Eskisehir: Anadolu University Publishing.

SOX. Sarbanes-Oxley Act. 2002. Accessed 13 Oct 2015.

Speckbacher, G., J.A. Asel, and A. Posch. 2010. Der Finanzbereich, n Krisenzeiten: Vom Performance Management zum integrierten performance-risk management. *Controlling & Management* 54 (2): 60–67.

Tchankova, L. 2002. Risk identification-basic stage in risk management. *Environmental Management and Health* 13 (3): 290–297. (MCB University Press).

TIBA. 2008. *Kurumsal Risk Yönetimi Raporu*. TIBA (Turkish Industrialists' and Businessmen's Association) Publishing.

Topcu, B. 2013. *İşletmelerde Kurumsal Risk Yönetimi*. Istanbul: Istanbul Chamber of Commerce-Academic Publications.

T.R. Prime Ministry State Planning Organization (PMSPO). 2006. *Kamu İdareleri İçin Stratejik Planlama Kılavuzu*. Ankara: T.R. Prime Ministry State Planning Organization (PMSPO).

Turker, I. 2011. *Güçlü Ve Özgür Bir Ülke İçin Muhasebe Kültüründe Devrim*, 92. TURMOB Publishing.

Uzun, A.K. 2010. Riskin Erken Teşhisinde Yönetim Kurulunun Rolü: "Risk Zekasına Sahip Kurum Yaratmak". *Journal of Active* 6 (7): 63–71.

Wallace, J., J. Hunt, and C. Richards. 1996. The relationship between organizational culture, organizational climate and managerial values. *The International Journal of Public Sector Management* 12(7).

Yildirim, O. 2015. Türk Bankacılık Sisteminde Basel Kriterleri. *Journal of Finance Political & Economic Reviews* 52 (569): 10–11.

Yuzbasioglu, A.N. 2003. *Risk Yönetimi ve Bankaların Denetimi*. Istanbul: Association of Risk Managers-Financial World.

Chapter 5
Decision-Making in Aviation Management: Multi-criteria Problem-Solving Strategy

Contents

Introduction to the Decision-Making Process

Decision-making is an essential part of both business and private life. Instantaneous and variable situations in aviation business are effective in making decisions. Organizational success cannot be achieved by ignoring individuals. Individuals as managers, make decisions according to their values. Managerial decision-making, therefore, depends strongly on the values.

Values include elements of individual contributions to performance at both community and corporate levels. An element of individual contributions covers the following qualifications of the human condition:

- Situational awareness level,
- Creativity,
- Capability,
- Experience and demography,
- Paradigm,
- Attitude,
- Interpretation style and approach, and
- Individual social responsibility.

The decision as a concept of business management and strategy means that one makes a "choice" from options. The core of Management is decision-making. Managers make a choice via their every decision-making. Value has an impact on effective and

A. Kucuk Yilmaz and T. G. Flouris, *Values, Ergonomics and Risk Management in Aviation Business Strategy*, https://doi.org/10.1007/978-981-15-1006-9_5

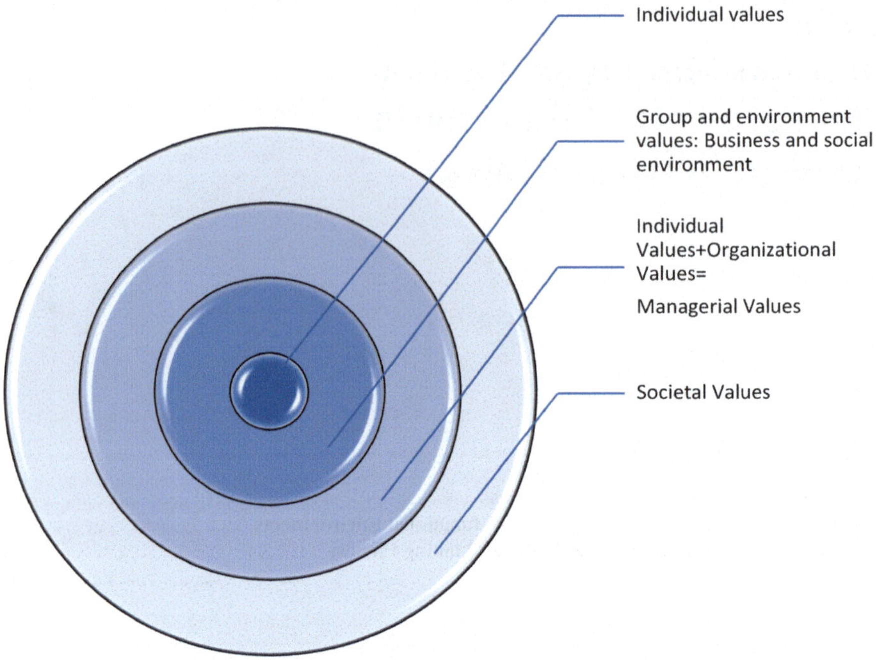

Fig. 5.1 Core value to societal values (Developed from Values for Decision Making Harrison, Ch. 4 Fred Wenstøp http://slideplayer.com/slide/8480077/ accessed at January 25, 2018)

timely decision-making. The values that individuals possess play a crucial role in decision-making. Individual values take places in core of the value cluster as seen in Fig. 5.1.

Strategic decisions taken in the aviation sector have international influence, and expert opinions should be consulted over the course of strategic decision-making. Regardless of the size, complexity or type of operation, there is no doubt that top management determines the company's safety culture (Civil Aviation Safety Authority Australia 2018, p. 3).

We assume that according to a universal approach in management and strategy, the factor of individual social responsibility is one of the main drivers/determinants to creating multi-criteria decision-making processes. Situational awareness level has the potential to affect individual social responsibility, but a high level of situational awareness does not mean high performance in both decision-making and social responsibility-based attitudes. Behavioral sciences can provide insights that can be translated into interventions to improve the safety culture (Flin 2013, p. 1).

Cognitive behavior CB applies itself to every decision we make and so it is important that we know what it is so that we can look out for it! Different people have different CBs and therefore deviations occur (i.e., different people will make different decisions based on the same evidence). People are generally not even aware that they have these biases until they are explicitly addressed (McDonald and Evans 2016, p. 2).

Fig. 5.2 The equation of Managerial Values (Adopted from Corporate Culture, Ethics, and Leadership by Lawrence Stokes http://slideplayer.com/slide/5757738/, January 25, 2018)

The typical business school model of optimized decision-making requires a brainstorming session during which options—the more of them, the better—are developed and considered. The evaluation criteria are constructed so that each option may be assessed, compared and prioritized. In the end, a solution is proposed that promises to be the best possible choice after hours, days or even years of deliberation (Albright 2015, p. 1). Generally, operators in aviation such as pilots, air traffic management professionals, even airport managers do not have time to apply this kind of process (Fig. 5.2).

Managers should consider individual social responsibility as start points to corporate performance determinants. To improve corporate performance, social responsibility and situational awareness issues may a good point to ergonomics-based risk management. If managers apply ergonomics-based risk management, they may close to effective decision-making in multi-environment of aviation. If individuals feel their values are consistent with both organizational values and aims, then they may present high individual performance to support corporate objectives.

The social responsibility concept is important for corporate performance especially in regard to stakeholder relationship management. According to Rađenović (2018), Social Responsibility is defined as the set of obligations (to behave responsibly) that an organization must protect and enhance the social context in which it functions. Areas of Social Responsibility are the following (Rađenović 2018, p. 13):

- Stakeholders: Customers, employees, and investors.
- The natural environment: Environmentally sensitive products, recycling, public safety.
- The general social welfare: Charitable contributions, support for social issues such as child labor and human rights.

Emotions are quite effective in decision-making and are experienced in the same way in this cockpit. In a landing phase, decision-making processes are usually based on rational elements such as the maximum wind speed of a given aircraft. However, emotional pressures can change rational logic by changing the decision-making criteria (Causse et al. 2013, p. 3).

Within the aviation system, there are various studies on different factors affecting situational awareness. The relationship between workload and situational awareness is examined in chapter 8 of the “Handbook of Aviation Human Factors” book by

Francis T. Durso and Amy L. Alexander, titled "Managing Workload, Performance, and Situation Awareness in Aviation Systems". (Durso and Alexander 2010, p. 217).

According to Mulenburg (2017), as managers, we get in our own way sometimes because we don't think enough and sometimes because we think too much. Thinking hard about the decision is not enough; we need to think about it in the right way. Rather than make us better decision-makers, a lot of experience in an area can sometimes blind us to alternatives because of our investment in what we've done before Mulenburg (2011, p. 12).

Human decision-making is a complex process that is strongly dependent on the environment in which the decision must be made. We all make decisions every day. Although there is no sure way to train someone to make the best decision, there are methods that improve decision-making by helping aviation professionals understand the processes underlying effective decision-making (SKYbrary 2010, p. 1).

Essentially organizational culture is about how people normally behave at the work site. You change the culture by changing behaviors and thus establish new norms for which behaviors are accepted by the workforce and which are not. The aim is to encourage workers to use behaviors that are known to be protective for safety, such as checking shared comprehension, speaking up, challenging unsafe actions, identifying errors, protecting others' situation awareness. And—to discourage unsafe behaviors such as violating procedures, distracting colleagues, poor communication, and not discussing decisions (Flin 2013, p. 1).

Human factors specialists also deal with physiological factors that could affect operator performance including workload, stress, vigilance, attention, pressure, sensory limitations, age, gender, g forces, oxygen deprivation, temperature, and many others. They also work with social factors including crew communication and teamwork, organizational influences, and cultural factors. To some extent, human factors specialists consider the impact of personality on performance. Finally, they work with cognitive factors including information processing, decision-making, language, and memory (Jensen 1997, p. 260).

Life is full of decisions. Some (e.g., deciding what to wear to work) are so routine that we are hardly aware we are making them, while others (e.g., changing jobs) take more effort because they have significant and lasting implications. Flying is also full of decisions. Many may appear to be routine, but even "small" decisions made in the cockpit can have a large impact on flight safety. Good Aeronautical Decision-Making (ADM) is, therefore, an essential pilot skill (Federal Aviation Administration 2015, p. 1).

Aviation-Specific Decision-Making in Multi-functional Environments

The majority of flight crew faults are a result of failures in the process. These processes may be in leadership, team coordination, and decision-making. As can be seen from the statistical data, the causes of accidents are almost the same, and these factors are directly or indirectly related to human factors such as human–human or human–machine interaction (Guler 2014, p. 19). Decision-making is a decisive factor. It may cause normal situations to turn into events. In this situation, the events turn into an accident (Plant and Stanton 2017, p. 24).

CDM in Aviation aims to improve operational efficiency at airports by reducing delays, improving the predictability of events during the progress of a flight and optimizing the utilization of resources (Capgemini 2017, p. 1). The activities of airlines and airports are complementary in nature, but the industry needs better coordination between all the aviation partners, i.e., Airport Operations (Airport Operators, Ground Handlers), Airlines and Air Traffic Controllers if operational efficiency is to be expected. Collaborative Decision-Making (CDM) enables the partners to share information and work together more efficiently and transparently with the common goal of improved overall performance, bringing a common situational awareness between all partners involved as well as refining the processes and information flows (Capgemini 2017, p. 1).

Recent studies on decision-making training suggest that the specific training approach may be most efficient when the decision-maker has had previous experience with similar situations. Attempting to cover the gamut of aviation decision-making contexts in a generalized manner is less efficient and may be less effective when decisions are time critical. Thus, it would appear as if it is important to emphasize context-based experiences in decision-making training (SKYbrary 2010, p. 1).

Poor situation awareness can lead to decisions that have fatal consequences (Vu et al. 2011, p. 7).

Non-Technical Skills (NTS) are the cognitive and behavioral abilities by which work is delivered safely and effectively and the main NTS are (McDonald and Evans 2016, p. 2):

i. Communication,
ii. Decision-making,
iii. Leadership,
iv. Situation awareness,
v. Stress management, and
vi. Teamwork.

Aviation knowledge acquired through training and experience is essential for proper crew decision-making. The crew is required to be knowledgeable concerning hundreds of rules, SOPs, and techniques in order to make sound "rule-based decisions". Clear, concise SOPs are essential for good rule-based decision-making (SKYbrary 2010, p. 1).

The FAA Aviation Safety Program developed a new framework for aeronautical decision-making and risk management: Perceive—Process—Perform (Federal Aviation Administration 2015, p. 1). Problems with in-flight decisions or planning include situations where a pilot elects to continue a flight with a known deficiency, continues a visual flight into adverse weather, or makes a poorly planned approach to an airfield (Bureau of Air Safety Investigation 1996, p. 6).

United Airlines is recognized as being the first company (in 1981) to explicitly address the NTS associated with working in a high-risk industry. This was in direct response to some of the findings from the investigation into the crash of Flight 173 (Denver to Portland: 28 December 1978) which found that human errors in situation awareness, decision-making, communication, and leadership led to the Controlled Flight into Terrain (CFIT) crash and 10 fatalities (McDonald and Evans 2016, p. 2).

According to Li et al. (2010), the processes of decision-making center around two elements: situation assessment, which is used as a precursor to generate one (or more) plausible courses of action and mental simulation to evaluate those courses of action for risk management purposes. However, only if a pilot recognizes there is sufficient time for making wide-ranging considerations will they evaluate the dominant response option by conducting a mental simulation to see if it is likely to work. If there is not adequate time, the pilot will tend to implement the course of action that experience (if any) dictates is the most likely to be successful (Li et al. 2010, p. 85).

Compare this with the "Miracle on the Hudson" (when US Airways flight 1549 from La Guardia to Charlotte successfully ditched in the Hudson River on January 15, 2009) where the National Transportation Safety Board (NTSB) cited NTS as being a major contributing factor in the outcome (5 serious injuries from total of 150 passengers and 5 crew) (McDonald and Evans 2016, p. 2).

Decision-making in aviation is explained as follows (https://www.skybrary.aero/index.php/Decision-Making_(OGHFA_BN) (SKYbrary 2010, p. 1):

"*Decision making is the cognitive process of selecting a course of action from among multiple alternatives. The decision-making process produces a choice of action or opinion that determines the decision maker's behavior and therefore has a profound influence on task performance. Decision making in an aeronautical environment involves any pertinent decision a pilot must make during the conduct of a flight. It includes both preflight go/no-go decisions as well as those made during the flight. In aeronautics, decision making is of particular importance because of the safety consequences of poor decisions. The U.S. Federal Aviation Administration (FAA) defines aeronautical decision making (ADM) as follows:*

ADM is a systematic approach to the mental process used by aircraft pilots to consistently determine the best course of action in response to a given set of circumstances. (FAA Advisory Circular 60–22).

Human decision making is a complex process that is strongly dependent on the environment in which the decision must be made. We all make decisions every day, such as the choice of what to have for breakfast or which road to take when driving to work. The extent to which safety considerations enter our decision making depends on the situation. Choosing cereal or bread for breakfast involves virtually no consideration of safety. Selecting a route to drive may involve some aspects of safety but is probably primarily based on travel time and, perhaps, scenery. Aviation is a complex, safety-critical endeavor. Many decisions made while flying can affect the lives of hundreds of people and have extraordinary economic consequences. Thus, even though some flight decisions are not strongly related to safety, it is best to view ADM as a safety-critical function.

Consequently, a successful decision is not necessarily the optimum or most rational decision. It is the decision the human being understands and knows how to apply effectively in the context of the situation".

Li and Harris (2006) state that "... many aeronautical decision-making mnemonic-based methods exist ...". They imply, however, that there is no empirical research that suggests that they are effective in improving decision-making. In this study, a short, ADM training course was constructed around two mnemonic methods, SHOR (Stimuli, Hypotheses, Options, and Response) and DECIDE (Detect, Estimate, Set safety objectives, Identify, Do, Evaluate). Forty-one pilots from the Republic of China Tactical Training Wing participated: half received a short ADM training course and half did not. After training, the procedural knowledge underpinning their Situation Assessment and Risk Management ability, two skills essential for successful decision-making, were evaluated using pencil and paper-based knowledge tests based upon several demanding tactical flight situations. The results show gains attributable to the decision-making training course in both situation assessment and risk management skills and the results strongly suggest that ADM is trainable and such a training course is effective in improving the bases of in-flight decision-making in their study" (Li and Harris 2006).

Li and Harris (2006) explained ADM studies as follows (Li and Harris 2006):

"Aeronautical decision-making (ADM) is defined by the FAA (1991) as 'a systematic approach to the mental process used by aircraft pilots to consistently determine the best course of action in response to a given set of circumstances' and Pilot judgement as 'the mental process that pilots use in making decisions'. Both definitions implicitly include both process and outcome. For military pilots operating in a hostile environment, the normal hazards of aviation are compounded by the enemy's intent for the destruction of the aircraft.

Risk and time pressure are situational variables that further constrain the decision process, as risk and time pressure may call for an immediate response whether or not the problem was fully understood. Minimal risk levels and fewer time constraints, in contrast, permit additional diagnostic actions or the deliberation of options.

The decision-making process centers around two processes; situation assessment, which is used as a precursor to generate a plausible course of action and mental simulation to evaluate that course of action for risk management. If a pilot recognizes there is sufficient time for making wide-ranging considerations, s/he will evaluate the dominant response option by conducting a mental simulation to see if it is likely to work. If there is not adequate time, the pilot will tend to implement the course of action that experience (if any) dictates is the most likely to be successful.

Risk management should be a key part of the decision-making process. Risk assessment feeds into decision making in two ways: during the assessment of the precipitating threats and in evaluating potential courses of action. A good decision-making process is one in which the decision maker successfully accomplishes the collection of information about a wide range of alternatives, carefully assesses the risks and benefits of each course of action and prepares contingency plans for dealing with known risks".

Li et al. (2010) state ADM research as follows (Li et al. 2010, p. 85):

"Flying a high-technology aircraft is not only an issue of skilled psychomotor performance but also of real-time decision-making involving situation awareness, choice amongst alternatives and assessment of risk within a limited-time frame (Endsley 1993, 1997; Prince and Salas 1993). Pilots must perform a wide array of tasks in addition to simply getting the aircraft from one point to another. As a result, pilots must learn to make decisions and develop judgments related to mission performance in addition to making those decisions related directly to flying the aircraft. Aeronautical decision-making (ADM) has traditionally been viewed as an intrinsic quality or as a by-product of flying experience (Buch and Diehl 1984). Jensen and Benel (1977) found that decisionerrors contributed to 35% of all nonfatal and 52% of all fatal general aviation accidents in the United States between 1970 and 1974. Furthermore, Diehl (1991) proposed that decision errors contributed to 56% of airline accidents and 53% of military accidents. More recent studies (Shappell and Wiegmann 2004) have found decision errors contributed to 45% of accidents in the USAF and 55% in the US Navy.

Experienced decision makers consider a large number of cues in building situation assessments, and under certain specific circumstances may take actions that appear contrary to those prescribed by checklist. Experts can see underlying causes and have more complex models of the problem space than novices.

For over 30 years the importance of aeronautical decision-making has been recognized as critical to the safe operation of aircraft. Decision-making is a complex cognitive process and is affected by situational and environmental conditions (Payne et al. 1988). Orasanu and Connolly (1993) have suggested that much decision-making occurs in an organizational context and that the organization influences decisions directly by stipulating standard operating procedures, and indirectly, through the organization's norms and culture. Maurino et al. *(1995) suggested that it is important to understand how decisions made by people at the sharp-end (pilots) are influenced by the actions of the people at the blunt-end of their operating worlds (i.e. the higher managerial levels in their organizations). However, there is little empirical work formally describing the relationship between organizational structures, psychological pre-cursors of accidents and the actual errors committed by pilots. Dekker (2001) proposed that human errors are systematically connected to features of peoples' tools and tasks, and as acknowledged more recently, their operational and organizational environment. Latent failures are spawned in the upper management levels of organizations which may be related to manufacturing, regulation and/or other aspects of management. As Reason (1997) noted, complex systems such as airlines are designed, operated, maintained and managed by human beings. As a result, it is not surprising that human decisions and actions are implicated in most accidents.*

In aviation, the Crew Resource Management approach helps to identify and address (mitigate) the potentially negative impact of Cognitive Bias in the workplace and thus amplify the application of positive Cognitive Bias (organizational culture) (McDonald and Evans 2016, p. 2).

It is important to remember that the pilot is part of a wider team and network of aviation personnel, many of whom have safety-critical roles where inadequate behavior and wrong decisions may impact immediately or decisively on the physical safety of passengers and crew and could ultimately lead to loss of life and resources. These people include cabin crew, air traffic control staff, flight instructors, Aviation Medical Examiners (AMEs), safety managers, aircraft engineers, maintenance personnel, baggage handlers, and dispatchers, among others (Bor 2017).

Multi-criteria Problem-Solving and Decision-Making Process

With respect to the importance of decision-making and the effects that it has by allowing ourselves the opportunity to investigate the applicability of an alternative decision solving model as in the Analytical Hierarchy Process (AHP) it will provide a platform to address complex problem in a more systematic and effective way (Zainuddin et al. 2012, p. 640).

Kadoić et al. (2017) state that:

"when researchers talk about multi-criteria decision making, many methods can be used. The most well-known multi-criteria decision-making method is the analytic hierarchy process (AHP). In that method, the decision-making problem is decomposed into a hierarchy. At the top of the hierarchy is the decision-making goal. The criteria are on the next level, which can be decomposed to the sub-criteria (and further decomposed to the lower levels). On the last level are the alternatives. By using pairwise comparisons (to be explained later in this paper), local priorities of alternatives as well as criteria weights are calculated. Then, it is possible to calculate the global priorities of alternatives and make decisions. In the decision-making problem field, if influences/dependencies exist between criteria, which the AHP does not consider, using the AHP might lead to a decision that is less than optimal. In those cases, using the analytic network process (ANP) is more appropriate. By using the ANP, we can model the dependencies and feedback between the decision-making elements, and calculate more precise weights of criteria, and local and global priorities of alternatives". (Kadoic et al. 2017, p. 1)

Saaty (2008) explained that:

"The Analytic Hierarchy Process (AHP) is a theory of relative measurement with absolute scales of both tangible and intangible criteria based on the judgment of knowledgeable and expert people. How to measure intangibles is the main concern of the mathematics of the AHP. In the end, we must fit our entire world experience into our system of priorities if we are going to understand it. The AHP reduces a multidimensional problem into a one dimensional one. Decisions are determined by a single number for the best outcome or by a vector of priorities that gives an ordering of the different possible outcomes. We can also combine our judgements or our final choices obtained from a group when we wish to cooperate to agree on

a single outcome. Analytic Network Process (ANP) is the common method to solve Multi-Criteria Decision Making problems and is also used to calculate priorities of factors. The Analytic Network Process (ANP) is a generalization of the Analytic Hierarchy Process (AHP), by considering the dependence between the elements of the hierarchy. Many decision problems cannot be structured hierarchically because they involve the interaction and dependence of higher-level elements in a hierarchy on lower level elements. Therefore, ANP is represented by a network, rather than a hierarchy" (Saaty, The Analytic Network Process 2008, p. 2).

Dağdeviren et al. (2006) indicated that:

*"The ANP method, developed by Saaty (*2001*) takes account of the relationships among the factors in the decision-making process and removes the necessity of modelling by adhering to a single direction of the problem. The problem of decision making in ANP method is modelled by a network structure and the dependencies between the factors and the internal dependencies within the factor are considered in the modelling phase. With this structure, the ANP method ensures that decision-making problems are solved more effectively and realistically"* (Dağdeviren and Kurt 2006, p. 248).

Sometimes decision-makers find difficulty assigning value to the criteria they have to assess. To solve the problem the weights of the criteria must be determined because criteria are not equally important. By determining the weight of the criteria, a value can thus be assigned to the criteria to indicate its importance relative to the other criteria under consideration. The larger the weight, the more the important or preferred the criterion. Decision-makers will then be able to identify the "best" alternative and order the alternatives in rank of preference (Zainuddin et al. 2012, p. 640).

AHP is a flexible approach and allows individuals or groups to shape ideas and define problems by making their own assumptions and deriving the desired solution from them. It takes into consideration the relative importance of factors in a system and enables people to rank the alternatives based on their goals (Ahmadi et al. 2010, p. 223).

According to Ecer et al. (2009) to:

"show a decision problem in the form of a network model, the problem is first divided into parts. Each of the parts is called a cluster and the subparts of the clusters are called factor. In the graphical representation of the network model, the clusters form node points. The interactions between the clusters are indicated by arrows and the direction of the arrow indicates the direction of effect. Because of the feedback and dependency properties of ANP, factors may be dependent on other factors as well as on themselves. Dependency between clusters is called external dependency and dependency within a cluster is called internal dependency. With internal and external dependencies, interactions both within cluster and between clusters are revealed. By defining the priorities, it is seen as an advantage of the ANP that bridge between the factors and aims, determine the priorities with a proportional scale, include the qualitative and quantitative criteria in the models, enable decision makers to reach consensus and a large number of decision-makers can take part in the decision process" (Ecer et al. 2009, p. 191).

Table 5.1 Pairwise comparison scale (Görener 2012, p. 195; Dağdeviren and Yüksel 2007, p. 103)

Intensity of importance	Explanation
1	Two criteria contribute equally to the objective
3	Experience and judgement slightly favor one over another
5	Experience and judgment strongly favor one over another
7	Criterion is strongly favored, and its dominance is demonstrated in practice
9	Importance of one over another affirmed on the highest possible order
2, 4, 6, 8	Used to represent compromise between the priorities listed above

The ANP method is comprised of four steps (Görener 2012, p. 195) (Dağdeviren and Yüksel 2007, p. 103) (İ. 2007) (Dağdeviren and Kurt 2006, p. 248):

Step 1: Model construction and problem structuring: The problem should be stated clearly and decomposed into a rational system like a network.

Step 2: Pairwise comparisons and priority vectors: In ANP, like AHP, pairs of decision elements at each cluster are compared with respect to their importance toward their control criteria. In addition, interdependencies among the criteria of a cluster must also be examined pairwise; the influence of each element on other elements can be represented by an eigenvector. The relative importance values are determined with the Saaty's scale (see Table 5.1).

Step 3: Supermatrix formation: The supermatrix concept is similar to the Markov chain process. To obtain global priorities in a system with interdependent influences, the local priority vectors are entered in the appropriate columns of a matrix. As a result, a supermatrix is actually a partitioned matrix, where each matrix segment represents a relationship between two clusters in a system.

Step 4: Synthesis of the criteria and alternatives' priorities and selection of the best alternatives: The priority weights of the criteria and alternatives can be found in the normalized supermatrix.

Since the aviation sector is highly variable and volatile, in aviation business managers generally have multi-criteria problems to make a decision in a timely manner. Kucuk Yilmaz (2017) has used Multi-criteria decision-making process in her last studies. Her research problem is dealt with as a "Multi-Criteria Decision-Making" (MCDM) problem because many criteria must be taken into consideration. In these researches, Kucuk Yilmaz used the ANP method based on BOCR criteria which are defined as criteria of benefit, opportunity, cost, and risk in relation to the criterion because of the relationship and interaction (Yazgan and Kucuk Yılmaz 2018, p. 1047).

Because the modeling of interconnected flight network is also interrelated with issues such as flight planning, crew, and fleet planning, strategies should be evaluated as risk-based and strategic human resource management must be accomplished successfully and effectively, as stated in Flouris and Yılmaz's article (2010). Connected flight is a second aircraft which a passenger should arrive on time to catch, and which will take him or her to the final destination. To determine flight destinations, graph theoretical measures were frequently used for the description of airline and aviation networks and transport networks in general. In this research, a qualified connection was explained as "a commercially sustainable, rantable, optimum, advantageous to compete, operationally feasible, and sufficient to flights (Flouris and Yilmaz 2010, p. 30). For this reason, the assessment and selection of the applicability of the developed interconnected flight network model for sustainability have been dealt with as a multi-criteria decision problem. The graph theory lists the possibilities of flight destinations without considering the benefit, opportunity, cost, and risk. In cases where statistical data is missing, ANP (Analytical Network Process) is a more effective method for use of multi-criteria decision-making problems dependent on concrete and abstract parameters requiring subjective evaluation, and for solving problems involving relations among system elements (Yazgan and Kucuk Yılmaz 2018, p. 1047).

Yazgan and Kucuk Yılmaz (Working Paper) implied that airline business management is set on airworthy strategy and airline sustainability is dependent upon corporate-based airworthy strategy since airworthiness is base to any airline business management and strategy. They also stated that an airline can ensize its corporate sustainability if it has both an airworthiness strategy and risk management. An important condition of surviving in the airline business is the ability of an airline to maintain airworthiness in regard to fleet, maintenance, and corporate risk management. However, Aircraft Maintenance Technician (AMT) has a dual role in aircraft maintenance systems as the source of failure in maintenance process via his volatility and unmanageable qualifications and secondly as a source of management to maintain airworthiness of the aircrafts in the airline. Situational awareness of managers about both limitations and qualifications of human factors is a vital determinant to the decision-making process in aviation. Although continuously improving in related literature, one of the biggest weaknesses of current methods of AMT error or performance, is the ability to model the reciprocal effects of the factors affecting the fault is limited.

For this reason, an Analytic Network Process (ANP) model is developed that considers the effects of mutual dependences among factors in their study. First, with the help of experts and extensive literature, 67 factors that contributed to AMT error are identified and grouped. Then, the factors identified as eligible to be accepted as criteria and sub-criteria that contributed to AMT error are determined. In their study, the weights of identified criteria that have an influence on AMT error are determined using the ANP method. ANP is a common method to solve Multi-Criteria Decision-Making problems and is also used to calculate priorities of factors. Criteria determined in their study are classified into three main clusters: individual-related criteria, working environment-related criteria, and organizational-related criteria. These main clusters include 15 sub-criteria such as communication, documentation (quality/updating/availability), peer pressure, etc.

The result of the abovementioned study by Yazgan and Kucuk Yılmaz shows that time pressure, organization's culture, and safety culture and supervision are the most important criteria that contributed to AMT error. Their weights are 0.207,

0.172, 0.102, and 0.094, respectively. There are many difficulties and limitations in measuring the factors that have an influence on AMT error. For this reason, the weights of criteria and sub-criteria necessary are determined by using ANP, and by this way, it is possible to make better decisions in this process as ANP is a multi-criteria decision-making technique that takes into consideration qualitative factors in decision-making problems. The factors taxonomy was created as a result of combining expert opinion with extant academic literature and the ANP model was developed by taking into account factor dependencies.

Yazgan and Ustun (2011) explained that the pilot selection process has been a focal point of many researchers in aviation literature. The selection of candidate pilots is very important because the training of pilots is very costly and time-consuming process. In their study, we try to determine the weights of selection criteria for civil pilots. Criteria determined in their study are classified into three main clusters: Technical Criteria, Non-Technical Criteria, and Job-Related Criteria. These main clusters include 15 sub-criteria such as personality traits, spatial ability, teamwork aptitude, etc., which are then weighed by using the Analytic Network Process (ANP) tool. ANP is a multi-criteria decision-making technique that takes into consideration also qualitative factors in decision-making problems. An ANP model including dependency between these criteria is developed; then pairwise comparisons of criteria are done by instructors. The result of their study shows that intelligence, decision-making, and problem-solving ability and psychomotor skills are the three most important selection criteria (Yazgan and Ustun 2011, p. 10).

Network design in airline management is a process in which decision-makers consider many factors together with corporate strategy. The direct or indirect effects of these factors on each other also reveal their relations. Due to relations and interactions between criterions, benefit, opportunity cost and risk modules defined as BOCR criteria based on ANP methods will be used in Yilmaz's Project (2017) (see Fig. 5.3). ANP is a multi-criteria decision-making technique that takes into consideration also qualitative factors in decision-making problems.

In order to make an optimum decision about flight network, it is suggested to select the optimum flight alternatives by following the suggested pre-selection process steps and then using the developed Analytical Network Process model. In this study, the Analytical Network Process was chosen as the most suitable choice among the alternatives of optimum flight routes, so that the Analytical Network Processor should be able to handle all the dependencies and feedback between the criteria and the qualitative, quantitative, abstract or concrete. It is the first and most comprehensive mathematical theory that makes it possible to use all kinds of data in the decision-making process and to make decisions as a group. On the other hand, today, airlines address the concept of sustainability in order to ensure the continuity of their development. The concept of sustainability has been built on three main dimensions: economic, environmental, and social. If the concept of sustainability is taken up by a business, it turns out that for a corporate's development to be sustainable, it must have not only economic but also environmental and social superior performance. After determining the relationships among all the elements included in the proposed

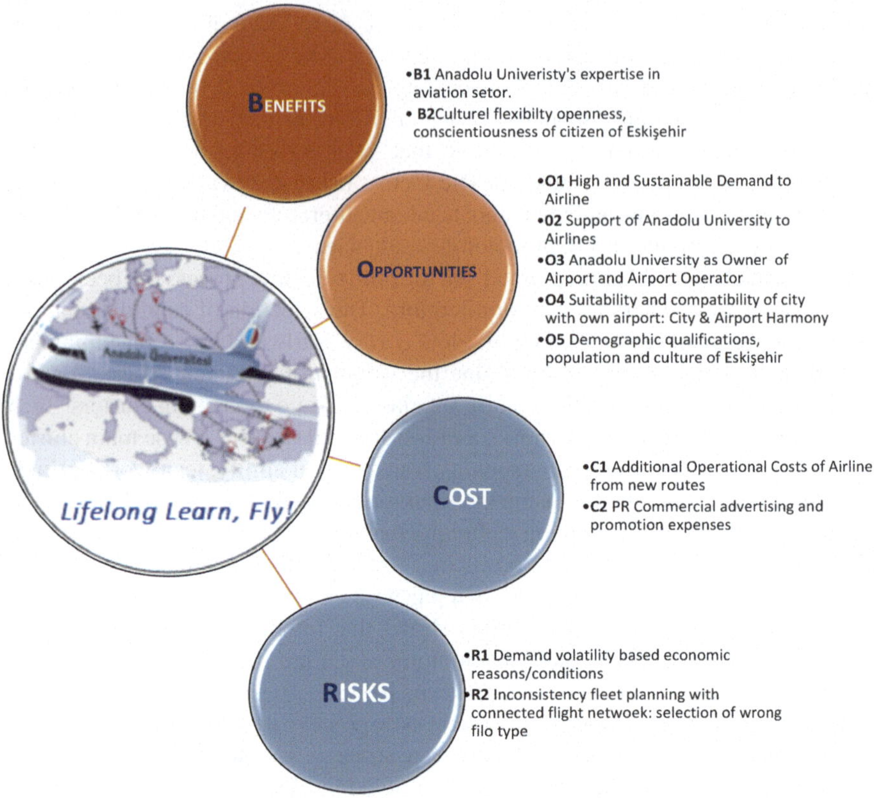

Fig. 5.3 Diagram for BOCR Criteria of Grid Flight Network at Anadolu University Airport AOE (Kucuk Yilmaz, A, Source and Need Equation II: AOE Hasan Polatkan Airport Network Modelling Scientific Project 2017)

ANP model and making related connections, pairwise comparisons were made by using expert opinions and the model was synthesized and the results were obtained.

The following follow chart, to achieve corporate performance in the way of corporate value and socially responsible style, managers consider their human resource value drives. Individuals have the potential to pose an effect on organizational culture. Ergonomics is a key issue in contemporary business management. Managers should have high and improved situational awareness level based on the mentality of enterprise risk management. So, they may achieve sustainability goals as value-based approach.

References

Ahmadi, Alireza, Suprakash Gupta, Ramin Karim, and Uday Kumar. 2010. Selection of maintenance strategy for aircraft systems using multi-criteria decision making methodologies. *International Journal of Reliability, Quality and Safety Engineering* 17 (3): 223–243.

Albright, James. 2015. How Pilots Intuitively Make Critical Decisions. *Aviation week*. 10 24, 2015, 1. http://aviationweek.com/business-aviation/how-pilots-intuitively-make-critical-decisions. Accessed 28 Feb 2018.

Bor, Robert, et al. 2017. Position statement Aviation and aerospace psychology: Pilot mental health and wellbeing. *The British Psychological Society*, 11 2017. https://www.bps.org.uk/sites/beta.bps.org.uk/files/News%20-%20Files/PP11%20WEB.pdf. Accessed 28 Feb 2018.

Bureau of Air Safety Investigation, BASI. 1996. Human Factors in FAtal Aircraft Accidents. 04 1996, 6. https://www.atsb.gov.au/media/28363/sir199604_001.pdf. Accessed 27 Feb 2018.

Bush, G L and SR Diehl. 1984. An evolutionary and applied perspective of insect biotypes. *Annual Review of Entomology* 29: 471–504. https://doi.org/10.1146/annurev.en.29.010184.002351.

Capgemini. 2017. Collaborative decision making in aviation. 07 2017, 1. https://www.capgemini.com/wp-content/uploads/2017/07/Collaborative_Decision_Making_in_Aviation.pdf Accessed 28 Feb 2018.

Causse, Mickaël, Frédéric Dehais, Patrice Péran, Umberto Sabatini, and Josette Pastor. 2013. The effects of emotion on pilot decision-making: A neuroergonomic approach to aviation safety. *Transportation Research Part C: Emerging Technologies* 33 (3): 272–281.

Civil Aviation Safety Authority Australia, CASA. 2018. *Aviation Safety Management An Operator's Guide*, p. 3. http://www.caa.lv/upload/userfiles/files/SMS/CASA/CASA%20SMS%20small%20operators.pdf. Accessed 28 Feb 2018.

Corporate Culture, Ethics, and Leadership by Lawrence Stokes.http://slideplayer.com/slide/5757738/. January 25, 2018

Dağdeviren, M., N. Dönmez, and M. Kurt. 2006. Bir işletmede tedarikçi değerlendirme süreci için yeni bir model tasarımı ve uygulaması. *Gazi Üniversitesi Mühendislik ve Mimarlık Fakültesi Dergisi* 21 (2): 247–255.

Dağdeviren, M., and İ. Yüksel. 2007. Personnel selection using analytic network process. *İstanbul Ticaret Üniversitesi Fen Bilimleri Dergisi, Year 6* (11): 99–118.

Durso, Francis T., and Amy L. Alexander. 2010. Managing workload, performance, and situation awareness in aviation systems. In *Handbook of aviation human factors,* 2nd ed. John A. Wise, David V. Hopkin and Daniel J. Garland, 217–247. Boca Raton, Florida: CRC Press.

Ecer, F., S. Açikgözoğlu, and F. Yaman. 2009. Analitik Ağ Süreci (AAS) ve Web Sitelerinden Yararlanarak Otel Seçimi. *H.Ü. İktisadi ve İdari Bilimler Fakültesi Dergisi* 27 (1): 187–207.

Federal Aviaiton Administration (FAA). 2015. The Art of Aeronautical Decision-Making, p. 1 https://www.faasafety.gov/files/gslac/courses/content/28/216/The%20Art%20of%20Aeronautical%20Decision.pdf. Accessed 27 Feb 2018.

Flin, Rhona. 2013. The power of behaviour: Non-technical skills. *Veiligheidskunde* 1.

Flouris, T.G., and A. Kucuk Yilmaz. 2010. The risk management framework to strategic human resource management. *International Research Journal of Finance and Economics Issue 36* (2010): 25–45.

Görener, A. 2012. Comparing AHP and ANP: An application of strategic decisions making in a manufacturing company. *International Journal of Business and Social Science 3* (11): 194–208.

Guler, Nurdan Kubal. PİLOTLARDA PSİKOSOSYAL RİSKLERİN BELİRLENMESİ. Ankara: ÇALIŞMA VE SOSYAL GÜVENLİK BAKANLIĞI İŞ SAĞLIĞI VE GÜVENLİĞİ GENEL MÜDÜRLÜĞÜ, 2014, p.19.

Jensen, Richard S. 1997. The boundaries of aviation psychology, human factors, aeronautical decision making, situation awareness, and crew resource management. *The International Journal of Aviation Psychology* 7 (4): 259–267.

Kadoić, N., N.B. Ređep, and B. Divjak. 2017. Decision making with the analytic network process. In *The 14th international symposium on operational research, Slovenia*, p. 1.

Li, W-C., and D. Harris. 2006. SHOR and DESIDE: Evaluating the effectiveness of ADM training using a flight simulator. In *Proceedings of the human factors and ergonomics society 50th annual meeting, San Francisco, CA*.

Li, Wen-Chin, D. Harris, Lun-Wen Li, Yueh-Ling Hsu, and T. Wang. 2010. Investigating accidents related to errors of aeronautical decision-making in flight operations. In *Proceedings of the 41st annual international seminar: investigating asia in mind–accurate speedy, independent, and authentic, Sapporo, Japan*, 82–88.

McDonald, Alan, and David Evans. Introduction to Non-Technical Skills (NTS) Introduction to Non-Technical Skills (NTS)—V011. *Corpress*. 2016, 2. http://www.corpress.uk/wp-content/uploads/2016/05/Introduction-to-Non-Technical-Skills-NTS.pdf. Accessed 28 Feb 2018.

Mulenburg, Jerry. 2011. Crew resource management improves decision making. *Insight Ask Magazine* 42: 11–13.

Plant, Katherine L., and Neville A. Stanton. 2017. The development of the Schema-Action-World (SAW) taxonomy for understanding decision making in aeronautical critical incidents. *Sefety Science Part A* 99: 23–35.

Prince, C., and Salas, E. 1993. Training and research for teamwork in the military aircrew. In E. L. Wiener, B. G. Kanki, & R. L. Helmreich (eds.), *Cockpit resource management*, 337–366. San Diego, CA, US: Academic Press

Rađenović, Saša. 2018. *Corporate culture, ethics and leadership*, 13. http://www.academia.edu/2362289/Corporate_Culture_Ethics_and_Leadership. Accessed 27 Feb 2018.

Saaty, T.L. 2001. *Decision making with dependence and feedback: The analytic network process*, 2nd ed. Pittsburgh, USA: RWS Publications.

Saaty, T.L. 2008. The analytic network process. *Iranian Journal of Operations Research* 1 (2): 1–27.

SKYbrary. 2010. Decision-Making Training (OGHFA BN), 1. https://www.skybrary.aero/index.php/Decision-Making_Training_(OGHFA_BN. Accessed 26 Oct 2010.

Vu, Kim-Phuong L., Thomas Z. Strybel, Vernol Battiste, and Walter Johnson. 2011. Factors influencing the decisions and actions of pilots and air traffic controllers in three plausible NextGen environments. In *Factors influencing the decisions and actions of pilots and air traffic controllers in three plausible nextgen environments*, ed. Kim-Phuong L. Vu, Thomas Z. Strybel, Vernol Battiste and Walter Johnson, vol. 37, 7. Long Beach, CA: NASA.

Yazgan, E, and K.A. Ustun. 2011. Application of analytic network process: Weighting of selection criteria for civil pilots. *Journal of Aeronautics and Space Technologies* 5 (2): 1–12.

Yazgan, E., and A. Kucuk Yılmaz. 2018. Multi criteria decision making process for modelling of network design to improve regional avitation in Turkey: Case of Anadolu University. *International Journal of Eurasia Social Sciences* 1047–1065.

Zainuddin, Nizamuddin, Abdul Ghani, Dayang Shalbia, and Adam Mohd Saifudin. 2012. Analytic Hierarchy Process (AHP) in multi criteria decision making: A case of locating the operations of low cost carrier in Malaysia. *World Academy of Science, Engineering and Technology* 72: 638–650.

Chapter 6
An Innovative, Human Behavior, and Social Psychology-Based Approach to Risk Analysis Tools and Techniques: Strategic Risk Mapping

Contents

Corporate Strategy and Risk

The purpose of the existence of businesses is to create value for their partners. Value creation is carried out through the use of resources covering human, capital, and technology. Businesses maintain their values by focusing on people, processes, systems, and activities. They create sustainable value through activities within the scope of product/service quality, production capacity, and customer satisfaction. The value is eroded by poor strategies and practices, inadequate information about risks and opportunities, and incomplete activities. The value is created, maintained, or degraded by management decisions taken by the organization to achieve its objectives and through strategy development for its activities. The well-designed and high-performance risk management system presents opportunities to add value to both stakeholders and policyholders while minimizing corporate threats.

Business exists to secure opportunities based on taking risks. No business is profitable without controlled risk-taking and its effective management. Consequently, risk management is a core function of all types of business (Acharyya 2013, p. 2).

The global competition and restructuring pressures not only increased the institutional risks but also had implications for management and organizational structure. Potential events are included within the scope of risk management. Uncertainty and risk are directly proportional, and as the uncertainty increases, the likelihood of the risk occurring increases. While uncertainty includes both negative and positive components, the negative component of uncertainty is a risk and the positive component

A. Kucuk Yilmaz and T. G. Flouris, *Values, Ergonomics and Risk Management in Aviation Business Strategy*, https://doi.org/10.1007/978-981-15-1006-9_6

is an opportunity. But the concepts of risk and uncertainty also have intertwined common features. In order to determine whether an event is a risk or not, the source and the effects of that event must be determined with the right tools and techniques.

Strategic Risk Mapping: Human Behavıor and Socıal Psychology-Based Approach

Risk management is a central part of the strategic management of any organization. It is the process whereby organizations methodically address the risks attached to their activities (AIRMIC 2010, p. 7). Holistic approach helps give organizations a true perspective on the magnitude and importance of different risks (Casualty Actuarial Society 2003, p. 6).

In business, defining the most efficient techniques for enterprise risk detection, using and categorizing them under certain groups within the management of defined risks is the main purpose of this stage.

Risk management techniques are determined in accordance with the strategy of the company and according to the objectives. A variety of techniques that require very different and different parameters are used to identify and identify risks. It may be advantageous to choose techniques that are compatible with the organization's self-determination. These techniques are interview, workshop, brainstorming, survey, and benchmarking. The organization structure, organizational capabilities, and resources should also be taken into account when choosing techniques for risk management.

Following the stage of choosing an appropriate technique for risk detection, risks must be categorized with their sources. For every business, the definition of the risk differs according to its measurement and management strategy with the way in which it handles the risks. Therefore, the stage of the risk categorization has no just one right way. While categorizing the risks, besides the risks that caused the business to lose money, the risks that have not caused any loss but may cause trouble in the future must be included in the categorization. Besides, for every risk that has been categorized, a key risk factor must be defined, the overlapping of the risk must be prevented. Also, while categorizing the risks, it must be thought in cause and effect relationship, the reasons for the possible loss of the business must be analyzed well. At the stage of risk identification, risk analysis, and risk categorization, negotiations with the top management are extremely important for the risk appetite. At this stage, it will be extremely beneficial to study the best sample applications (benchmark) in the sector.

At first, making a preanalysis, gathering the risks that have similar characteristics together, taking the risks that have less importance of the content will be beneficial in risk analysis for the business. After that, a detailed analysis must be made. But the development of risks that were left out of the content must be recorded and observed. The businesses must make a current situation analysis with respect to the risk analysis. In order to relieve the risks, the weak and strong sides of the current process, equipment, and applications of the business must be analyzed well.

The first step in measuring the risks is to detect the losses the business is liable to face and to evaluate the possibilities of occurrence and the intensity of these losses. An event may have more than one outcome for a business and many effects on making various business goals real. Therefore, while defining the importance levels of the risks, just their effects and possibilities shouldn't be considered. Their importance levels must be defined by gathering their possible effects on the business and their accrual possibilities together by using the statistical analysis and calculations (TIBA 2008). The accrual possibility in the future of an event is similar to the repetitions experienced in the past. But, while predicting the accrual possibility of an event, taking the changing product and services with marketing and market conditions into consideration will be beneficial for a healthy prediction. While predicting the accrual possibilities of the frequent events, it will be a right approach to proportion the repetition number that happened at a certain time in the past to the total accrual number. But, while predicting the possibility of infrequent events to occur in the future, it will be appropriate to create a make scenario analysis. With a scenario analysis technique, which is used mostly for the uncertain and doubtful situations and which has subjective features, the accrual possibilities of every scenario developed for unexpected events and the dimension of the operational risks taking their potential effects into consideration are tried to be defined. The importance level of the events is calculated according to their effect and accrual possibility. The importance level of the events is the result that shows the importance of the risks and their criticality levels (Kucuk Yilmaz 2007).

The risks must be analyzed carefully before being measured. There are types of risk analyses that differ depending on the risk to be analyzed, the aim of the analysis, the level of the accessed information and sources. Risk analysis types are qualitative, quantitative, semiquantitative or, as a combination of them, combined analysis. With respect to complexity and cost, it is possible to count them from top level to the lowest one as: quantitative, semiquantitative, and qualitative. Also, for analysis of the suitability of the responses to be given to the risks in ERM, sensitivity analysis can be used, too.

Qualitative Analysis

It is an analysis type that defines the accrual possibilities of the events and the levels of their potential effects as the results that emerge with the personal judgements of the analysers using the scales of words. Qualitative analysis is arranged according to needs. In this analysis type, different definitions for different risks can be used (TIBA 2008).

It is possible to state the conditions in which qualitative analyses are used as the following:

- In situations where the risk level cannot meet the time and effort for detailed risk analysis.
- At the stage of preparation made for risk detection that needs more detailed analysis.
- If the qualitative risk analysis method is thought to be adequate for the decisions to be made.
- If the needed sources are inadequate for quantitative analysis.
- If the structural features of the risk make this analysis type necessary.
- If acquiring and analyzing the data is not suitable in terms of the cost.
- When the risks don't make measuring possible, the qualitative risk analysis method is used.

In the qualitative risk analysis method, data, related to the experiences of the past, is used as much as possible.

Semiquantitative Analysis

In this analysis type, different from the qualitative analysis type, numbers take place of the words used in scales. With semiquantitative analysis, supplying an opportunity for the application of more extended rating scales is aimed. Rating, as in the qualitative analysis, is defined with the personal judgements of the analyser. Thus, for risks, rating at the scale doesn't contain the effect and possibility prediction's rated levels. Semiquantitative risk analysis may be inefficient in showing the differences between risks whose potential effects and accrual possibilities are extremely high (TIBA 2008). Semiquantitative analysis, which provides an order of magnitude for only analytical goals, ensures prioritizing the risks in detail in addition to the results attained with qualitative analysis. But it doesn't give real rates as in the quantitative analyses (Gunes 2009).

Quantitative Analysis

Quantitative risk analysis is a method that applies to quantitative methods when calculating the risks. Quantitative methods used in the quantitative risk analysis may be complicated techniques like simulation models as well as being basic techniques such as probability and reliability theorems. In a quantitative analysis, numerical values are given to the possibility of a dangerous event and to the values as the effects of the danger. These numerical values are given with mathematical and logical methods. Thus, the risk value is found. There were also several common methods and principles interviewees mentioned when managers analyze and communicate risk at their organizations. Managers agree that these methods were important to ensure decision-makers understood risk analyses and were enabled to make risk-informed decisions (USA Department of Homeland Security 2010, p. 5).

Risk = the possibility of a dangerous event = the effect of the danger.

The formula is the basic formula of the quantitative risk analysis. Actually, risk may both measure and analysis with integrated approach quantitatively or qualitatively. Managers may decide what to do about the risk according to measurement results.

Sensitivity Analysis

Flexibility has vital qualification to do best analysis according to parameters. Under normal circumstances, it is possible to find the effects of any changes in the sources or constraints by resolving the linear programming model. However, resolving this way is often unnecessary, because it is possible to reach a different optimal solution with the same fundamental variable. Here, sensitivity analysis tries to determine the effect of such a change from the optimal solution table before it is resolved again. Sensitivity analysis examines the effect of changing the coefficient values determined in a linear programming problem on the optimal solution of the problem. It is examined whether the coefficients in the model are uncertain and how they will affect the optimal solution by changing in later periods. If it is observed that there will be a difference in the optimal solution as a result of this change, the problem must be solved again. In the sensitivity analysis, changes in the objective function and constraint coefficients and source values and the change in the optimal solution if a new variable and a new constraint are added are examined. Sensitivity analysis is used for defining the flexibility of the model in some certain scenarios and defining the effects of the uncertainty on hypothesis and the data used. Also, it is used for the analysis of the suitability of the responses to be given in both risk management, project and quality management process applications.

Prioritizing the Risks

Risk priority of businesses' is defined with respect to their vision and missions. Before deciding on how the risks will be managed, the risk appetite and risk tolerance borders of the business must be known well. The biggest aim of prioritizing the risks is to decide on which risks must be addressed first.

With this respect, there are three reasons for measuring the risks:

- Defining and calculating the effect the business' goals made,
- Defining the risk tolerance, and
- Prioritizing the risks.

While detecting the importance levels of the risks, they are categorized as the risks at low, medium, and high levels. At the end of this categorization, responses to be given to the risks are defined. While an immediate response must be given to the risks at high level of importance, the risks at less importance level are evaluated and an emergency plan is developed. While deciding on the responses to be given to the risks at medium levels, the risks important at low levels are observed periodically. Prioritizing the risks means ordering the risks in view of their effect on accrual time and the institution's success. The levels of the risks' effect and possibility are the biggest signs of their importance levels. First, their accrual possibilities and potential effects on the business are detected. Later comes the stage where the needed precaution is taken for the risk by detecting its importance level. A point that must be given attention to is that not only the risks that have certain importance but also the risks that are considered unimportant for the business shouldn't be ignored. The risks that are considered unimportant must always be under control. That they continue to be unimportant especially in consideration of the changing environmental conditions and external events must be ensured (HKICPA 2005).

A risk mapping strategy builds on the organization's vision to provide the organization with a well-defined pathway for the future. This strategy helps move away from the focus on individual risk analysis component missions to a much broader and integrated goal structure (World Custom Organizations 2015, p. 5). Risk assessment is a vital part of risk management (Yildiz et al. 2014, p. 148). Risk mapping is not a new concept, but one which several international organizations have looked into and where they have advocated a series of approaches in different sectors (health, education, etc.) (World Custom Organizations 2015, p. 5).

Correlations among risks and an enterprise-wide approach are critical (IMA 2007, p. 14). There is a need to understand the risks being taken when seeking to achieve objectives and attain the desired level of reward. Organizations need to understand the overall level of risk embedded within their processes and activities. It is important for organizations to recognize and prioritize significant risks and identify the weakest critical controls (AIRMIC 2010, p. 3).

Risk mapping is a cost-effective tool to incorporate risk awareness and institute risk management into a company's management and operational processes. As the process is used management will, over time, become comfortable in its role as a risk manager and begin to incorporate risk management into all aspects of its role within the company (Wilkinson et al. 2003). A risk mapping strategy builds on the organization's vision to provide the organization with a well-defined pathway for the future. This strategy helps move away from the focus on individual risk analysis component missions to a much broader and integrated goal structure (World Custom Organizations 2015, p. 8). Organizations gradually moved from the traditional silo toward a holistic perspective when integrating their risk management tools and techniques at the corporate level (Acharyya 2013, p. 8).

In the ISO Guide by AIRMIC, the risk management process can be presented as lists of coordinated activities in which the components listed below are usually present. This list represents the 7Rs and 4Ts of (hazard) risk management:

- recognition or identification of risks,
- ranking or evaluation of risks,
- responding to significant risks: tolerate, treat, transfer, and terminate,
- resourcing controls,
- reaction planning,
- reporting and monitoring risk performance, and
- reviewing the risk management framework.

A holistic approach helps give organizations a true perspective on the magnitude and importance of different risks (Casualty Actuarial Society 2003, p. 6). A risk map helps companies to identify and prioritize the risks associated with their business. It is a tool to model risk assessment and give guidance for risk transfer decisions. A risk map is often presented as a two-dimensional matrix with the likelihood versus risk impact (Bozzelli 2018, p. 1). Strategies for risk mapping will vary from organization to organization. Organizational objectives arise out of the institutional risk culture. These objectives help determine the organization's risk tolerance level (World Custom Organizations 2015, p. 7).

As a step toward operationalising their definition of ERM, COSO (2004) produced their ERM Integrated Framework, which discusses ERM according to the following aspects (Taylor and Wang 2013, p. 4): internal environment; objective setting; event identification; risk assessment; risk response; control activities; information and communication; monitoring.

The main steps involved in value-based risk management include: a. identification (determination) of risk and its sources, b. evaluation and analysis of corporate risks, c. prioritization of risk to both resource allocation and selecting handling strategies, and d. developing a risk map, performance analysis of ERM implementation results, gap analysis ideal aims with practice, control and improvement practices to ERM system performance.

In the first stages of the ERM cycle, risk management techniques tend to be rather qualitative than quantitative. At later stages, or when more information on specific risks has become available, the use of quantitative techniques increases (Treasury today 2007, p. 1).

It is important to use appropriate techniques and methodologies for risk assessment, risk analysis, risk map generation, risk management, high-performance implementation, and ideal-application gap. Risk management as a field is a management discipline that has its own techniques and principles that must be understood by the business organizations (Chauke and Sebola 2018, p. 2).

The identification techniques are based on working groups called brainstorming, the nominal group technique, and Delphi (Chapman 1998, p. 335).

- Common techniques include (Taylor et al. 2011):
  - Surveys,
  - Workshops,
  - Management interviews,
  - Environment scans,

- SWOT analysis, and
- Results of audits.

Risk analysis aims to provide a corporate risk profile. A risk profile proves very useful to the decision-making process. Risk analysis provides the opportunity to understand which events may affect the targets. By way of analysis, the likelihood of the impact of the risk, the likelihood of occurrence and also the relationship with other risks are also determined.

Risk analysis has two types. The first is Qualitative Risk Analysis, which is the process in which the probability of realization of defined risks and the effective power are evaluated. In particular, by applying the opinions of experts, the analysis aims to identify both types and source of the risks and their impacts In order to perform qualitative risk analysis, you need a risk management plan, defined risks, probability and impact scaling used in your organization and the assumptions defined at the beginning of the project. Using tools and techniques, such as risk probability and impact research, probability/impact matrix generation, detailed analysis of assumptions, and data accuracy ranking, you can expose the project's overall risk threat ranking, trends, and prevention ideas of risks.

The second type is Quantitative Risk Analysis. This is the study of determining the threats of risks with more numerical values by taking lessons from the past. At this stage, inputs in the qualitative risk analysis are needed. All types of risk analysis use the following tools and techniques in general means:

- Sensitivity Analysis.
- Decision Tree Analysis.
- Simulation.
- SWOT Analysis.
- Management Interviews.
- Possible Error Types and Effects Analysis Method (FMEA):
  - L Type Matrix Method: Risk = Probability × Violence.
  - Fine-Kinney Method: Risk = Probability × Frequency × Violence.
  - Hazard Analysis Method.
  - Event Tree Analysis Method.
  - Risk Assessment Decision Matrix Method.
  - Error Tree Analysis Method.
  - Risk Map Method.
  - Human Error Analysis Method.
  - If so Analysis Method.
  - Reason-Result Analysis Method.

The output of the prioritization stage can take various forms (Treasury today 2007):

- Risk matrix chart: This type of graph represents each risk on a two-dimensional graph with one axis indicating the potential severity of a risk and the second axis

the likelihood of the risk occurring. Depending on the position of the risk on the chart it can be identified as a lower or more significant risk.
- Risk mapping: Again, individual risks are plotted on a graph according to potential impact and probability of occurrence. In addition, iso-risk curves are drawn on the graph. These lines visually separate low-risk areas from areas representing significant risks.
- Probability-impact tables: P-I tables follow the same principle to assess the relative importance of risks. The probability of occurrence and potential impact are assessed using a scoring system for each attribute. Both scores are then multiplied to arrive at a single P-I risk score which will enable risks to be directly compared. The higher the P-I score, the more significant the risk.
- Other methods include "heat maps" in which individual risks are color coded to indicate their priority. The use of a single indicator has the advantage that risks can be further categorized or classified.

In an ERM approach, it is not sufficient to develop probability distributions for individual risks alone and then manage each risk individually. It is the essence of ERM that risks which are interrelated are managed accordingly from a portfolio perspective. This allows risk managers to take advantage of natural hedges and to manage risks more efficiently. Therefore, it is necessary to capture the correlation of the identified risks (Treasury today 2007).

Risk Mapping Methodology: Notechs Based Perspective

Risk mapping is a cost-effective tool to incorporate risk awareness and institute risk management into a company's management and operational processes. As the process is used management will, over time, become comfortable in its role as a risk manager and begin to incorporate risk management into all aspects of its role within the company (Wilkinson et al. 2003).

The risk mapping process is part of a systematic, comprehensive methodology to identify, prioritize, and quantify risks to gather all relevant data. Other methods that can be used for capturing information include structured interviews, surveys (written and electronic), or a combination of these (World Custom Organizations 2015, p. 9).

Risk mapping is the visual presentation of identified risks in a way that easily allows them to be ranked. This presentation often takes the form a two-dimensional grid with frequency (or likelihood of occurrence) on one axis, and severity (or degree of impact) on the other axis; the risks that fall in the high-frequency/high-severity quadrant are typically given highest priority risk management attention (Casualty Actuarial Society 2003, p. 24). Risk maps include plotting intersection points between measures of frequency (on an x-axis) and severity (on a y-axis). Each point represents the relationship between the frequency of the exposure and the severity of the exposure for each risk measured (World Custom Organizations 2015, p. 7). But in this research, risk map which has three dimensions has been developed. Integration assumed a vital third dimension of risk mapping. This new mapping approach is consonant with contemporary based needs in today's business environment.

A risk map is a data visualization tool for communicating specific risks an organization faces. The goal of a risk map is to improve an administration's understanding of its risk profile and seek clarification of the nature and the impact of the risks. Risk maps can be a useful tool for explaining and communicating various risks to senior management and employees (World Custom Organizations 2015, p. 6).

Risk maps can also be illustrated by a heat map, using colors to illustrate the level of risks individual branch offices are exposed to (World Custom Organizations 2015, p. 7).

The objectives of risk mapping are identified by WCO's research as follows:

- Identify risks and how they are interconnected;
- Provide a mechanism to develop a robust risk management strategy;
- Compare and evaluate current risk handling and aid in selecting appropriate strategies;
- Show the remainders of risks after all risk mitigation strategies have been put in place; and
- Communicate risk management strategy to both management and employees (World Custom Organizations 2015, p. 8).

A risk map helps companies to identify and prioritize the risks associated with their business. It is a tool to model risk assessment and give guidance for risk transfer decisions. A risk map is often presented as a two-dimensional matrix with the likelihood versus risk impact (Bozzelli 2018, p. 1).

Risk maps can help an organization determine how to respond to risk. As organizations see the greater risks, they can plan a response (IMA 2007).

A "control strategy"/ "risk treatment" is a plan to reduce the severity of the organization's exposure to risk. A control strategy may include removing risk drivers, reducing the likelihood of events, or reducing the severity of the consequences (World Custom Organizations 2015, p. 10).[1]

Definitions used during the risk map generation are critical. What is "important" to one work unit or individual may not seem "important" to another (IMA 2007). Risk assessment is to evaluate any operational, project or business risks systematically.

In her article, Yilmaz (2019), has developed a novel taxonomy of risks, which presents risk factors by developing two main groups (Yilmaz 2019, p. 660):

i. Group of unalterable/impenetrable risk factors.
ii. Group of affectable/alterable/ penetrable risk factors.

The first group includes employee, individual social responsibility factors, and individual factors. Here, an individual social responsibility factor is a new category and fresh approach to the field. The second group includes penetrable factors, such as environmental organization-related and task-related.

[1] http://www.wcoomd.org/-/media/wco/public/global/pdf/topics/integrity/instruments-and-tools/risk_mapping_guide_june_2015.pdf?la=en.

NTS complement the technical skills of the flight crew (as well as cabin and ground crew, engineers and air traffic controllers) and contribute to reliable and effective performance in the complex work systems typical of the aviation industry (Flight Safety Australia 2016, p. 2).

The NOTECHS framework consists of four main categories: Cooperation, Leadership and Managerial Skills, Situation Awareness, and Decision-Making, each of them being subdivided into elements and behavioral markers (Flin et al. 2003). According to research by Patey, key categories of notches are listed as following (Patey and Winter 2015, p. 3):

i. Situation awareness,
ii. Decision-making,
iii. Communication,
iv. Team working,
v. Leadership,
vi. Coping with stress, and
vii. Coping with fatigue.

As seen in the above list, NTS are mental, social and personal management skills contributing to safer and efficient operations (Flight Safety Australia 2016, p. 2).

Widely Used Enterprise Risk Management Standards

Because of reasons such as inadequacy of risk management, it's focusing on certain risks, perceiving just the threats when the risk is mentioned, ERM standards started to be used. With ERM, while the businesses are protected from the possible negative effects of the risks in their working area, they look for the ways to get positive contributions from the risks for their businesses. If the risks are managed well, the businesses are not affected by the risk's negative sides or effected at the lowest level. Besides, "the added values" that the risks will provide for the businesses can be at unignorable extents.

Just one ERM standard may not give the same results for all of the businesses. An ERM model that is in accordance with a business' structure may cause new potential risks rather than a benefit for another business. Thus, various ERM standards were developed. Out of the ERM standards, there are four standards most widely used:

- AS/NZS (Australia and New Zealand Standard) 4360.
- FERMA (Federation of European Risk Management Associations) ERM Standards.
- COSO—ERM Standards—Integrated System.
- ISO (International Organization for Standardization) 31000 Standards.

Australia and New zealand Standard

AS/NZS was developed by the Joint Standards Australia and Standards New Zealand Committee OP-007 in 1999. It has the feature of being the first official standard in risk management and documentation. AS/NZS was updated in 2004. According to the perception of this standard, risk management is a supplementary part of good management (http-18).

AS/NZS has five fundamental components:

- Determination of the content: The stage of defining which systems are important for the risk management.
- Detection of the risks: Defining which risks are seen in the determined systems at the stage of content determination.
- Analysis of the risks: It is a stage of analyzing the determined risks. At this stage, if considered necessary, supportive controls, if any, are defined.
- Calculating the risks: It is a stage of defining the increasing risks.
- Handling the risks: It is a stage where the ways to relieve the risks which the businesses may face are defined.

AS/NZS formed a basis for the international ISO 31000 standard published in 2009. Following the publication of the ISO 31000 standard, AS/NZS 4360 defined the international standard officially and AS/NZS published the Risk Management Principles and Guidebook AS/NZS ISO 31000:2009 (Greenberg ve Lowrie 2010).

Australia and New Zealand Standard is a management model that may consider to new implementation of risk management systems. This standard looks both suitable and productive for organizations which want to transform their traditional risk management into enterprise risk management via understanding and require Sarbanes–Oxley coherence.

FERMA Risk Management Standard

FERMA, founded by the prominent risk management associations in Europe, among which is the Turkey Enterprise Risk Management Association, is a federation active in the risk management field.

Risk evaluation factor, one of the factors of FERMA Risk Management Standards, is the stage of general risk analysis and evaluation process. Risk analysis factor is composed of four separate stages. First of these stages is the risk detection stage. At the risk identification stage, the market, social, political, and cultural environment of the business must be analyzed well. This stage aims to define to what extent the business is exposed to uncertainty situations. The step of risk detection must be carried out systematically in order to define all of the business' important activities and the risks based on these important activities. All the variables related to the business activities and the possible risks must be defined and categorized clearly.

The second stage is the stage of defining the risk. At this stage, pointing out the risks in a table will be useful to provide that the risks are seen clearly. Taking every risk's possibility and effects, which are shown in the table, into consideration, risks that must be studied more in detail can be prioritized. Risks that may be effective at the decision-making stage, can be categorized as strategic, tactical, and operational risks. Risk analysis factor's third stage is the stage of risk prediction. Right predictions of the risks are extremely important at the stage of the decision-making process of the business. Risk predictions can be made in quantitative, semiquantitative or qualitative ways with respect to their accrual possibilities and possible effects. For instance, with respect to the threats and opportunities, the effects may be low, medium or high. The accrual possibility, similarly, may be low, medium, and high. At the risk profile stage, the last stage of the risk analysis factor, according to the results obtained from the risk analysis process, a risk profile for the business is created. This risk profile, created to specify all the risks and reveal their relative importance levels, is used as a means to prioritize the risk management studies.

FERMA Risk Management Standard's third factor is risk management action. Risk management action contains factors such as risk control/reduction, ignoring the risk, transferring, and finance.

Reporting the risks and communication factor are extremely important for an effective risk management. In a business, the directors and employees at different levels need various information in the risk management process. Besides, a business must give information regularly to its shareholders about the risk management policies and the productivity of the risk management studies to attain its goals.

Observation and revision of the risk management process, the last factor of the FERMA Risk Management Standard, is the reporting and revision structure necessary for defining the risks clearly, evaluating and applying the suitable actions. For defining the opportunities, policies and the standards must be supervised continuously and the performance of the standards must be revised.

COSO Enterprise Risk Management

COSO can be accepted as the oldest risk management system. It was developed for improvement by combining the financial reporting process quality with an inner control system. This system was established in 1985 as a platform for the National Commission on Fraudulent Financial Reporting. In 1992, it was approved by the SEC as a standard for the inner control system. With the "Inner Control Integrated Framework" report, published in 1992 by COSO, the definition and the standard of the inner control was defined (Gupta ve Thomson 2006).

In the 2000s, the big business scandals and as a result, the emergence of various new risks with the slowdown of the economy caused the point of view related to the risk management to change. The deficiencies of the current risk management techniques started to appear more (Arslan 2008). In 2004, COSO published the "ERM—Integrated framework" report. This report is a kind of guide for the businesses on the subjects such as the efficiency and the objectivity of the inner control, risk management. According to the COSO model, inner control is a process that ensures the attainment of the strategic targets that the business has defined and applied by all the enterprise employees starting from the top managers. COSO has goals such as the efficiency of the activities, the reliability of the financial reporting, and regulatory compliance (Adopted from COSO 2004).

COSO inner control system became an industrial cornerstone and took place as a model advised for the supervision of the public companies' management systems in the Sarbanes–Oxley laws (Charette 2010). The businesses started to comprehend the fact that they shouldn't ignore not only the financial risks but also the other risks. While the COSO's ERM integrated system has an extensive content of inner supervision, it also looks at the subjects related to ERM with a broad perspective. The COSO ERM model not only presents satisfactory solutions for the needs of the inner control mechanisms at the organizations but also gives advice on the application of a more extensive and effective risk management process (Moeller 2014).

The COSO ERM system is a system based on making a balance between the operational strategies' goals and the risks related to these targets and providing a position in which this balance yields maximum value for the business (Adopted from COSO 2004). This system signifies the organizational targets and risk management systems in a cube-formed, three-dimensional matrix. Top of the matrix represents the four different target levels as strategy, activities, reporting, and compliance. The side face of the matrix represents the units of the organizations at different levels such as branch, unit, section, and general enterprise. The front side of the matrix is composed of eight different ERM components such as interior environment, goal setting, event description, risk evaluation, risk responding, control activities, information and communication, and observation (Fig. 6.1).

Interior environment: The directors', employees', and all the organization's perception of the risk management and the way they handle the risk management, risks in their working area, the business' risk appetite and the ethical values are defined in the interior environment.

- Objective setting: An organization must set its targets clearly. It is extremely important that the businesses define the risks related to these targets in accordance with their risk policies, risk appetite.
- Event description: Internal and external events that could potentially hinder the organization's strategic objectives must be defined. Besides, risks must be separated from the opportunities. The opportunities must be associated with the management strategies or goal-setting process.
- Risk evaluation: The risks must be categorized according to their effects and similarities. In order to respond to the risk, the categorization process is extremely important.
- Risk responding: The management department is responsible for the risk responding process (Adopted from COSO 2004). If the business prefers the risk accepted choice, it does nothing and accepts the risks as the way they are. The effect of the relevant risk is mild, or even if its effect is not mild, it means that the business

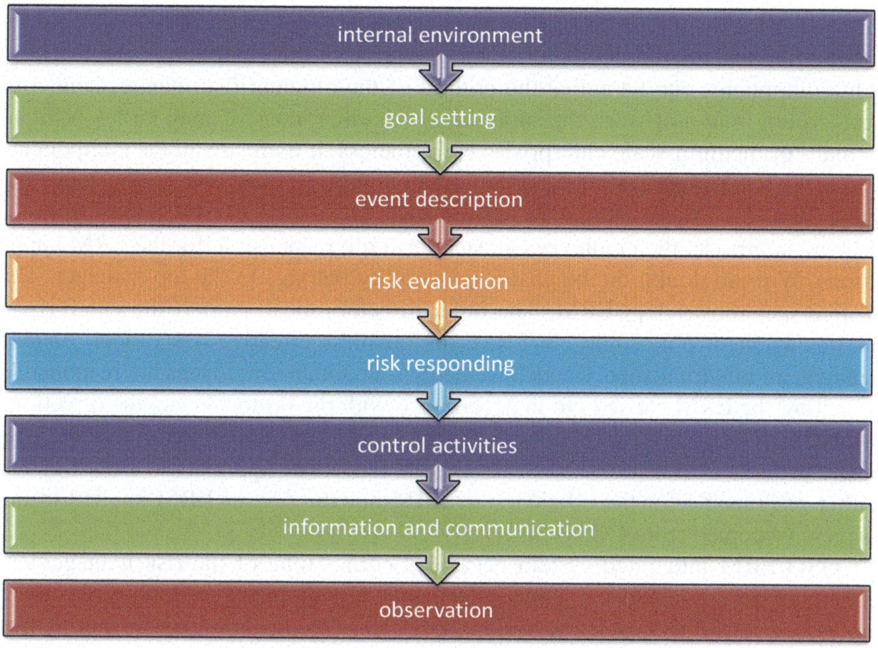

Fig. 6.1 ERM components (Adopted from COSO 2004)

accepts taking this risk. In the stage of reduction, the second stage, the business applies the strategies it developed to/or reduce the effects of the risk. If it prefers the sharing choice, it shares with third persons by spreading and transferring the risks or by making various agreements and/or by making insurances for financial losses it gives necessary responses.

In regard to evasion which is another choice, the business minimizes the risk to zero by not taking place in the relevant activity.

- Control activities: Control activities are carried out for the detection of the efficiency of the business' risk responses and the appropriate application of the risk policies after being formed.
- Information and communication: Information and communication is an extremely important process. Relevant information must be defined and conveyed to the related units for the manager and employees to fulfill their responsibilities with good communication skill. In a successful organization, effective communication is achieved both vertically and horizontally.
- Observation: Implemented ERM activities are documented. The observation process is extremely important for the detection of the risk management application's efficiency. At the end of the observation, if necessary, relevant changes are made in the processes (Adopted from COSO 2004).

The measuring of the COSO ERM activity efficiency applied in an organization is determined by evaluating the efficient operation of the eight components. These eight components can be called the criteria of the efficient risk management. But these criteria may not work the same in all the enterprises. It may be less official in small- or medium-scale enterprises. Nevertheless, if there are all the components even in the small organizations and they are operated, efficient risk management can be the case.

In an enterprise, the employees at each level are responsible for the ERM applications. With no doubt, the biggest responsibility belongs to the top manager. The top manager must adopt ERM. The other directors must support the enterprise's risk management philosophy. In ERM, the business effective risk officer, finance manager, and internal supervisors have a key role. Other employees are responsible for getting the ERM carried out in accordance with the protocols and the directions formed. Suppliers, business partners, external supervisors, and shareholders like customers provide useful information for an efficient ERM application. But, they are neither responsible for the efficiency of ERM nor the part of ERM applied in the business (Adopted from COSO 2004).

COSO ERM integrated system became a cornerstone of the risk management schemas of the organizations. Although the government managers don't give enough importance to the COSO ERM system, enterprise credit rating organizations like Moody's Investors Service, Standard & Poor's, Fitch Ratings put forward the ERM applications as a criterion while evaluating the enterprises (Charette 2010).

ISO 31000 Standard

The ISO 31000 Standard is a standard that can be applied by all the businesses that are active in the public or private sector regardless of their size or activity area (Kizildag 2011). The purpose of the ISO 31000 Standards, which is, especially at the crisis periods that the businesses active at a global scale can live frequently, guaranteeing the management of the risks in a systematical and disciplined way and the business' sustainability, was published by ISO. Besides, the ISO 31000 Standard aims to integrate the risk management applications into the current management systems and to provide a situation in which risk management applications operate in harmony with respect to the business' needs. ISO 31000 is presented with the documents below:

- ISO 31000: Principle and Norms.
- IEC (International Electrotechnical Commission) 31010: Risk Management—Risk Evaluation Techniques.
- ISO/IEC: Risk Management—Words.

ISO 31000 is composed of three complementary components as risk management principles, risk management framework and risk management process. Risk management principles form a guide to the rise of the risk management framework, the second component. With the application of the risk management frameworks in the businesses, risk management process emerges as the third component (Misiura 2015).

These standards are based on these principles:

- Top manager, responsible for the risk management, must observe and check the risk management applications continuously.
- Risks must be handled not only at the strategic management level but also at the operational management level. According to the ISO 31000 Standards, risk management must be negotiated by the managers at all levels starting from top managers to the managers at lower levels.
- ISO 31000 Standards aim to define all the internal and external risks that concern an organization. Defined risks affect all the risk management applications (Morris ve Pinto 2010).

After the plans are made in an organization, they are integrated into the ISO 31000 standards at the current management system at the stage of application.

In the ISO 31000 risk management standards, initially, the content must be created. After that, the risk evaluation process is launched. At the risk evaluation process, internal and external risks that concern the business first are defined. After defining, risks are analyzed. The risks that can affect the business most are prioritized. Therefore, the defined and analyzed risks are valued. Every valued risk is given an appropriate response alternative. But, at every stage, there is always a continuous communication with each director at each level. Besides, the top manager also observes the process at each level. If necessary, feedback is given. ISO 31000 Standards integrated into the current management system with its current situation are included in the stage of the application of the plans that the business made in accordance with its policies. Afterward, it is revised, and the results are developed. If there is a change in the policy or strategy of the business, the plans to be applied are revised. This cycle continues in this way.

ISO 31000 Standards need the steps shown in under the page that are interrelated with each other. First, the directions and the responsibilities of risk management are formed. In order to manage the risks within the directions and responsibilities formed, a layout of the risk management that is in accordance with the perception of risk management is created. After the stages of the layout of responsibilities for risk and system come to an end, the application process of the risk management system, the layout of which was designed, starts. At suitable steps, necessary arrangements are made to develop the system. That created risk management framework must support the risk management process. The risk management process applied in the whole business should create value in the business. Besides, this process must be supplementary of the organizational process. At the same time, by analyzing the potential threat and opportunities carefully, the risk management process must also be a part of the decision-making process.

Risk management process, advised by the ISO 31000 Standards, is composed of five steps that constitute the main factors of the ISO system and are interrelated with each other.

These steps are:

- Creating the content,
- Evaluating the risk,
- Responding to the risks,
- Observing and revising, and
- Communication and consultation.

The operation of the risk management process advised by the ISO 31000 Standards resembles other risk management systems with respect to their structure. The steps of the risk management process are interrelated with each other and are continuous in the form of a loop. The businesses, first, must make analyze the current situation related to the internal and external targets of the business to define the risk factors of their activity, and to define and evaluate the risks. Risk criteria must be detailed taking the business' strategic and operational targets into consideration. Which responses must be given to the related risks must be defined by determining the risk tolerance and risk appetite levels.

Risk criteria must give the opportunity to evaluate and respond to the risk factors. All the stages of the process must be observed continuously and revise. Also, the internal and external shareholders must be informed of the risk management process continuously. With the help of it, the shareholders not only guarantee that all the employees of the business are responsible for the risk management activities, but they also learn the basis of the decisions given by the management and make sure that they are compatible with the legal necessities (Misiura 2015). A response precaution taken for the risk factor that concerns the businesses can bring about other new risks. Therefore, the decision-makers must act accordingly and perceive the potential effects the risks can have on the business' targets while taking precautions as a response to the risks. Also, the risk management shouldn't be considered as a separate management process in a business and should be integrated into the current management process.

Conclusion

We believe that Risk management is an integral part of good management and decision-making. The institutional perspective of risk management also takes into consideration issues of strategic importance, such as organizational culture and leadership.

Value-based Enterprise risk management is a vital part of business management and strategy. It is continuously processed, and it is not a one-time event. It is highly probable that the risk management system, which is designed with the organization culture (values) in mind and compatible with the strategy and which can be updated continuously, is formulated with flexibility. From the economic perspective, the value maximization of the entire firm is an overarching corporate goal (Acharyya 2013,

p. 3). It is important that entities will have to adhere to sound enterprise-wide risk management methodologies and framework (Chauke and Sebola 2018, p. 7).

Risk management must be integrated into the culture of the organization and this will include mandate, leadership, and commitment from the Board. It must translate risk strategy into tactical and operational objectives and assign risk management responsibilities throughout the organization. It should support accountability, performance measurement, and reward, thus promoting operational efficiency at all levels. Achieving a good risk-aware culture is ensured by establishing appropriate risk architecture, strategy, and protocols (AIRMIC 2010, p. 7).

References

Acharyya, M. 2013. The benefits of implementing enterprise risk management: Evidence from the non-life insurance industry. In *Centre for finance and risk. The business school*, 1–26. Bournemouth University, Casualty Actuarial Society, Professional Risk Managers' International Association, Society of Actuaries.

AIRMIC. *Alarm, IRM*: 2010 https://www.theirm.org/media/886062/ISO3100_doc.pdf.

Arslan, I. 2008. *Kurumsal Risk Yönetimi*. Ankara: Ministry Of Finance Strategy Development Presidency.

Bozzelli, R. 2018. Blog risk mapping: A corporate strategic need? https://www.24vision.solutions/risk_mapping_a_corporate_strategic-need.html, 25 Sep 2018.

Casualty Actuarial Society, C. 2003. Overview of enterprise risk management. https://www.casact.org/area/erm/overview.pdf.

Chapman, R.J. 1998. The effectiveness of working group risk identification and assessment techniques. *International Journal of Project Management* 16 (6): 333–343.

Charette, R.N. 2010. *Enterprise risk management*. In P. Simon, (ed.). The next wave of technologies: opportunities from chaos. Hoboken, NJ: John Wiley & Sons.

Chauke, K., and M. Sebola. 2018. *Risk management: Can it be a Panacea for state-owned enterprises Ills?*, 291–298. Saldahna Bay: South Africa, Stellenbosch University.

COSO. (2004). Eterprise risk management-integrated framework. Committee of Sponsoring Organizations of the Treadway Commission (COSO).

Flight Safety Australia. 2016. https://www.flightsafetyaustralia.com/2016/03/non-technical-skills-can-they-be-taught/. Accessed 1 Nov 2018.

Flin, R., et al. 2003. Development of the NOTECHS (non-technical skills) system for assessing pilots' CRM skills. *Human Factors and Aerospace Safety* 3 (2): 95–117.

Greenberg, M., and K. Lowrie. 2010. From the Editors. *Risk Analysis* 30(12): 873–874.

Gunes, S. 2009. Kurumsal Risk Yönetimi ve Türkiye'de Farkındalığına İlişkin Bir Uygulama. Istanbul: Istanbul Technical University Of Science, Unpublished Master's Thesis.

Gupta, P.P., and J.C. Thomson. 2006. Use of COSO 1992 in management reporting on internal control. *Strategic Finance* 10: 28.

HKICPA. 2005. *Internal control and risk management basic framework*. Hong Kong: Hong Kong Institute of Certified Public Accountents.

IMA, I.o.M.A. 2007. *Enterprise Risk Management Tools and Techniques*. https://erm.ncsu.edu/library/article/enterprise-risk-management-tools-techniques. Accessed 2018.

Kizildag, D. (2011). Yönetsel Açıdan Risk Yönetimine Bir Bakış: ISO 31000 Risk Yönetimi. Ankara: Seckin Imprint.

Kucuk Yilmaz, Ayse. 2007. Application of analytic network process in the enterprise risk management an example of the selecting best operator in the airport business. Europea

Moeller, R.R. (2014). *Executive's guide to COSO internal controls: Understanding and implementing the new framework*. Hoboken NJ: John Wiley & Sons, Inc.

Morris, P., and J.K. Pinto. 2010. *The Wiley Guide to Project Control*. Hoboken: John Wiley & Sons.

Patey, R., and Winter. 2015. Human factors and non-technical skills: What do I need to know? s.l. Federation of State Boards of Physical Therapy.

Taylor, C., E. Babin, and M. Reid. 2011. Enterprise risk management tools and techniques, s.l.: s.n.

Taylor, G., and S. Wang. 2013. ERM and optimal control. http://www.businessandeconomics.mq.edu.au/our_departments/Applied_Finance_and_Actuarial_Studies/acst_docs/seminar_series/Taylor.pdf. Accessed 29 Nov 2018.

TIBA. 2008. Kurumsal Risk Yönetimi Raporu. TIBA (Turkish Industrialist Misiura, A. (2015). Enterprise Risk Management in the Airline Industry- Risk Management Structures and Proctices. London: Brunel University Brunel Business School, Unpublished Doctoral Thesis. s' and Businessmen's Association) Publishing.

Treasury today. 2007. Enterprise risk management—risk identification and measurement. http://treasurytoday.com/2007/02/enterprise-risk-management-risk-identification-and-measurement. Accessed 29 Nov 2018.

USA Department of Homeland Security, O. o. R. M. a. A. 2010 Office of risk management and analysis, risk management practices in the public and private sector: Executive summary, p. 5, s.l.:s.n.

Wilkinson, M., D. Ingram, and C. Ehrlich. 2003. Best practices for life insurance company risk management, 2004. http://us.milliman.com/common/wireframes/InsightSummary.aspx?Pageid=26579&id=1836&pg=9.

World Custom Organizations. 2015. World custom organizations guide to corruption risk mapping. http://www.wcoomd.org/-/media/wco/public/global/pdf/topics/integrity/instruments-and-tools/risk_mapping_guide_june_2015.pdf?la=en.

Yildiz, A., et al. 2014. A knowledge-based risk mapping tool for cost estimation of international construction. *Automation in Construction* 144–155.

Yilmaz, A.K., yse Kucuk Yilmaz. 2019. Strategic approach to managing human factors risk in aircraft maintenance organization: Risk mapping. *Aircraft Engineering and Aerospace Technology* 91 (4): 654–668. https://doi.org/10.1108/AEAT-06-2018-0160.

Chapter 7
Introduction: Crises Management in Aviation Business and Strategy

Contents

Crisis Management in Aviation Business

All the businesses may face crisis situations at large or small scales since their establishment. The crisis that may be at a small scale for a business may be at a large scale for another one in the same sector. The more prepared businesses are for a possible crisis, the less painful the process will be. Crisis situations are a kind of examination for the businesses. While the businesses that go through this examination successfully continue their routine works, the businesses that face the crisis unprepared are probably at the brink of bankruptcy due to the process they have to handle with great loss. Therefore, the preparations made before the crisis will supply a great deal of support for the businesses during the crisis. In consideration of this information, it is beneficial to explain what the crisis is, what are its effects on the businesses, what must be done before, during, and after the process.

A. Kucuk Yilmaz and T. G. Flouris, *Values, Ergonomics and Risk Management in Aviation Business Strategy*, https://doi.org/10.1007/978-981-15-1006-9_7

Every business should have a crisis management plan in order to cope with unexpected unwelcome events. Anticipating a crisis may make it less traumatic and costly. Unfortunately, many businesses mistakenly assume that crises will not blight their doorsteps. Not only is this assumption overly optimistic, it is certainly a formula for an ineffective response when a crisis does occur (Spıllan and Hough 2003, p. 398).

Organizations must work in harmony with the others around them and must be innovative and open-minded in order to attain their goals and survive. Besides, working in harmony with their subsystem, they must shape their structure and long-term strategies in accordance with the demand and expectation of the surroundings (Can 1997, p. 143).

Otherwise, it is inevitable to face a crisis situation losing the advantage of competition in their sector. The airline industry operating in a technology-intensive sector comes alive in a dynamic environment. Therefore, airline businesses must follow technological developments closely and implement the necessary modifications and innovations in time. A possible delay in their implementation of the necessary modifications and innovations may result in a possible crisis. In the event of such a crisis situation, the survival of the business is only through a strong crisis management. Since they live on a very low profit margin, an airline business run by the managers not capable of a good crisis management may end up with the risk of bankruptcy in the event of a possible crisis situation.

The Crisis Concept and Types of Crises

Crises have no borders or boundaries. They can happen anytime, anywhere, and to any organization—profit, not-for-profit, public, or private. The interconnectedness of the global economy and its political realities can magnify the ripple effect of any single crisis, making it a common feature of corporate life. A crisis affecting one organization can, among other things, cause layoffs and closings among that organization's suppliers, customers, and partners; bring about a loss of investor confidence that can cause a dip in the stock market, and even bring about environmental damage and psychological angst (Klann 2003, p. 22).

According to Can, crisis is a situation of tension in which an organization's goals can be seriously endangered if it is not addressed immediately and effectively (Can 1997). According to another definition, the crisis is a series of events that have highly bad consequences (Hale et al. 2005, p. 112). Also, it is possible to define crisis as surprising events that may harm the environment, the premises, and people's lives greatly. Almost all the definitions of a crisis contain an element of surprise. The event that triggers a crisis is not expected or with a small chance, it is expected to happen sometime in the future. Therefore, the date of the crisis to happen is a surprise. Since the crisis is not expected to happen, the businesses may lose control in the situation for a short time (Stephens et al. 2005, p. 391). In the center of all the explanations of crisis, there is a situation in which one or more stakeholders suffer. Because of the adverse effects of the crisis on the stakeholders, businesses have also legal and ethical responsibilities for its stakeholders (Alpaslan et al. 2009).

A crisis is an undesired, extraordinary, often unexpected and timely limited process with ambivalent development possibilities. It demands immediate decisions and countermeasures in order to influence further development again positively for organization and to limit the negative consequences as much as possible (Regester 2001, p. 181)

Crises are often turning points in organizational life. They represent opportunities to establish a reputation for competence, to shape the organization and to tackle important issues. In most crises, because time is at a premium and resource allocation critical, company executives need strategic guidelines on what kinds of action are needed (Regester 2005, p. 196).

It is possible to come across different classifications of the crisis in different sources. There lies the same reality underlying all of the classifications. The reality that it endangers an organization's senior goals and future and must be interfered immediately forms a basis for all types of crisis. Nevertheless, it is possible to categorize the crisis under four headings as the most general and common ones:

- The crisis caused by the natural disasters (flood, earthquake, etc.).
- The crisis caused by the mechanical problems (plane crash, product defect, etc.).
- Human-related crisis (terrorism, political, sabotage, etc.).
- The crisis caused by the managing decision/indecision (wrong decisions, delay in decision-making, etc.) (Chris 1999, p. 23).

No matter which heading it belongs to, all the crises have uncertainty. Minimizing the uncertainty and if possible, the elimination of it in a short time is of great importance while giving decisions in the business. The adverse effects on the business may be minimized with sound decisions given in a short time. At this point, it is important how prepared the businesses are for the crisis situations.

Although the crisis has many definitions, the characteristics of these definitions are the same. Every crisis has a surprise lying underneath. Because of the weak predictions a crisis that is sometimes not expected, sometimes may confront us as an expected event happening sooner than expected. When we evaluate crisis in terms of organizational aspect, inability to expect the crisis situation, the weakness of the organization's prediction and prevention mechanism, lack of necessary information and time to take the control of the situation to be overcome, the pressure and tension it has on the managers since it needs to be treated at once are all basic characteristics of the crisis. Besides, in crisis time, in order to overcome the crisis and to compare the road maps to be followed at the crisis time, due to the lack of time and knowledge, decisions may be given in nervous atmospheres. Therefore, it is possible for every organization to face a crisis in its life cycle endangering its life (Can 1997). The managers must be conscious and educate their personnel accordingly. The managers of the airline businesses that have a delicate balance must treat the crisis management with necessary seriousness and delicacy. The strategic success to the managing crisis situations has two fundamental keys; these are: to well preparation as proactive style and perform crisis management well at the time of the crisis.

Crises are often turning points in organizational life. To determine a crisis situation, the question must be asked whether the organization still has the ability to achieve important corporate goals. However, only those goals that exert considerable influence over the future survival of the company are of significance. The initial specifications of these high-ranking goals include solvency, that is, the ability to fulfill business payment obligations, and success expressed through minimum profit or return on investment. The advantage of this narrow version of the term crisis was the simple definition of crisis conditions with a company. Its financial base allows the simple derivation from accounting through a target/actual comparison. However, this advantage of simple definition is confronted with the disadvantage that the actual causes of deviation from the corporate goal, which occur earlier, are not covered. For this reason, the inclusion of the company's success factors that form the basis of solvency and success as a further criterion is important (Regester 2012, p. 205).

In any crisis, the most important of all the key external audiences are the media—print publications of all types, the broadcasting outlets and, now, the new technologies involved in the World Wide Web. Planning how the media should be dealt with in a crisis is the task of the communications member of the crisis team. Handling the situation can only be done effectively if you have a clear idea of how each branch of the media family work. Each of them disseminates information (good and bad, accurate, and inaccurate) so fast and to so many audiences that you need procedures in place in order to control the information they receive from you. Just as importantly, you also need parallel systems to find out what information they are getting from other sources. Every journalist knows that the faster you get on to and ahead of a story or an issue the better. If your business or organization is in the center of a newsworthy incident or event you need to have a similar mental attitude and the ability to act swiftly and decisively. Efficient media handling requires specialist skills and a detailed knowledge of what is required (Ruff 2004, p. 45).

The Factors that Cause Crises in the Business Environment

Many factors that would cause a crisis can be specified. Many factors such as uncertainty, getting too little data, lack of communication, incoordination in or out of the organization, the variability of the political situations, being unplanned, and lack of time can cause a crisis (Dincer 1998, p. 248). If we want to study the factors that cause a crisis in the businesses more systematically, it is suitable to categorize these factors under two headings: Internal Factors and External Factors. Especially considering that airline businesses perform in the global arena, the fact that it is inevitable for the events happening outside the business to affect the airline businesses directly or indirectly comes out. The businesses become more vulnerable when their control over the outer environment declines. If the internal factors are added to the decline in the control competence of the outer environment, it will be inevitable for this business to face a crisis.

External Factors

We can define the factors that are outside the business and that the business cannot control totally as the external factors which cause a crisis in businesses. As uncertainty and chaos increase, the possibility of a crisis for businesses will increase. The more dependent businesses are on the external environment, the higher the effect of the external factor that caused a crisis will be (Genc 2004, pp. 148–150). Thus, the control of the business over the environment can be assessed as a scale of its endurance against a crisis. It is possible to collect the external factors, which cause a crisis in the businesses, under the following headings:

- Political and economic factors.
- Advancement in technology, profession, and working area.
- The increase in the number of rival businesses and the effect of the rivalry.
- The difficulty in supplying the source.
- The developments in the international environment (Sen 2011, p. 84).

Political and Environmental Factors

The political developments are one of the most important factors that affect the businesses with open system directly. The political developments that happen in a country directly affect the businesses. Businesses perform their activities within the framework of changing political developments. Furthermore, international policy shows up as an important factor affecting the businesses operating on a global basis. A political tension between two countries affects directly the businesses that work with these countries and the airline businesses that launch flights to these countries. Therefore, the administrators of the businesses shouldn't be indifferent to the political developments happening inside and outside the country. The businesses that follow the political developments closely direct the work to take precaution beforehand taking the signals of a forthcoming crisis into consideration. The uncertainty that feeds the crisis most is relieved through this, and if the crisis is unavoidable, the possible effects it will have on the business will be relieved, too.

Organizations are a subsystem of the economic system. Therefore, they are affected easily by every kind of a trivial alteration, instability or uncertainty that can occur in the economic system they belong to. Factors such as the situation of the natural resources, the level of profiting from these resources, the structure and the situation of the sector they belong to, the characteristics of the rivalry intensity in the sector, constitute the economic environment of an organization. Any adverse situation that may happen in these factors may cause businesses to face a crisis (Peten 2003, p. 79). Thus, the managers of the businesses should perceive well and follow the developments in the economic environment closely. Having superior situational awareness of the economic environment, businesses will decrease the possible effects of a crisis, if it is unavoidable, partly, and will also eliminate some of them, rather than getting trapped in a crisis abruptly and surprisingly.

Advancements in Technology, Profession and Working Area

Technological advancements are of particular concern to the businesses performing at the national and international platforms. Especially, the aviation sector is a technology-intensive sector. Therefore, a little development in the technology affects many areas ranging from the passengers' comfort, the airplanes' effects on the environment such as "carbon emission, noise pollution, etc.", fuel saving, to many other areas that contribute to the business. This situation forces the airline businesses to follow the advancement in technology closely. Besides, the aviation sector is a sector in which educated personnel works. Technological advancements are integrated into the business with the help of the educated personnel. An airline business' investing in an innovation with a belief that it will be beneficial for it, following the technology closely, makes it necessary to invest in the education of the personnel who will use and work with that technology as well.

In the aviation sector, the speed of the development in business life makes the capacity of the employees inadequate. The necessity and the obligation to know the newly developed equipment and systems before the changing and developing technology poses a pressure even a threat to the individuals. If the employees' education level is not at an expected level before the technological developments, this situation is a "potential crisis and stress" factor and creates an emotion of inefficiency among the employees. The most important characteristic of the crisis caused by the technological problems is that it happens unexpectedly and damages the safety of life and property to a great extent (Karaca 2003). In the aviation sector, the rules of which have been written with blood, safety is always of high importance. Therefore, the education requirement of the personnel should be invested in time and in needed amount before the technological developments. Thus, for the businesses not to suffer from the problem caused by the technology, it is highly important for the businesses in the aviation sector, which is a technology-intensive sector, to follow the technological developments closely and invest in the education their personnel in order to continue their existence.

The Increase in the Number of Rival Businesses and the Effect of the Rivalry

The law and legislation are taking form according to the necessities has caused one or more business' oligopoly structure to change, has caused more than one business to be founded in the same sector, and therefore has caused a rivalry and made this rivalry become rigid in time. The increase in the number of rival businesses made it obligatory for the businesses already active in the sector to take extra precautions. Being prepared for the crisis situations that can be faced unexpectedly while carrying out ERM efficiently is of great importance for the businesses to make themselves stronger at their rivals' weaker sides and to have rivalry superiority over their rivals.

In the aviation sector, a similar situation is the case. With liberalization, new regulations in the airline transport came up. After these regulations, in the following years, a significant increase in the number of the airline businesses was observed. The increase in the number of the airline businesses in the aviation sector drew attention to the rivalry between the airline businesses performing at global basis. The airline businesses working with low profit margin had a fierce competition in the geography where they were active. In a possible unexpected situation, airline businesses shouldn't delay their routine. Airline businesses have fragile structures for the crisis. Thus, they should carry out ERM efficiently and be prepared for a possible crisis. A crisis situation on a global basis may affect the airline transport directly or indirectly no matter what the cause is, the economic, the political, or different reasons. As a consequence of globalization, there are a lot of airline businesses from different countries active in the same geography. This situation increases the rivalry in the region. The rise of the rivalry parallel to the increase in the number of the rival businesses makes it necessary for the businesses to take extra precautions. Every area that is given service has its own risk factors. Managers, the people responsible for the crisis and risk must take the characteristics of the market given service into consideration in their crisis and risk management works.

The Difficulty in Sourcing

The difficulty in finding the raw material, labor, and financing sources may form a base of the crisis for the businesses. The businesses' difficulty in finding the raw material that they use in production, the sharp increases in the cost of the raw material, difficulty in the supply of imported raw materials are a few of the situations that lead the businesses into trouble (Sen 2011).

When we study the case in consideration of airline businesses, the sharp increase in the fuel prices, the increase in the cost of maintenance, the difficulty in the supply of spare parts come up as the case that leads the airline businesses into trouble urging their budget. Besides, the obligation of the typical airline sector to employ competent personnel is another obstacle that airline businesses face. In airline businesses, the personnel is to have education relevant to their working area at specific periods. For each mission, competent personnel educated differently are employed. The cost of the competent personnel is, naturally, high for the airline business. The businesses shouldn't avoid this cost, should employ the experts for the professions. Infringing upon the flight and land safety while economizing on the small costs may cause irreparable damage in the airline businesses.

Also, difficulty in the availability of financial credit, the sound rise in the cost of labor, the frictions in the trade union relationships are the other factor that affects the businesses adversely (Dincer 1992). Airline businesses generally purchase the airplanes they own with credit. Those that keep their credit rating high will find finance easily when they need to. Because of the problem it has with finding financing, an airline canceling an aircraft order or decreasing the number of flights in its target area is a sign of its weakness in the sector and a forthcoming crisis. No airline business wants to end up in such a situation. On the other hand, the high cost of labor is an expected situation in airline transport. But the unexpected sharp rise in the cost of labor may put the businesses' cash flow into trouble. This situation may retard the business' regular payment. It is not possible for a business failing to pay regularly to have a high credit rating. Therefore, the businesses must have some cash or assets to change into cash in a short term for unexpected situations.

Besides, the risk of cambium is another factor that causes the businesses to face a crisis in terms of finance. While the airline businesses sell their flight in their own currencies, they have to pay for the cost of fuel, maintenance, and some spare parts for which they have to spare a great deal of budget in foreign currency. The sharp change in the foreign currencies may cause the businesses to face a cash shortage. Therefore, the airline businesses make various deals with the relevant businesses about the fuel, maintenance, and spare parts and take precautions against the crisis that may be caused by the risk of cambium.

Developments in the International Environment

Globalization is the case that affects all the businesses active in the national and international platform directly or indirectly. Therefore, the businesses cannot define their area of activity in the national economy and the national borders. The effect of the globalization that is felt all over the world makes it obligatory for the businesses to define their area of activity in terms of the service and industries across the world (Genc 2004).

The change and uncertainty happening in the international environment are the developments that concern the businesses active in the international market. A political crisis that may happen between two countries, conflict and state of war, special treaties and sanctions must be the developments that the businesses, active in the international platform, have to follow closely. For example, a terror operation directed by a foreign government or an organization may cause a lot of crises in the target country (Dincer 2002). All the airline businesses that give service to the relevant area may get affected directly by the terrorist attacks, political conflicts or the state of war not only financially but also psychologically. Therefore, the administrators of the businesses and those in charge of decision-making should follow the political and economic developments in these geographies closely.

In national and small-scale businesses, the factors such as culture, language, political system, financial environment, and the law system are shared, which gives such businesses great advantages over the businesses active in the international area. The businesses active in the international platform have to manage the economic, political, cultural, legal legislation and many other risk factors in all the countries they perform (Sen 2011). Since airline businesses perform at the international market, the risk factors they have to manage are far more than those of the small-scale businesses' active on the national basis. The managers of airline businesses must be able to examine the cultural, economic, and legal dynamics of their geography well while following the international developments closely.

Internal Factors

In addition to the external factors that cause the businesses to face a crisis, there are internal factors that they can control more. Businesses become vulnerable to the crisis when their capability to conform with the change in the environmental factors weakens. In order to conform with the change in the environmental factors, the decision-makers must analyze the business and the environment well. Therefore, in order to manage internal factors, deciding which strategies will be fruitful for the business after the analysis of the decision-makers will be of high importance in consideration with the crisis management.

When we take all the factors that cause the crisis, the internal factors are claimed to have a more effective role (Tuz Vergiliel 1996, p. 8). Although external factors are variables that cannot be controlled, a good analysis of the environment can make it possible to predict well and give right decisions (Dincer 1998). Through this, the uncertainty that the businesses cannot control will be decreased and realistic and right decisions for the future of the business will be given with the help of right predictions. Besides a careful analysis following the outer environment closely, managing the internal factors that cause the crisis well, and conforming with the environmental changes in a short time will help the businesses get rid of the crisis situation in a relatively short time. The internal factors that cause crisis can be studied under five following headings:

- Factors related to the managers,
- Organizational factors,
- The factors caused by the production system,
- Life stage factor, and
- Other factors (Sen 2011).

Factors Related to the Managers

The managers of the business must analyze the geography where they are active. They must observe the other businesses performing in the same geography and in the same sector closely, identify their rivals' strengths and weaknesses correctly, and must not neglect these points when they are giving decisions. Business will start to have loss in short or middle term as long as they are indifferent to the demands of the customers. The managers' inadequate environment analysis, their indifference to the demands of their customers and the reactions of their rivals, and failing to produce necessary strategy will create strategical gap in the business. This gap will increase their possibility to face the crisis.

Lacking a crisis plan that must be prepared in consideration of their organizational culture, customers, suppliers, the position of their rival businesses, credit foundations, and various internal and external factors will intensify the crisis increasing the stress and pressure of the crisis on the businesses' administrative and organizational structure. The mobility of the businesses that have no crisis management plan will weaken at the time of the crisis and the businesses may become vulnerable.

Within the framework of the prepared crisis management plan, the businesses should form a crisis management team, and define their duties and responsibilities in terms of the crisis management. The businesses that have no crisis management plan and have not appointed the personnel in charge of the crisis management will have accepted the adverse effects of the crisis on the business beforehand.

For successful crisis management, the businesses must be run by successful managers. Just like people want to be treated by the best doctors at the best hospitals within the bounds of possibility, so do businesses at the time of the crisis; they want to be directed by the best managers. Similarly, if the people try to direct the factors that can make them ill by giving attention to their vaccination, clothing, food, and drinks well, the businesses should look for the ways not to face the crisis, if it is inevitable, to get rid of it at once by managing the factors that they assess as the reasons of the crisis well. At this point, the managers have a great duty. The inadequate characteristic features of the managers mean the crisis is unavoidable for the business in the changing environmental conditions.

We can signify the features of the incompetent managers that can cause the businesses to face the crisis as the following:

- Weakness in the prediction and instinction that is so important for the crisis management.
- Being unable to perceive the difference of the new problems failing to comply with the changing situations and the tendency to apply the old solutions to them.
- Being unable to comply with the environmental conditions' changing speed.
- Being unable to understand that the trouble that is faced is a problem.
- Not being well informed about the changes in the surroundings.
- One of the most important features is the manager's personality. Since crises have subjective characteristics, it is of high importance to perceive the crisis. The situation that can be perceived as a crisis by some decision-makers may be perceived as a trivial problem by the others. Therefore, the characteristics of a manager are of high importance in the perception of the crisis.
- The role of the top manager is another highly important subject. Since the top managers have a tendency to see themselves as a strategist, they might ignore the

responsibilities such as motivating the personnel, the organizational culture in the business, belief and values, indoctrinating the personnel (Sen 2011). This situation not only triggers the crisis but prolongs the period at the time of the crisis as well.

Organizational Factors

Among the internal factors, the organizational factors are more effective on the managers, employees, technical reasons, budget, and cash flow. Factors such as the organizational structure and malfunction, the inadequacies of the budget and finance, the managers' inadequacies and incompetence, the incompetence of the personnel can be assessed as the organizational factors (Baydas et al. 2004, p. 241).

At the top of the factors that increase the effects of the crisis on the business' administrative and organizational structure comes organizational factors. As their scales get bigger, businesses have a more bureaucratic structure. As a result, they react less to the environmental developments. The increase in the scale of a business creates a structure that diminishes the personnel initiative and gives importance to the formal methods to increase the control and efficiency. The organizations should form formal methods and written laws to maintain control. But giving too much importance to the formal politics and written laws may eliminate the dynamism in the organization. This situation will diminish the organizational flexibility of the business.

By the administrative and organizational structure, we mean the subjects such as the management and leadership styles of the managers, authorization and responsibilities, the superior and subordinate relationship between the employees, the formal and informal communication and decision-making in the organization.

The inability of a business' organizational structure to show enough flexibility prolongs the process to comply with the newly formed conditions. Besides, there arouses a resistance against the change among the personnel. The inadequacies caused by the structure of the organization and its operation with poorly analyzed environmental conditions form a basis for the business to face a crisis (Genc 2004).

When we consider the case from the aspect of the aviation sector, the airline businesses must comply with the changing and developing conditions immediately, and therefore must have a flexible structure. Especially, the continuous and fast flow of information at the time of the crisis is of high importance for the business to get rid of the crisis situation in a short time. The existence of the competent managers, the contribution of the personnel at the time of the crisis, and peace at work are among the most important points when struggling against the crisis.

Factors Caused by the Production System

Businesses may continually face unexpected danger and opportunities due to the uncertain surroundings and dynamic environmental conditions. For the businesses to continue their existence depends on their action style and ability to perceive and take advantage of the opportunities. Thus, businesses should give importance to the strategical production activities in the face of changing environmental conditions. By strategical production, we mean the production and the services which will lead the business to success in their area against their rivals and help them comply with the changing conditions in time (Taymaz 1996, p. 20).

Some research done on the reasons for the crisis period experienced by the businesses active in Turkey shows that the crisis is caused especially by the economic and financial problems at the macro level. Besides, there are some other reasons such as everlasting strikes, the problem of the raw material and the suppliers, loss in the foreign market, rise in the cost of input, the rivalry because of the existence of the other businesses active in the same market, the access of the alternative products to the market, legal regulations, etc. All the reasons mentioned can be assessed as the reasons that can trigger a possible crisis if not treated in time (Ozgen and Turk 1996, p. 32).

Life Stage Factors

Like all the other organisms, a businesses' life stage consists of five parts: birth, growth, maturity, recession, and fall. Businesses sometimes run the risk of experiencing a crisis more than necessary at their growth stage. Similarly, at their recession stage, they face crises too often. But, whatever their area of activity is, failing to meet the needs of the physical, financial, and manpower sources that the wish of taking advantage of the environmental opportunities and chances accompanies may mean a new crisis for the business. On the other hand, the stage of maturity is the stage where the organizations should watch the developments closely and take careful decisions (Genc 2004).

In considering the life cycle, the target of an organization is to attain the stage of maturity and preserve this stage. Preserving the success is more difficult than attaining success. With this consciousness, businesses should move more delicately at the stage of maturity. The flexibility of businesses to keep pace with the developments in the environmental factors at the stage of maturity presents itself as a very important characteristic. As is flexibility, the business' maintenance of its balance is important, too. Apart from the flexibility, those businesses that maintain their balance go through a possible crisis keeping pace with the environmental changes easily (Dogan 2003).

The stage of the recession where the fear and loss that threatens the continuity of the business, where the sale and profits tend to decline is also a suitable period for a crisis (Dincer 1998). Wrong decisions that save the day taken as a result of the wrong politics carried out in the recession period may be the decisions that form a basis for the fall of the businesses in the short or long term. When giving these decisions, the pressure of time may play a big role. Nevertheless, the managers and the decision-makers should be more careful while giving decisions than they do at the other stages in order to continue their existence.

Besides, there are some opinions that claim all the businesses definitely face a crisis at the end of each stage. According to Garnier, the businesses face the leadership crisis at their establishment stage, the delegation crisis at their growth stage, the bureaucracy crisis at their maturity stage, the crisis caused by the wish of revival at their recession stage. At their recession stage, if the managers don't analyze the environmental factors well, and don't give necessary decisions for the businesses' needs, the stage of fall will be inevitable. On the other hand, those businesses that cannot go through the crisis special to each stage may sometimes skip to the stage of fall without experiencing the recession stage (Uzun 2001, p. 20). Therefore, no matter which stage the businesses are at, the managers and decision managers should be conscious that their decisions will affect the existence of the business in short, medium or long term.

Other Factors

At the crisis period, the uncertainty and time pressure are among the most important factors. The managers are expected to give the right decisions at the time of uncertainty for the businesses to continue their existence. For the managers to give right decisions, it is of high importance to relieve the uncertainty, to supply the flow of information, to form a continuous communication network. The managers should consider the organizational factors while trying to decrease the effects of the environmental factors on their decisions. It is an expected situation in which the decisions are in harmony with the climate and culture of the organization. It is not surprising that a decision made at the time of a crisis will have different results for the two different businesses active in the same sector.

The businesses' failing to establish an early warning system analyzing the internal and external environmental factors means that they will face the crisis defenselessly (Sen 2011). Lack of a crisis plan, not defining the role and responsibilities of the personnel at the time of a crisis beforehand will mean that, with the effect of time pressure, decisions that save the day will be given in the face of a possible crisis. In that case, many businesses may pass to the stage of fall even without experiencing some stages of the life cycle.

The Effects of the Crisis Period on the Businesses

The fastest effect of the crisis on the business‘ functions is related to the time. Time pressure makes it hard for the businesses to do their job at the time of the crisis. The managers may have to give hard decisions that can affect the destiny of the business. Some decisions that are given in a very short time may have an important role in shaping the business' future.

As a second effect, the stress that emerges with the time pressure can be signified. Most of the decisions given under stress can be wrong. Managers might not be able to take the right decisions in a short time and under pressure and as such, their ability to solve the problems and self-confidence might diminish. On the other hand, stress has effects on the employees, too (Sen 2011). With the effect of the stress, the business‘ coordination may get into trouble owing to the conflict and friction among the employees. Such a situation in which the right decisions must be given in a short time may deepen the crisis period that the business faces.

The Effects of the Crisis on the Management Function

The crisis period may cause many permanent effects on the business and its employees. The effects of the crisis on the management function can be categorized under four headings: the obligation to make decisions fast, tension that emerges in the business, causing the mistrust of the business, and the rise in the tendency to centralization. Besides, in the crisis period, a malfunction in the organizational communication appears, the resistance against the change increases in the business, some sections start to move independently owing to the incoordination that appears (Ozdeveci 2002, pp. 99–101).

When the relevant literature reviewed, lack of crisis plan is appeared as main reason of failuring in crisis management process. Additionally, crieses causes for both the physiological breakdown of personnels, the loss of trust between the management and the employees, the increase in the tendency to centralization and as the most powerful reason for the crisis to deepen, lack of the crisis plan appear (Oncul et al. 2003, p. 100).

Taking action in a crisis can be fraught with risk. A strategy is needed for deciding when to define a situation as a crisis, when to take action and to work with others in solving the crisis. Such a strategic sense is in itself a great advantage when tension develops. The ability to keep cool when everything is collapsing is a quality valued in leaders, especially since apparent confidence by the leader is so reassuring to subordinates. Advance planning makes it more possible to concentrate on the actual problem when it peaks and provides a framework for action (Regester 2005, p. 212).

The Effects of the Crisis on the Production Function

From a general point of view, production function means the production of the goods and services without defect, at the time, amount and quality determined earlier. For this function to be fulfilled depends upon the activities' place and process in which they are carried out. The process generally can be defined as the list of the activities that turn the inputs such as manpower, machinery, material, and technology into a valuable output, in other words creating the added value for the business. According to another definition, the production function process is the process or the processes that produce the outputs which fulfill the customers' needs, using the sources determined earlier (Guvemli 2001, p. 59).

From the aspect of the aviation sector, the production function is the process in which the passengers fly to the places they want to travel safely, without any trouble and retard. In case of a possible crisis at the airline businesses, the production process may be interrupted owing to the crisis' deepness. Situations such as delayed flights, the strike of the competent and educated personnel, the inability of the managers to give critical decisions in a short time owing to the pressure upon them, the rise in the customers' complaints and displeasure will deepen the crisis situation that the airline businesses face. Besides, since the difficulties in supplying the maintenance and spare parts will hinder the airplanes' safe flight, they will deepen the crisis affecting the production function process.

The Effects of the Crisis on the Marketing Function

At the time of the crisis, a general decline in demand is the case. Searching for the market will take more time. While there emerge new problems in finding the domestic market and getting into the foreign market, decline in the orders will be observed. On the other hand, as a natural feature of the crisis, time pressure's showing its effect too much will increase the cost of market search (Guvemli 2001).

One of the biggest cost items of the airline businesses is the cost of the advertisement. Since the businesses work with low profit margin, they want to sell flights at high level. With this aim, in order to make themselves known in the global market, they form various marketing strategies. Putting these strategies into practice can be costly for the business. The airline businesses run the risk of that cost. On the other hand, the airline businesses must pay attention to the flight and land safety while performing their activities. The cost of a crisis caused by the lack of flight and land safety may be too much for the airline business. The high cost of advertising and marketing may have no meaning and yield. People want to travel safely and comfortably. After a plane crash owing to the insecure flight of an airline business, it will be realistic to expect the demand for the flights to decline in short or medium term. In such a case, the income of that business will decrease correspondingly. The bad reputation of the business in the international market, whose plane has crashed owing to the insecure flight will make the great budget that the business has for the advertising and marketing meaningless.

The Effect of the Crisis on the Finance Function

It is inevitable for the crisis to affect the businesses' finance function. Every kind of crisis that the businesses face may affect the businesses' financial structure, liquidity and profitability more or less. In order to overcome the crisis with little loss, the managers must take action carefully especially about the points related to the finance.

Because of the problems that the banking sector may have at the time of the crisis, the financial structures of the businesses are affected badly. Banks failing to collect their debts in time causes them to cash their liquidity, face financial problems and have capital loss. Because of these, the credit that the businesses may get from the banks decreases, the opportunity to find domestic and foreign sources gets limited, and the sourcing cost increases.

On the other hand, the problems that increase at the time of the crisis hinder the businesses' plans and cause them to have liquidity trouble. The businesses that have cash inflow trouble will have trouble in cash outflow as a consequence (Erkus 2001, p. 38)

That the crisis has an effect on profitability is an important reality. One of the biggest effects of the factors that affect a business' profitability is their cost. Because of devaluation, the rise in the expenditure of the businesses that work especially on the imported input and the rise in the cost of finance that emerges with the rise in the interest rates meet us as the factors that boost the expenditure of the businesses at the crisis period. Furthermore, there are some factors that are effective on the businesses' competitive power and therefore their profitability at the crisis time. While a rise in the rivalry at the market is observed during a crisis, a sharp decrease in the businesses' competitive power is also observed owing to the decline in their market size. The businesses at the crisis period may greatly discount even the sale prices of some products because of various factors (Muslumov 2001). Since generally the airline businesses operate with very low profit margin, they look for the ways to differentiate the service they give preferring non-price competition. But, the businesses at the crisis period, in order to supply urgent cash flow to the businesses in a limited time, may prefer offering a discount on flights. Besides, the businesses that cannot add their expenditures to the product they have sold or service they have given, will decrease their profitability, and therefore will lose money from their profits.

The Crisis Management at the Businesses & the Behaviors of Managers

Crisis management for businesses starts with the pre-crisis period. Businesses in the globalizing world market, may sometimes not have a vision about their activities related to the future. They may focus too much on the factors thinking they can cause a crisis and neglect the others. The factor that is not given enough importance may cause the businesses to face the risk of bankruptcy in medium or long term. The businesses should focus on the whole picture rather than focusing on one factor. The more capable they are of eliminating the uncertainty, the more successful they will be at the time of the crisis. Thus, the businesses should be prepared for the crisis period. Being prepared for the crisis period means making preparations in the pre-crisis period. At this point, the managers have important responsibilities. The managers must believe in the need for crisis management and persuade the employees of it. The formation of the crisis management team, the preparation of the crisis management plan and defining the authority and responsibilities of the personnel at the time of the crisis are the things that must be done in the pre-crisis period. The managers are responsible for getting the needed work done and following them in the pre-crisis period. Crisis management is the fruit of the preparations made in the pre-crisis period. The better the preparations are at this period, the better the management will be at the crisis time.

At the crisis time, the decisions of the managers are an important factor that can change the businesses' destiny. Hasty decisions shouldn't be made because of time pressure. The fact that the decisions made in a short time affect the destiny of the businesses shouldn't be neglected. The managers must have self-confidence, but they also must value the ideas of the employees and the managers expert in their field. The managers' giving decisions just by themselves may cause the business to find itself in a worse situation. Thus, at the crisis time, when giving decisions, the ideas and opinions of the employee's expert in their field must be valued, taking the target position into consideration in the medium and long term, everybody must act carefully.

The role of the crisis management team is one of command and control, so we shall now turn our attention to the people who would be required to "roll their sleeves up", provide information and carry out instructions, in the event of a crisis. To this end, every function (other than those deemed to have no emergency role during a crisis) needs to have an established action team. An action team needs the same things as the CMT (Batchelor 2003, p. 57):

- A leader,
- A deputy,
- Team members,
- Action plans,
- Somewhere to operate from, and
- Access to essentials.

Leading in a crisis can be extremely difficult and challenging. Managers who have led in such circumstances describe the experience as highly developmental—a benchmark in their professional careers. But what does effective leadership during a crisis look like? There may be as many descriptions of leadership, and crisis leadership, as there are executive coaches and management gurus. In some of its educational activities, CCL has described leadership as a process of influence in which managers interact with direct reports and others in the organization in collective pursuit of a common goal. Given the emotionally volatile environment that surrounds a crisis situation, and that can contribute to ineffective or even counterproductive behavior, a useful working definition of crisis leadership may simply be this ability to influence others (Klann 2003).

Crisis Management at the Businesses

The airline businesses must fulfill the pre-crisis preparations well. At this point, the managers of the airline businesses have important responsibilities. The business managers must form a crisis management team and share the responsibilities. The civil airline business is active in a dynamic area that has many variables. Cem Mehmet Kozlu, one of the old general managers of TA (Turkish Airlines) claims that running an airline business means crisis management in a sense (Kozlu 2013, p. 320).

Crisis management is composed of various stages that contain the pre-crisis period. Each of these stages has processes that must be given importance. We can assess the crisis management process at five stages: Crisis management starts with the pre-crisis period. The businesses shouldn't focus on just one factor, but rather on the whole picture. Focusing on just one factor will cause the negligence of the other factors. In such a case, the businesses may find themselves in a crisis situation facing the conditions they do not wish. The businesses that focus on the whole picture can get the signals of the crisis better perceiving the conditions of the market. Getting the signals well will help the business to get more prepared relieving the uncertainty. In this way, the businesses will decrease the adverse effects that the crisis will cause to a great extent. Getting the signals of a forthcoming crisis will guide the businesses to the necessary precautions that must be taken in order to protect themselves. If the crisis is inevitable, these precautions will play an important role in controlling the crisis before it deepens by decreasing its adverse effects on the business. After the crisis, the businesses pass into the process of normalizing. At this stage, business activities start to return to their pre-crisis position. After the crisis, the businesses criticize the examination they went through at the time of the crisis. They record whether they were successful or not at the crisis management, their faults, their good sides at crisis management and the lessons they took from the process to the memory of the business. This experience is a kind of guide that will enlighten the businesses in the face of similar crisis situations. The experience and the lessons taken is a kind of rare treasure for the businesses. The businesses, thanks to the lessons they took from the process will not repeat the faults when they face a similar crisis situation.

Behaviors of Managers

At the time of the crisis, the position that everyone has his eye on is the management position. The managers are expected to give satisfactory explanations to their shareholders and media, make the best decisions with limited information in the shortest time when the circumstances allow. Therefore, the managers must act delicately before the crisis occurs and form a good crisis management team. They should take the signals of the crisis before it is too late by following the agenda and the developments well and should make necessary preparations. They must take all the necessary precautions to avoid the crisis as well as possible in order to continue the business' existence. They must share all the duties and responsibilities among the employees well at the pre-crisis period. At the pre-crisis period, no employee should have a question about his duty in his mind. When a crisis emerges, maybe the first thing a manager must do is to determine the dimension of the crisis (Tack 1994). At the time of the crisis, lack of authority shouldn't be allowed to happen, a hierarchy must be formed (Drucker 1999, p. 213). Besides, the crisis process must be planned well, and right decisions and directions should be given by a good information flow through continuous communication. At this point, the importance of the coordination among the units becomes evident. All the units must work in coordination with a good communication network. Also, at the crisis time, all the processes must be in control of the managers. It is not a surprising situation that uncontrolled situations bring about new crises. The managers at the position of the leadership during a crisis are expected to be flexible, competent to comply with the conditions and give hard decisions if necessary (Muffet-Willett and Kruse 2009, p. 249). The most important duty that the managers have after the crisis is to take lessons from it.

When the crisis process starts, the first reaction of the airline business must be proper and consistent. When it is released to the public for the first time by the business, it will be a right and expected explanation to say that the pain and sorrow of the individuals, the institutions or establishments suffering from the airline business' crisis situation are shared while making a statement. The press agent that will give an explanation in the name of the airline business may have to be the one from the top management team who has education on media depending on the dimension and the nature of the crisis. But the selection of the press agent must be done carefully. In some crises, selecting the CEO (Chief Executive Officer) as a press agent can cause the crisis to be exaggerated (Rose 2008, p. 17). Furthermore, in some cases, the airline business' CEO's appearance can be seen as a sign showing that the top management of the business takes the crisis seriously and follows the situation closely (Anon 2010). One of the most difficult duties of a press agent is to guarantee that the explanation made in the name of the business reaches the target group. In order to achieve this, the website of the airline business, visual and written media should be used well (Grundy and Moxon 2013, p. 57).

Uncertainty, doubt and limited time are the characteristics of the post-crisis period. At this period, the media will try to question and find the guilty that has caused the crisis. Besides, the post-crisis period is seen as the period at which the airline business will present the relevant reason and explanation (Ray 1999). Also, at this period, all the shareholders must be informed of the up to date information. All the efforts that made for recovery and the adjusting precautions must be shared with the shareholders without delay. The shareholders must be supplied with up to date information (Coombs 2007, p. 136).

It will be right to state that while some businesses face the risk of bankruptcy even in the face of a small-scale crisis owing to their scales, the businesses that have overcome the crisis have no tolerance for another crisis.

The Outcome of the Crisis for the Businesses

The target of an organization at the crisis period is to relieve the severity by taking the crisis under control and if possible, to terminate it. Crises are at the chaotic situations. Crises are also complicated concepts . Decision making in crises times has extra important. The maked decisions in crises times may have effects on the sustainability of organization in the short, medium, and long term. in this view, decision making in crises times has strategic qualification (Ritchie 2004, p. 679). The crises shouldn't be seen as a threat or danger, the fact that they can cause positive results in consideration with new opportunities shouldn't be ignored. The businesses that overcome the crisis with little loss thanks to the successful and competent managers, should also assess the good sides of the results that affect the business in the short, medium, and long term. The managers should be able to evaluate the events and developments with a multi-perspective approach. In consideration of this information, the crisis has not only negative but also positive outcomes for the businesses.

The Positive Outcomes of Crises for the Businesses

It is a mistake to claim that crises only have bad outcomes for businesses. At the post-crisis period, the managers should focus on their personnel motivating and appreciating their self-confidence. That kind of behavior will increase the personnel's sense of belonging to the business. The worst time of a business is the crisis time. At this period the feeling of unity and solidarity among the personnel gets stronger. All the employees take the responsibility to help the business overcome the crisis at once. The crisis period will make the relationship of personnel become stronger to help the business overcome the crisis with less harm. The feeling of unity and solidarity and the sense of belonging within the personnel will increase. The businesses that come out as a family and a unity after a crisis continue their activities in a stronger form.

Crises are also important in that they show the weak and fragile points of a business. The businesses, when everything is going well, may not want to waste much time checking out their position. But they will have to face their weak points at the crisis time. They form the necessary strategy on how to react in the face of the problems by eliminating their weak sides as well, just like the frogs that are left into a bowl of hot water at certain periods (Sen 2011).

The crises are a kind of experience for the businesses. Since they will know what to do in the face of such a case, the possible adverse effects of a crisis in a similar situation will be diminished. With the consciousness that the experience is the lesson taken from the past, businesses may make better-directed, more constructive, and more consistent decisions for the future of the business with the help of the experience they got from the crisis they faced before. Therefore, a crisis experienced in the past will have positive effects on the business' decision-making process.

The Negative Outcomes of the Crisis for the Business

For the crises to have negative effects on the businesses is an expected situation. Most of these effects are caused by the tension that the individual events bring about owing to the pressure and stress. After the crisis, the employees may act in a fearful, tired, mistrustful and overreacting way (Tack 1994). After these behaviors, the breakdown of the bilateral relation of the personnel, the increasing level of stress, decrease in the decision-making time with time pressure and the increase in the rate of making mistake are the expected situations. The faulty decisions can form a basis to prolong the crisis process.

The need to supply the continuous, fast, and versatile flow of knowledge at the crisis time may make the existing organization structure inadequate. The decline in the competence of the business‘ data collection may cause the tendency to give a decision and centralize in control. This situation may end up with decision-making with insufficient and defective information (Erdil 1994, p. 216). A decision made with insufficient and defective information can cause the business' situation to deteriorate by making the crisis deepen. For the businesses to deteriorate trigger the friction and conflict among the personnel by affecting their motivation badly. The problems in the unity and solidarity within the personnel, there comes out many new troubles. At the periods when the fear prevails the situation, the feeling of trust within the personnel may be lost, too. The loss of trust can cause many communicational problems among the personnel (Cuceloglu 1996, p. 270). The businesses that have to deal with many problems at the crisis time may pass to the stage of fall due to the loss of their personnel's support.

The businesses' failing to pass the exam successfully at the time of the crisis may result in having a weak position against their rivals, having cash shortage, having a rise in the cost or failing to find finance due to a possible decline in their rate of credit when looking for finance. The fact that, at the time of the crisis, inability to find the needed finance in a short time results in their terminating the activities accelerating the speed of fall of the businesses is an expected situation for the businesses.

At the post-crisis period, the businesses may still be under the effect of the crisis period (Tack 1994). Even if the crisis ends, it will take time to reassure the personnel. The long period of the crisis will increase the deepness of its psychological effects on the personnel. Grouping within the personnel may start, a rise in the number of approaches like "I have warned before." can be observed. Such behaviors of some employees which are effective on the whole personnel will cause problems in the mutual trust of the employees (Turkel 2001, pp. 28–29). Humans are creatures that are affected by their surroundings and each other easily. The bad impression of the people with negative opinions which they may have on the other employees trying to fulfill their responsibilities under some of the pressure and stress factors that the crisis brings about may form an easy basis for the crisis to deepen more. The people that have to interfere in the crisis in time and to the purpose and give the right decisions for the business with good-evaluation must stay away from the people with bad opinions. In the post-crisis period, the existence of pessimistic people will prolong the recovery process.

With not only visual but also social media, the written press has an undeniable power. Especially the big scale businesses find themselves under the media's watch at the crisis time even if they do not want. The steps that the businesses take at the crisis time must be healthy, the decisions they give must be consistent. A faulty step and a decision inconsistent with the general principles of the business given to save the day may arouse a big reaction in the media. The power of media plays a dominant role with regard to the businesses like the airline businesses that are active in an oligopoly market. At the airline businesses, in a possible crisis situation, the media will search the events to find out who is responsible.

A crisis, if not managed well and efficiently, with the decisions deepening the crisis for the business, may cause the airline business to have a bad reputation in the international market. This situation may cause the value of the business' trademark to go down. Because of this power of the media, the loss of value will result in the customers' preference of the possible rival businesses rather than that airline business. Correspondingly, the power of rivalry in the area where the airline business is active at the crisis time will decrease significantly.

The Relationship Between Crisis and Opportunity

Every crisis situation may lead the businesses into unexpected. This uncertained conditions can create surprise for organizations. These surprises will include threats and opportunities. Managing crises are vital for the minimizing threats and seizing opportunities in sustainable way.

The businesses, if they evaluate the conditions well, may provide a competitive advantage against their rivals, overcoming the crisis situation at once. For this, the businesses must analyze their conditions (in other words the facilities and the abilities in hand) well and must provide solutions that will benefit the business in the long term according to the developing conditions.

The crisis may not always be domestic. While sometimes the crisis situation affects just one business, sometimes more than one business may face the same crisis. In these situations, the businesses should be aware of not only their own opportunities and abilities but also their rivals' opportunities and abilities. They must give decisions that will make them at least one step ahead by analyzing their rivals' decisions well. They should be able to gain not only the confidence of their customers but also the confidence of the potential customers who have not preferred their business for their travel yet.

The businesses must evaluate the situations they are in well, instead of the steps taken to save the existing position, they must give decisions that will affect the business well in the long term. They must analyze the geography, the conditions in which they are active, their opportunity and abilities well. The businesses active in different geographies, facing different conditions but experiencing similar crises, although they carry out the same style of policy, while one business increases its value by turning the existing crisis into opportunity, it is possible for the other business to face the risk of bankruptcy, failing to overcome the crisis. The decisions to be given for the same crisis situation can change according to the conditions.

Sometimes it is the rival businesses that face the crisis. The business managers must always be open-minded. The decision-makers must follow the market and the developments of aviation that happen at a global scale as a natural reality. For example, the opponents of a business which is expected to have a cash shortage may turn the situation into an opportunity thinking that the order of plane of this business will be canceled.

The Preventability of the Crisis

A crisis is an undesirable situation for all businesses. The surprise lies in the nature of the crisis; sometimes an unexpected event, sometimes an expected event in an unexpected time causes the crisis. But, if the agenda is followed closely, the developments of the aviation sector is analyzed well and the necessary preparations are made in time, this expected negative situation will be prevented from turning into a crisis. The prevention of a possible crisis is only possible through an efficient ERM. Besides, we should keep in mind that every crisis causes new crises at the same time. It will be inevitable for the airline businesses to lose trust of the society if they cannot control the crisis well. The loss of trust that a business faces can be at a big scale as to cause a financial crisis at first and then the bankruptcy of the business if right and to the point decisions are not given at the post-crisis period.

Every crisis, in fact, causes new crises. The surprise lies on the basis of the crisis. At the crisis time, unexpected events are faced and the businesses may find themselves in new conditions in the face of developing situations. Every new condition may mean new risks for the businesses. The businesses must analyze the new conditions well and must prevent the other crisis and crises by taking extra precautions according to the new conditions. Consequently, they will be able to manage the new risks they face well as well as getting new opportunities for the business through managing the existing crisis well.

The most undesirable and maybe the biggest the crisis of an airline business is the crisis situation that emerges as a result of a plane crash that belongs to their fleet. The managers are expected to give the rightest decisions with a little information in a short time about the crisis situation that happens unexpectedly. The airline businesses give an important proportion of their budget to the advertising in order to sell their flights. While an airline business gives an important proportion of its budget to advertising in order to get known, it has to give the needed share for flight insurance. Flight insurance is a very extensive subject. The businesses must spare the needed sources for the education of the personnel especially the pilots, flight team, and the maintenance team. The aviation sector is education intensive sector. The businesses must follow the developments of the sector closely. They must take necessary precautions to boost the level of the personnel's knowledge, ability, and competence as well as maintaining them.

An airline, very used to razor-thin profits margins from its operation, constantly strives for the optimal utilization of their fleet aiming toward use maximization. The desire to use the planes of the fleet actively brings about the condition to take care of the maintenance. A plane crash due to the lack of education of the personnel and the poor maintenance of the planes means a bad reputation for the business that spares a big proportion of its sources to advertising in order to get known. For the passenger profiles close or far from the aviation sector, this business will be at top of the list that will not be preferred for travel. The businesses that give an important part of their sources for a good reputation must be careful to show necessary care for the flight safety in order not to face bad scenarios. Thus, the businesses will decrease the level of the risks that may affect them adversely and will take necessary precautions for possible crises.

References

Alpaslan, C. M., S. E., Green, I. I. Mitroff, and C.M. Alpaslan. 2009. GrCorporate Governance in the Context of Crises: Towards a Stakeholder Theory of Crises Management. *Journal of Contingencies&Crises Management,* 17(1), pp. 38–49.

Anon. 2010. http://www.theguardian.com/business/2010/feb/09/pr-view-toyota-reputation-management. Accessed 17 Aug 2014.

Batchelor, P. 2003. *Surviving a corporate crisis: 100 things you need to know*, 57. London: GBR: Thorogood.

Baydas, A., İ. Bakan, and A. Ozyilmaz. 2004. *Kriz ve Kriz Yönetimi, Çağdaş Yönetim Yaklaşımları-İlkeler, Kavramlar ve Yaklaşımlar*. Istanbul: Beta Imprint.

Can, H., 1997. *Organizasyon ve Yönetim*. Ankara pp. 498: Siyasal Imprint.

Chris, F. 1999. *Marketing communications*. Spain: Prentice Hall Europe.

Coombs, W.T. 2007. Attribution theory as a guide for post crisis communication research. *Public Relation Review* 33 (2): 135–139.

Cuceloglu, D. 1996. *İçimizdeki Biz*. Istanbul: Sistem Imprint.

Dincer, F. M. 2002. *Ekonomik Krizlerin Türkiye'de Ekonomi ve İstihdam Üzerindeki Etkileri.,* Sakarya: s.n.

Dincer, O. 1992. *Stratejik Yönetim ve İşletme Politikası*, 2nd ed. Istanbul: Timas Imprint.

Dincer, O. 1998. *Stratejik Yönetim ve İşletme Politikası*, 580. İstanbul: Beta Imprint.

Dogan, D. 2003. *İzlenimler/Genç Bir İş Adamının Yaşamından Kesitler*. Istanbul: Sarnic Imprint.
Drucker, P. F. 1999. *21. Yüzyıl İçin Yönetim Tartışmaları*. Istanbul: Epsilon Imprint.
Erdil, O. 1994. *Belirsizlik Dönemlerinde Stratejik Yönetim ve Çevre*, 216. Kusadasi: Dokuz Eylul University Business Faculty Publications.
Erkus, H. 2001. Şubat 2001 Krizinin Malatya Sanayi İşletmeleri Üzerinde Ortaya Çıkardığı Etkiler. *Journal Of Economic Reviews* 38 (8): 37–48.
Genc, N. 2004. *Yönetim Organizasyon-Çağdaş Sistemler ve Yaklaşımlar*, 264. Ankara: Seckin Imprint.
Grundy, M., and R. Moxon. 2013. The efectiveness of airline crisis management on brand protection: A case study of British Airways. *Journal of Air Transport Management* 28: 55–61.
Guvemli, O. 2001. Krizin İmalat Sanayiine Etkileri İstanbul Sanayi Odası'nın 2001 Yılı İlk Yarısı İçin Durum Tespiti. *Journal of Accounting and Finance* 12: 59–61.
Hale, J.E., R.R. Dulek, and D.P. Hale. 2005. Crises response communication challenges. *Journal of Business Communication* 42 (2): 112–134.
Karaca, Y., 2003. *Ekonomik Kriz Dönemlerinde Uygulanan Pazarlama Stratejileri.*, Eskisehir: Anadolu University, The Institute of Social Sciences.
Klann, G., 2003. *Crisis Leadership: How Military Lessons and Corporate Experiences Can Help Leaders Find Opportunity in Times of Chaos.* Greensboro, NC, USA: Center for Creative Leadership: ThriftBooks-Green Earth Center for Creative Leadership.
Kozlu, C. 2013. *Bulutların Üstüne Tırmanırken THY, Bir Dönüşüm Öyküsü*. Istanbul: Remzi Imprint.
Muffet-Willett, S.L., and S.D. Kruse. 2009. Crisis leadership: past research and future directions. *Journal of Business Continuity and Emergency Planning* 3 (3): 248–258.
Muslumov, A. 2001. *Türkiye'de Ekonomik Krizlerin Halka Açık KOBİ'lere Etkisi*, 55. Nevsehir, Small And Medium Enterprises Development And Promotion Administration-Erciyes University Faculty Of Economics Administrative Sciences.
Oncul, S., H. Tagraf, B. Filizoz, and S. Ekici. 2003. Sivas Sanayi İşletmelerinin Şubat 2001 Krizine Genel Yönetsel Tepkileri. *Journal of Cumhuriyet University Faculty of Economics Administrative Sciences* 4 (1): 99–120.
Ozdeveci, M. 2002. Krizin İşletmelerin Yönetsel ve Örgütsel Yapısı Üzerindeki Olumsuz Etkileri ve Kayseri Sanayi İşletmelerinde Yapılan Bir Araştırma. *Journal of Erciyes University Faculty of Economics Administrative Sciences* 19: 99–101.
Ozgen, H., and H.M. Turk. 1996. Türkiye'deki Sanayi İşletmelerinin Kriz Yönetimi Sorunlarının Çözümlenmesi Üzerine Bir Araştırma. *Journal Of Management, Issue* 7: 25–42.
Peten, O. 2003. *Administrating's management of crisis. The public survey investigating influence of economic crisis on marble companies in Afyon by the year 2001.* Afyon: Afyon Kocatepe University, The Institute of Social Sciences.
Ray, S.J. 1999. *Strategic communication in crisis management: Lessons from the airline indusrty.* Westport CT: Quorum Books.
Regester, M., 2005. Risk issues and crisis management: A casebook of best practice. 3rd ed., 196. London: GBR: Kogan Page, Limited.
Regester, M., and J., Larkin. 2001. *Risk issues and crisis management.* London: The Institute of Public Relations.
Regester, M., and J., Larkin. 2012. *Risk issues and crisis management*, Kogan Page; 6th ed. (6 Nov 2012). London: The Institute of Public Relations.
Ritchie, B.W. 2004. Chaos, crises and disasters: A strategic approach to crisis management in the tourism industry. *Tourism Management* 25: 679.
Rose, M. 2008. CEO as crisis spokeperson? Think again. *Public Relation Strategist* 14 (4): 16–19.
Ruff, P. 2004. *Managing communications in a crisis*, 192. Abingdon, Oxon, GBR: Ashgate Publishing Limited.
Sen, F. 2011. *Kriz Yönetimi ve Kriz Döneminde Yönetici Davranışlarının İşletme Başarısına Olan Etkisi.* Kutahya: Dumlupinar University, The Institute of Social Sciences.
Spıllan, J., and M. Hough. 2003. Crisis planning in small business: Importance, impetus and differences. *European Management Journal* 21 (3): 398–407.

Stephens, K.K., P.C. Malone, and C.M. Bailey. 2005. Communicating with stakeholders during a crises. *Journal of Business Communication* 42 (4): 390–419.
Tack, P.B. 1994. *Kriz Zamanı Yönetim*. Istanbul: Bilgi Imprint.
Taymaz, E. 1996. Kriz ve Üretim Teknolojileri. *Journal of Science and Technology* 23: 18–30.
Turkel, S. 2001. Olağan Üstü Durumlarda İşletmelerde Yönetim Sorunları. *Journal Of Isveren* 5: 28–29.
Tuz Vergiliel, M. 1996. *Kriz Dönemlerinde İşletme Yönetimi*, 194. Bursa: Ekin Imprint.
Uzun, D. 2001. *An evaluation of crisis preparedness of five star hotels*. Mersin: Mersin University, The Institute of Social Sciences.

Index

A. Kucuk Yilmaz and T. G. Flouris, *Values, Ergonomics and Risk Management in Aviation Business Strategy*, https://doi.org/10.1007/978-981-15-1006-9

E

F

G

H

The manufacturer's authorised representative in the EU is Springer Nature Customer Service Centre GmbH, Europaplatz 3, 69115 Heidelberg, Germany. If you have any concerns regarding our products, please contact ProductSafety@springernature.com

Printed and bound by CPI Group (UK) Ltd, Croydon, CR0 4YY
25/09/2026
02222900-0006